Cyber Warfare – Truth, Tactics, and Strategies

Strategic concepts and truths to help you and your organization survive on the battleground of cyber warfare

Dr. Chase Cunningham

BIRMINGHAM - MUMBAI

Cyber Warfare – Truth, Tactics, and Strategies

Producers: Andrew Waldron, Jonathan Malysiak
Acquisition Editor – Peer Reviews: Divya Mudaliar
Content Development Editor: Ian Hough
Technical Editor: Aniket Shetty
Project Editor: Tom Jacob
Copy Editor: Safis Editing
Proofreader: Safis Editing
Indexer: Priyanka Dhadke
Presentation Designer: Pranit Padwal

First published: February 2020

Production reference: 1210220

Published by Packt Publishing Ltd.
Livery Place
35 Livery Street
Birmingham B3 2PB, UK.
ISBN   978-1-83921-699-2

www.packt.com

This book is dedicated to all those digital warriors who operate in a never-ending game of digital cat and mouse. Warriors like Shannon Kent, Blake Mclendon, and countless others who have given all while taking the fight to the enemy. May God bless those select few that are engaged with the enemy in a boundaryless battlefield. Keep up the good fight brothers and sisters!

packt.com

Subscribe to our online digital library for full access to over 7,000 books and videos, as well as industry leading tools to help you plan your personal development and advance your career. For more information, please visit our website.

Why subscribe?

- Spend less time learning and more time coding with practical eBooks and Videos from over 4,000 industry professionals
- Learn better with Skill Plans built especially for you
- Get a free eBook or video every month
- Fully searchable for easy access to vital information
- Copy and paste, print, and bookmark content

Did you know that Packt offers eBook versions of every book published, with PDF and ePub files available? You can upgrade to the eBook version at www.Packt.com and as a print book customer, you are entitled to a discount on the eBook copy. Get in touch with us at customercare@ packtpub.com for more details.

At www.Packt.com, you can also read a collection of free technical articles, sign up for a range of free newsletters, and receive exclusive discounts and offers on Packt books and eBooks.

Foreword

The last fifty years have witnessed a tremendous revolution. This revolution continues to rage all around us, threatening to redefine international borders; destroying long-cherished businesses and institutions; disrupting our social fabric and norms; challenging our privacy; and calling into question what is right and what is wrong. Often referred to as the "Information Revolution," this revolutionary technological transformation continues its relentless march around the globe.

As the Information Revolution transformed the world and the advent of the World Wide Web brought internet access into homes around the world, pundits came to adopt the "Cyber" moniker from William Gibson's 1984 novel *Neuromancer* to describe the new domain of human experience. As the World Wide Web continued its expansion in the 1990s, "Cyber" soon became a prefix added to words highlighting the impact of digital technology to everyday activities. Soon, internet cafes were rebranded as "Cyber Cafes," offering internet access to those who didn't have a computer or internet access. The explosive growth of internet connectivity throughout society saw new terms like cyberspace, cyberpunks, cyberbully, cybercrime, cyberstalker, cyberporn, and other like terms added to the lexicon.

It wasn't long before this newly minted "cyber domain" became a source of potential conflict, earning the interest of the world's military powers. For example, during my Air Command and Staff College classes in 1994, I penned a monograph positing a unified cyber command and describing how cyber capabilities could be used as an instrument of national power in lieu of kinetic strikes. Such thinking was not unique in military circles.

For example, in 1999, two Chinese People's Liberation Army colonels, Qaio Liang and Wang Xiangsui, wrote a seminal book on military strategy, *Unrestricted Warfare*, which highlighted how China could leverage non-traditional means to attack an opponent, including leveraging attacks in the networked digital world. Not long after, in December 2005, the United States Air Force added "cyberspace" as a warfighting domain to its mission statement, highlighting the importance of cyber operations in military doctrine. With that Air Force mission statement, "Cyber Warfare" came of age.

The infamous Prussian general and military theorist Carl von Clausewitz said, "War is politics by other means." A century later, the noted humorist and philosopher Julius "Groucho" Marx said, "Politics is the art of looking for trouble, finding it everywhere, diagnosing it incorrectly, and applying the wrong remedies." I submit that both Clausewitz and Marx's statements apply to today's so-called "Cyber Warfare."

Sadly, we have seen too many people declaring themselves as experts in "Cyber Warfare." I contend that anyone who says they are an expert isn't. The cyber domain is vast, incorporating numerous skills and specialties. During my decades of experience in the cyber domain, I have witnessed many so-called "Cyber Experts" whose non-technical background often leads them to fall victim to superficial analyses that invariably lead to inaccurate conclusions that are often passed on as gospel to others.

Fortunately, we have those like Dr. Chase Cunningham who indeed can and should be considered a "Cyber Expert." With deep experience in cyber operations, forensics, research, and domain leadership, he understands the broad cyber domain and is able to (to paraphrase Groucho) discern what is trivial versus what is real trouble. He uses his real-life experience to diagnose it properly, and has the technical heft to apply the right remedies. In an era rife with self-declared cyber experts, Chase Cunningham is the real deal and presents this much-needed book to help the reader truly understand Cyber Warfare.

In my book, *Cybersecurity for Executives: A Practical Guide*, I state that cybersecurity is a risk management issue and not just a technology problem. I highlighted that people, process, and technology are all critical parts of any cybersecurity program. In this great book, Dr. Cunningham provides outstanding analysis and description of the cyber domain in a manner that even a cyber-neophyte (Yes, I note the irony of me deliberately using a cyber-prefixed word) would understand.

The chapters presented are crisp and clear; each worthy of a college class. In Chapter One, he describes the continually evolving threat landscape and the strategic implications of this dynamic threat environment. Chapter Two is logically placed in the discussion as Dr. Cunningham explains why the traditional castle moat-like perimeter defense model has become obsolete and how this challenges our strategic risk and investment decisions. From there, in Chapter Three, he discusses how adversaries are adapting their tactics, techniques, and procedures to gain a strategic advantage to achieve their goals as well as what we can and should do to thwart them.

Those who do not have deep technical background will benefit to pay particular attention to the next three chapters. Chapter Four discusses influence operations, where attackers seek to manipulate the reader's views and persuade them to make certain decisions favorable to the attacker's objectives. This cyber warfare topic is highly relevant in today's hotly-contested political environment where charges of influence operations in the 2016 US presidential election remain part of the daily discourse. Chapter Five presents a fascinating discussion of how "DeepFakes" and Artificial Intelligence/Machine Learning technology are the next cyber battleground. Chapter Six demonstrates how cyber adversaries are increasing sophisticated in their operational employment of advanced campaigns. Here Dr. Cunningham forecasts what are the most likely courses of action and identifies what remain "science fiction."

The next three chapters provide practical analysis and guidance of great value. Chapter Seven highlights the importance of strategic planning to thwart future cyber threats. Chapter Eight discusses the types of cyber tools that are used to conduct cyber operations.

Some readers may be surprised to find that many are what I call, "dual-use tools," that is, tools that can be used for both offensive and defensive purposes. Chapter Nine is a seminal discussion of how tactics, when properly applied, enable strategy in cyber warfare.

At the beginning of this foreword, I stated that the Information Technology revolution threatens to redefine international borders; to destroy long-cherished businesses and institutions; to disrupt our social fabric and norms; to challenge our privacy; and call into question what is right and what is wrong. As he concludes this book, Dr. Cunningham addresses these conditions, discusses the future of cyber warfare and forecasts how it will impact society, governments, and technology. I believe his projections are noteworthy, and ones we all should be paying particular attention to. As such, *Cyber Warfare – Truth, Tactics, and Strategies* is a necessary handbook for all who seek to understand cyber operations and the world we live in.

"Si vis pacem, para bellum." ("If you wish peace, prepare for war." Quote from Publius Flavius Vegetius Renatus.)

GREGORY J. TOUHILL, CISSP, CISM
Brigadier General, USAF (ret)

About the reviewer

Glen D. Singh, CEH, CHFI, 3xCCNA (cyber ops, security, and routing and switching) is a cyber security instructor, author, and consultant. He specializes in penetration testing, digital forensics, network security, and enterprise networking. He enjoys teaching and mentoring students, writing books, and participating in a range of outdoor activities. As an aspiring game-changer, Glen is passionate about developing cyber security awareness in his homeland, Trinidad and Tobago.

Glen is also the lead author of the following books:

- Learn Kali Linux 2019
- Hands-On Penetration Testing with Kali NetHunter
- CompTIA Network+ Certification Guide
- CCNA Security 210-260 Certification Guide

> I would like to thank Divya Mudaliar for having me as part of this project, Tom Jacob and Ian Hough for their continuous support during this journey, and the wonderful people at Packt Publishing, thank you everyone.

Contributors

About the author

Dr. Chase Cunningham focuses on helping senior technology executives with their plans to leverage comprehensive security controls and the use of a variety of standards, frameworks, and tools to enable secure business operations. His work focuses on integrating security into operations, leveraging advanced security solutions, empowering operations through artificial intelligence and machine learning, and planning for future growth within secure systems.

Dr. Cunningham served as a director of cyber threat intelligence operations at Armor. He was the computer network exploitation lead for Telecommunication Systems and the chief of cyber analytics for Decisive Analytics. Dr. Cunningham is a retired U.S. Navy chief with more than 20 years' experience in cyber forensic and cyber analytic operations. He has past operations experience, stemming from time spent in work centers within the NSA, CIA, FBI, and other government agencies. In those roles, he helped clients operationalize security controls, install and leverage encryption and analytic systems, and grow and optimize their security operations command systems and centers.

Chase holds a Ph.D. and M.S. in computer science from Colorado Technical University and a B.S. from American Military University focused on counter-terrorism operations in cyberspace.

> I want to thank all the visionaries and innovators that I have had the luck of coming across over the years. Those insightful leaders who help shape our collective future and hopefully lead us all to a more secure and prosperous future.

Table of Contents

Preface

This book is for all those cyber security professionals who seek to know the truth behind the history of cyber warfare and are working to secure their infrastructure and personnel for the future. The aim of this book is to cover the topics around cyber warfare tools, tactics, and strategies.

Who this book is for

This book is for any engineer, leader, or professional with either a responsibility for cyber security within their organizations, or an interest in working in this ever-growing field. In particular, CISOs, cyber security leadership, blue team personnel, red team operators, strategic defense planners, executives in cyber security, and cyber security operations personnel should benefit from the insights and perspectives offered in this book.

What this book covers

Chapter 1: A Brief History of Cyber Threats and the Emergence of the APT Designator – This chapter will dive into the real history of cyber threats and their emergence in the space and provide some background on nation state APT designations.

Chapter 2: The Perimeter Is Dead – In this chapter, we'll go through all the intricacies and details that prove that the perimeter-based model of security failed years ago.

Chapter 3: Emerging Tactics and Trends – What Is Coming? – This chapter will be a journey down the rabbit hole into the future of cyber warfare tools and tactics and will provide examples of the new trends in this ever evolving space.

Chapter 4: Influence Attacks – Using Social Media Platforms for Malicious Purposes – In this chapter, we will cover the ways in which social media and influence can be weaponized for cyber warfare tactics.

Chapter 5: DeepFakes and AI/ML in Cyber Security – In this chapter, you will learn about the reality of AI and ML in cyber security and delve into the practical applications of these often-misunderstood technologies.

Chapter 6: Advanced Campaigns in Cyber Warfare – In this chapter, we will get into the types of attack campaigns and their real-world implications.

Chapter 7: Strategic Planning for Future Cyber Warfare – In this chapter, we will break down the specifics around how to better plan for cyber warfare and why strategy matters in digital combat.

Chapter 8: Cyber Warfare Strategic Innovations and Force Multipliers – This chapter is going to provide specific examples of what tools and technologies there are on the market that can help exponentially increase an organizations defensive posture.

Chapter 9: Bracing for Impact – In this chapter, you will be offered examples of how to apply tooling, tactics, and strategies to brace for the impact of a cyber attack and ways in which your organization can better respond when things go awry.

Chapter 10: Survivability in Cyber Warfare and Potential Impacts for Failure – In this chapter, we will cover essential ideas for defensive strategic planning and provide real-world examples of what may happen when cyber warfare tactics go big.

Appendix: *Major Cyber Incidents Throughout 2019* – A list of recent major cyber incidents throughout 2019, categorized by the class of attack, as presented in *Chapter 6*.

To get the most out of this book

- Existing cyber security planners and strategists will gain insight into the reality of the space and will be better able to understand how future innovations part of that future state will be.

- This is not a how-to guide; the author does not wish to provide readers with knowledge that could potentially be turned to malicious purposes, but rather this book aims to provide the reader with a new perspective, to see and prepare for what is coming, rather than to be blinded by the threats that are more imminent.

- Cyber security experience is assumed; however, the book also features introductory concepts, which even beginners can take advantage of.

Download the color images

We also provide a PDF file that has color images of the screenshots/ diagrams used in this book. You can download it here: `https://static. packt-cdn.com/downloads/9781839216992_ColorImages.pdf`.

Conventions used

`CodeInText`: Indicates code words in text, database table names, folder names, filenames, file extensions, pathnames, dummy URLs, user input, and Twitter handles. For example: "`Changeme.py` focuses on detecting default and backdoor credentials, and not just common account credentials."

Bold: Indicates a new term, an important word, or words that you see on the screen, for example, in menus or dialog boxes, also appear in the text like this. For example: "The first, and arguably most important, technology is commonly called **Software-Defined Networking (SDN)**."

Get in touch

Feedback from our readers is always welcome.

General feedback: If you have questions about any aspect of this book, mention the book title in the subject of your message and email us at customercare@packtpub.com.

Errata: Although we have taken every care to ensure the accuracy of our content, mistakes do happen. If you have found a mistake in this book we would be grateful if you would report this to us. Please visit, http://www.packt.com/submit-errata, selecting your book, clicking on the Errata Submission Form link, and entering the details.

Piracy: If you come across any illegal copies of our works in any form on the Internet, we would be grateful if you would provide us with the location address or website name. Please contact us at copyright@packt.com with a link to the material.

If you are interested in becoming an author: If there is a topic that you have expertise in and you are interested in either writing or contributing to a book, please visit http://authors.packtpub.com.

Reviews

Please leave a review. Once you have read and used this book, why not leave a review on the site that you purchased it from? Potential readers can then see and use your unbiased opinion to make purchase decisions, we at Packt can understand what you think about our products, and our authors can see your feedback on their book. Thank you!

For more information about Packt, please visit packt.com.

1

A Brief History of Cyber Threats and the Emergence of the APT Designator

"I think most people today understand that cyber clearly underpins the full spectrum of military operations, including planning, employment, monitoring, and assessment capabilities. I can't think of a single military operation that is not enabled by cyber. Every major military weapon system, command and control system, communications path, intelligence sensor, processing and dissemination functions – they all have critical cyber components."

— *Gen. William L. Shelton, Commander, Air Force Space Command*

Hackers aren't what Hollywood shows us

The common perception of a "hacker" is usually that of some individual at home or working in a basement somewhere, cloaked in a cheap hoodie and ingesting copious amounts of caffeine, while hammering away at code sprawled across at least three different monitors or displays.

In these Hollywood representations, the malicious actor is usually smiling and talking to themselves as they craft unique singular exploits that might be used to take down a bank or some world-ending computer system. These overhyped mythical "hackers" are almost always introverts and technical geniuses that are anti-social, anti-government, and often woefully ignorant of the totality of their actions.

In truth, this is not the reality behind the keyboard in the real world of cyber warfare operations. Certainly, in some instances, there must be a "hacker" somewhere that is a representation of this stereotype, but more often than not, the personas behind some of the most malevolent and vicious attacks in cyberspace look nothing like this. In many cases, those malicious actors are wearing a uniform and are paid, protected, and trained by their government – or in some cases, governments. They are exceptionally bright, well trained, highly focused, and creative individuals that have found a niche in their ability to engage in espionage and combat operations anywhere in the world, with any adversary. They are the tip of the digital spear for what is to be the dominant combat environment for the future, and they are the front-line warriors that are constantly engaged in a game of binary cat and mouse that rivals all other wars.

The command of cyberspace in the 21st century is as decisive and impactful as the command of the sea was in the 19th century and the command of the air in the 20th century. Cyberspace is, in all truth, the battlefield on which the war of the future is currently being fought. It is the arena for the New Cold War. An arena in which every nation on Earth, every criminal enterprise, and indeed almost every human on the planet, holds interests and resides. Never in the history of man has there been a location in which global conflict is actively raging in the same space as every business and organization on the planet.

With only about 50 years of history behind it, the internet and global connectivity are expanding at an extraordinary speed. More connections and more data were created and shared or distributed in the last 5 years than in the whole of human history previously.

Cyberspace is now the new platform for political, economic, military, and cultural interactions and engagements. This will be the domain wherein impacts on social stability, national security, economic development, and cultural communication will be made in the next century.

Computer security and the study of computer threats and exploitation have not always been at the forefront of computer science, however. It has only been in the last few decades that the need for, and the power of, cyber espionage and warfare tactics have been realized at an international level. In order to understand the power and efficacy of these digital warriors and the operations in which they hone their craft, it is imperative that we understand where computer exploitation came from, and analyze the evolution of this space; an evolution from a focus on innovation by any means necessary in order to benefit businesses and the consumer, to one of strategic combat on a global scale.

There are a variety of "early instances" of cyber threat activities and operations, and if you were to cobble together 50 different experts on the topic, you would likely have 50 different incidents to discuss as the beginnings of cyber warfare. It is therefore pointless to argue over the absolute particulars of specifics on what was the first or most influential of these attacks throughout time. What is important is to point out and detail a few major exploits and threat activities that stand out as seminal points in time to help us better understand the reality of this space and its evolution toward its future state.

For clarity's sake, in common definitions, a cyber-attack and cyber-defense could be conducted at any scale: from the state level by the military to a major organization, right down to the personal level involving a singular individual. It could be a simple hacking attack, focused mainly on nuisance type outcomes, or the attack could be a long-term, multi-year, large-scale state-launched operation that is aimed at damaging the physical infrastructure of an enemy state. There is no unequivocal "gospel" definition of a cyber-attack, or a cyber threat operation or operator.

However, in most circles familiar with the topic area, it generally refers to *an unauthorized intrusion into a computer or a computer network in such forms as tampering, denial of service, data theft, and server infiltration.* Additionally, there is no real consensus on what constitutes the actual "first" ever cyber-attack, be it by a nation state or a lone operator. Many cite the Morris Worm as one of the first real attacks, while others cite the attacks on the federal network in the early 1980s as the first real appearance of dedicated cyber threat actions. Regardless of the specific chosen threat action in history, in truth, there are so many possible referenceable actions that have occurred that there is no real right answer. What is more important to understand is the reality that the ways in which attacks have occurred in and around cyberspace have evolved from their earliest iterations, and that they are continuing to change and adapt as technology develops.

The Battle of the Beams

One of the earliest attacks leveraging communication- and electron-related conduits was not on a computerized system; those did not exist at the time. While not often widely considered as a direct part of cyberspace operations, signals espionage – an early form of cyberspace warfare, due to its use of communication media and electronic systems – was used to achieve specific operational objectives as far back as World War 2. In one of the earliest instances of leveraging a specific communication medium as a means of conducting espionage for warfare-focused outcomes, the United States and Great Britain launched an attack that would befuddle and confuse the German adversaries for years.

In what would come to be known as "the Battle of the Beams," German bombers navigated from continental Europe to Great Britain by following a radio signal transmitted from a point of origin (Manners, 2016). The German pilots would know they were above their targets when they intercepted a second beam, also transmitted from continental Europe. That system ensured that German night raiders found their targets in the dark and returned home safely – until it was "hacked," that is.

British engineers discovered the German use of radio-frequency telemetry and coordination for the German combat runs and developed countermeasures that would modify the German command signals.

By broadcasting similar signals at precise times on specific German frequencies, British cyber warfare operators fooled the German bombers, causing them to drop their ordnance at a location chosen by the British. Additionally, the British cyber-attacks made return trips nearly impossible for the Germans, many bombers never finding their home base, and a few even landing at Royal Air Force fields, their pilots thinking that they had returned home (Manners, 2016). This use of the frequency spectrum (a critical portion of what is now commonly referred to as cyberspace) created effects that illustrate the operational power of cyberspace half a century before it was to be considered a warfighting domain.

Modem hacks

The first focused instances of computer threat research and exploitation studies actually began during the 1970s and were not even related to computers; they were instead noted as a problem in the telephone-switching network. The phone system was growing so fast and becoming so large that the system had to be integrated and automated to survive. This first automated phone system was built to serve a large test environment, and immediately many problems were discovered. Calls originated and ended on their own, phone numbers were allocated to persons without phones, and a myriad of other issues came to light.

These initial issues were not actually considered a threat as much as they were thought to be a problem for the owners of the systems and those administering the networks. In the 1980s, the modem became the powerhouse means of connecting and managing the large networks that were becoming more and more commonplace, and as such modems became the primary point of compromise from which systems could be hacked.

While there are many different opinions about the first real virus on a computer system, the reality of this becoming a problem for computers did not become prevalent in public literature until the computer became a household item in the mid-1980s. During the "age of modems," groups like the 414s, a group of modem hackers whose name came from their area code, were identified and arrested by the FBI (Hansman, 2003).

The 414 group targeted and exploited the phone networks and modems of Los Alamos National Laboratory and a center for cancer research, using a combination of malicious code and a deep understanding of the flaws in the automation technology that was used by the phone companies at that time. Not long after this first noted computer threat campaign was finalized, the federal government passed the Computer Crime and Abuse Act (CISPA 2010). This legislation detailed what constituted a protected computer and the resulting punishment for those who sought to conduct malicious actions against any protected system (Grance, Kent, & Kim, 2004).

Anti-virus growth

Only a few innovative and industrious companies understood the possible maliciousness that could be wrought by activities such as those conducted by hackers and hacker groups.

Consequently, it was during this time that companies such as Symantec and IBM began to research and study viruses and malware to isolate and mitigate the threat. The malware and anti-virus company McAfee was established during this era. John McAfee noticed that many of his friends' and associates' computers were acting abnormally and running very slowly. After some research, he was able to discern that programs had either been installed and were intentionally causing detriment to the system, or programs had begun to simply degrade and harm the system on which they were running.

After some technical research and development, McAfee was able to write specific technical signatures for the anomalies within those programs, and the signature-focused malware and anti-virus system was born (Hutchins, Cloppert, & Amin, n.d.). McAfee's system of signature recognition and anomalous behavior detection was immediately recognized as a pivotal point in mitigating and detecting these newly recognized threats. Overnight, companies began to follow suit and corporate defensive cyber security operations were effectively "born."

It was not until 1987 that the federal government began to take notice of this type of activity and instituted the first **Computer Emergency Response Team (CERT)** (Grance et al., 2004). By the early 1990s, the rate of annual computer virus detection grew to over 1,000 instances per month. As the detection and isolation of computer viruses became a practice area within computer science, the detection and signature generation for viral programs also increased exponentially. By 1995, more than 250,000 viruses or variances of viruses had become commonplace. All of these incidents of early exploits and attacks paled in comparison to the growth of cyber threats that would emerge in the early 21st century.

The dawn of Advanced Persistent Threats (APTs)

The field of specific targeted cyber threats and especially cyber threat research did not truly exist in any real formality prior to the early 2000s, beyond that of what was in practice within the US government and other nation state agencies. The first mentions of cyber threats and cybercrime outside of government arenas appeared in 2001 during an unclassified briefing from the National Security Agency (Werlinger, Muldner, Hawkey, & Beznosov, 2010). This report was actually supposed to be focused on the issue of securing a network as large as that of the **Department of Defense (DoD)**. However, thanks to leaks and the unclassified nature of the report, the spread of the threats that were becoming common knowledge within the DoD came to light in public circles.

Certain aspects of the report alluded to a highly trained and motivated cyber threat that was likely already deeply embedded in many DoD networks and was actively targeting commercial businesses as part of their plan to proliferate their attacks in the future.

The term APT, or Advanced Persistent Threat, came to light for the first time during a discussion at the Air Force Intelligence Agency (Iracleous, Papadakis, Rayies, & Stavroulakis, n.d.). The discussion involved a group of Lieutenant Colonels trying to determine which term to use to classify the new type of computer hacker, the ones who were very well trained and very successful and were in all likelihood funded and trained by nation state adversaries or well-financed criminal organizations. Since these attackers were advanced, persistent, and certainly a threat, the term APT was born and then quickly became the industry norm term for foreign government cyber operators and skilled threat teams. While this single term is used to categorize and identify a rather wide swath of possible threats, it is worth noting that APT is now used by almost every cyber warfare magazine and cyber-security official, from think tanks all the way to the White House.

In order to truly be considered an APT-specific attack, there are a few general criteria that are accepted by some (but not all) analytic groups across both industry and cyber operations personnel. For these groups, both the totality of the operation that took place and the means by which the group conducted the attack must generally fall into the following three categories for the attack to be even considered as a likely APT attack or exploitation event:

- **Advanced** – Operators behind the threat must have a full spectrum of intelligence-gathering techniques at their disposal. These may include computer intrusion technologies and techniques but also extend to conventional intelligence-gathering techniques such as telephone-interception technologies and satellite imaging.

While individual components of the attack may not be classed as particularly "advanced" (for example, malware components generated from commonly available do-it-yourself malware construction kits, or the use of easily procured exploit materials), their operators can typically access and develop more advanced tools as required. They often combine multiple targeting methods, tools, and techniques in order to reach and compromise their target and maintain access to it. Operators may also demonstrate a deliberate focus on operational security that differentiates them from "less advanced" threats.

- **Persistent** – Operators give priority to a specific task, rather than opportunistically seeking information for financial or other gain. This distinction implies that the attackers are guided by external entities. The targeting is conducted through continuous monitoring and interaction in order to achieve the defined objectives. It does not mean a barrage of constant attacks and malware updates. In fact, a "low-and-slow" approach is usually more successful. If the operator loses access to their target, they will usually reattempt access, and most often, successfully. One of the operator's goals is to maintain long-term access to the target, in contrast to threats that only need access to execute a specific task, such as run-of-the-mill hackers and those seeking financial gain via computer hacking.

- **Threat** – APTs are a threat because they have both capability and intent. APT attacks are executed by coordinated human actions, rather than by mindless and automated pieces of code. The operators have a specific objective and are skilled, motivated, organized, and well-funded. This funding has typically been known to come from either a host nation's government or from an extremely well-funded nefarious group, such as mafia or crime syndicates. However, in some cases there has been an indication that funding may have come from one or more of these providers and there are even cases where the source of funding appears to be interwoven between criminal enterprises and host nation agents.

In most of the circles that study or classify cyber-security threats and APTs there are normally a few major players in the space that have relatively specific targets, tactics, and procedures or TTPs (Targets, Tactics, and Procedures):

- **Russia** – Mainly focused on improving the Russian power position across the globe. They are typically noted as engaging in long-term threat operations that often include the use of spies and human assets to conduct their operations. Added to that, the Russian APT is known to be extremely well funded and capable of engaging in kinetic cyber action (physical strikes on infrastructure or assets that result in destruction) when needed, as noted in the attacks on Estonia and Crimea. The Russian APT also has significant focused technology and capability in the area of targeted influence and disinformation campaigns and sees the proliferation of social media and consumer interactions as an avenue for exploitation.

- **China** – The Chinese APT groups are the most successful at the theft of intellectual property via cyberspace operations. This is done via a concerted focused national effort within the Chinese military and government, with strategic plans aimed at "leapfrogging" the enemy via their operations. This leapfrogging approach to gaining an advantage is a national-level area of focus for the Chinese. Chinese leaders are open in detailing their strategic plans in that they aim to enhance their capability in science and technology wherever possible. The Chinese APT is willing to engage in espionage all the way down to implanting hardware and chips within manufactured devices that are built in China, and they are known to use American and British internships and education programs to embed their operatives within research and development groups at companies and government institutions.

- **North Korea** – The North Korean APT is not usually as persistent as they would like. Due to limited connectivity in the country and sanctions that are in place on travel and logistics, the North Korean APT groups are mainly noted for launching attacks on those entities that disparage or damage their national image.

- While they do have a dedicated cyber operations group with extensive training (most often gained in China), their ability to conduct any significant operation beyond basic ransomware attacks is limited. As noted during the SONY exploit operation, attacking weaker targets of opportunity is their most common activity.

- **Israel** – Unit 8200 is the elite of the elite for the Israeli cyber group. This unit is comprised of their most well trained and experienced cyber operations personnel and they are well funded and focused in their operations to counter perceived threats. Often, Unit 8200 engages directly with the Iranians in cyber threat operations, but it is logical to think they are under attack by the majority of Middle Eastern nation states as well as the usual suspects that the United States and NATO countries encounter. The Israeli cyber operations group conducted one of the first kinetic responses to a cyber-attack this year when they bombed an Iranian-affiliated hacker group building after the hacker group was discovered to be responsible for an attack on an Israeli asset. In many research circles, this extermination of the hacker group via missile attacks was seen as one of the most significant responses to cyber threat operations and demonstrates that there are literal life and death outcomes of actions in cyber warfare.

APT exploitation and targeting also follow a well-defined methodology and practice of attempting to maintain anonymity both during and following exploitation or compromise. Again, this is likely due to several factors, the primary of which is that the host nation funding and guiding the operation does not wish to have it known that they are participating in such a covert and possibly damaging attack.

However, the preceding definitions for APT and the clarification of the usage for this classification of attack are still not adopted across the entirety of cyberspace. For many different agencies, companies, and governments, the definition of any APT exploitation event is extremely difficult to concretely define. Consider that an organization such as NATO has more than 28 different countries working within its combined operations center.

Each one of these different groups has been actively targeted and independently hacked or exploited by different APT groups and actors, but there are literally no reporting criteria or vehicles across NATO that succinctly and definitively detail the need for an APT designation; each country and each group that has been reporting or analyzing their relative exploitation event determines APTs differently. Even within different agencies of the US government, attempting to specifically detail an APT exploitation event or hack cannot be done well. The **National Security Agency (NSA)** has its own specific set of criteria for determining an APT attack while the CIA and FBI have their own criteria, most of which do not cross-reference each other and none of which possess the same rules for delineating specifics on these items.

The lack of a cohesively uniform definition for APT operations and exploitation provides a great example of just how fluid and dynamic this area of study currently is and has been. Further, this example shows how the lack of consensus and broad term definition is so prevalent within cyber operations and analysis that even defining one of the most important terms used in the industry is difficult at best, as it is almost impossible to clearly identify and isolate any one threat group, the generic APT term is used across such a wide spectrum.

Early APT attacks

In the mid to late 2000s, a large section of the computer and internet industry was focused solely on increasing the speed and interoperability of their networks and the usability of their products, all while paying little, if any, real attention to security or cyber threats. It wasn't until the discovery of a coordinated and large-scale attack that concern for the future of computer, and later cyber, security became a serious consideration for both developers and persons in places of political power. This first real cyber threat attack at a significant scale was the discovery of the Zeus Botnet in 2007 (Singh & Silakari, 2009). This attack targeted the US Department of Transportation, among other things, and was responsible for extracting large amounts of data from government systems.

A broad range of data, including passwords for master control systems, system administrator passwords, network and control mapping systems, and proprietary code samples, were all taken (Singh & Silakari, 2009). While there were many previous computer viruses and different variations of computer threats prior to this, the discovery of the Zeus Botnet and the engineering and powerful programming capabilities of those behind the threat group led to the development of the term *cyber* and brought the dedicated study of cyber threats into its own area of focus.

In the realm of kinetic cyber warfare operations, the first real shot across the bow occurred in 2007. Russia was engaged in a low-action but highly tense dispute with the nation of Estonia. While the dispute was not of much international significance beyond basic news coverage, the follow-on cyber-attack and planning certainly was. As the political and societal sabers began to increase their rattling, the government of Russia maneuvered its physical forces into place for an invasion of Estonia. As the offensive ground operations began, nearly every aspect of internet-based infrastructure in Estonia was attacked by **Distributed Denial of Service (DDoS)** attacks (Goodchild, 2009) and was shut down, or at least severely degraded.

Everything from banking systems, government websites, state-sponsored media outlets, and electrical systems to any other connected system that was of military or strategic importance was taken "offline" by these attacks. Billions of packets were launched simultaneously from tens of thousands of computers and servers located within and outside of Russia as part of this campaign. As the Estonian systems began to crash and communications and coordination were interrupted, the Russian military moved into position and forced its will on the Estonian government. While officially none of the cyber-attacks were either attributed to or acknowledged by the Russian military or government, the implications and trail of evidence indicated that a coordinated cyber-attack was launched in conjunction with this military operation. This was one of the first and most powerful examples in the modern era of warfare of how a relatively simple, yet coordinated cyber-attack could not only hamper communications but also severely impede a defending system and cause a real loss of command and control for those under attack.

Confusion in cyber defense

In more recent history, the definition of cyber threat and any attempt to systematically or intelligently further demarcate the differences between what constitutes a cyber threat has become difficult at best. Consider the use of malware in relation to cyber security and cyber threats. While malware is certainly considered a subset of a cyber threat issue, it is not by itself an identifying term. Typically, research and academic work within the cyber field now discuss malware as a piece of the cyber problem, and any research or discussion of the malware term breaks down into an immediate classification of the malware type itself. Additionally, terms and definitions, such as social engineering and exploitation, have become a piece of the collective definition of cyber threat research.

They are not typically considered as specific corollaries to any set of cyber threat groups or certain operations. These terms and their uses, within cyber research, evolve on a nearly daily basis and have become more a study of tying specific cyber actions or operations to a group of cyber threats, instead of the collective research determining with any specificity what certain terms can be tied to which cyber threat. It is the language equivalent of trying to catch rain in one's hand; the medium simply moves too quickly and is reformed according to its own whims.

US and allied cyber defense establishment

It would not be until the mid-1990s that a formal, dedicated warfare fighting unit would be established to gain command and control of national security-related infrastructure, and leverage operations that would increase the ability of the United States to defend national interests in cyberspace. In Europe, the establishment of any actual functional warfighting entity that could operate at the covert or clandestine level in cyberspace would not take shape until the mid-2000s with the formalization of the NATO cyber task force and the British **Government Communications Headquarters (GCHQ)** cyber security units.

It would be even later when, in 2009, a singular military command body was established to take any offensive action in security cyberspace at the national level. This was done with the establishment of the US Cyber Command headquartered at the NSA in Ft Meade Maryland.

An important point of note on the evolution of this space, and the establishment of these new component commands and the authorities and capabilities that they now encompass, is that this occurred almost entirely in a defensive effort, not an offensive one. The establishment of the totality of these warfighting entities was almost singularly built on the premise of defending their respective national assets and infrastructures. It wasn't until the late 2000s that real cyber offensive capabilities came into real practice or use. This slow but important evolution from a focus on information warfare, gaining knowledge and information on the adversary, to cyber warfare, or conducting kinetic and non-kinetic attacks on the adversary, indicates a subtle shift in mission over time, based on the realization of the change in the battlespace: from one of information as a commodity necessary to the national intelligence community to one of attack and defense of the systems used to process, store, and transmit information and critical infrastructure.

The cyber shot heard round the world

The establishment of international command centers and operations groups focused on cyber security operations was a needed practice in cyberspace defense. The growth and formalization of those organizations, however, did not remain solely focused on defensive postures for long. In the early part of the 2010s, these groups began to be exposed as they engaged in a New Cold War in cyberspace. This clandestine back and forth would soon result in the leaking of some of the most powerful nation state-level weapons in cyberspace becoming commodities on the internet. Commodities that any person, anywhere could access and aim at their intended targets. One of the first, and most impactful, of these nation state cyber weapons to become public was Stuxnet – a US cyber weapon.

While there is no "official" declaration of the Stuxnet worm being a result of any specific US cyber operation, it is widely accepted that this is where the weapon originated. Stuxnet was a direct result of the tensions between the United States and the Iranian government's development of nuclear capabilities that took place in the late 2000s and early 2010s. In order to stop the development of potential nuclear weapons by an openly threatening regime, the US would unleash a new weapon of mass destruction, one built from code.

The development of Stuxnet began in the early 2000s, possibly 2003 or 2004, and took anywhere from a few months to a year to develop. Analysis of the code that operates within Stuxnet indicated that the level of sophistication required for this type of weapon could only come from the global superpower in cyberspace at the time, namely, the US. Given the assumption that the US is that superpower, the only place that has the capabilities to develop that advanced code to enable a weapon as complex as Stuxnet is the NSA.

Prior to late 2009 or early 2010, the NSA did not have a specific mission set that was solely focused or tasked with offensive cyber operations capabilities. Most of the missions within the NSA directorates prior to the establishment of US Cyber Command in 2010 operated as loosely-connected mission sets that often focused specifically on intelligence collection and dissemination. The development of the Stuxnet weapon was in actuality the result of an amalgamation of intelligence collection on possible targets in Iran, and the realization that there was certain vulnerable hardware running in the Natanz nuclear plant that could be exploited.

The NSA's intelligence collection apparatus had managed to collect open source technical information on the providers for the nuclear plant that openly advertised what specific hardware was in use within Natanz. The companies that provided support and hardware to the Natanz nuclear site in Iran noted that they serviced Siemens S7 **programmable logic controllers (PLC)** as part of their contract with an affiliate provider.

This information, combined with other intelligence resources that were collected via other methods, would be critical to the development and deployment of the Stuxnet worm.

The operation to get Stuxnet installed and launched on internal systems within the nuclear facility was most likely the result of a combined human spying operation via contacts that the CIA had in Iran. Those assets were provided with a USB device that contained the early version of Stuxnet, and with the simplicity of simply inserting that USB into a device that was connected to the Natanz network, the first shot across the bow was fired. The malware worked its way deep into the core of the Natanz network and ultimately found its target: those PLC controllers that control critical functions within the centrifuges that are used for enriching uranium. Slowly and covertly, the malicious code did its job and degraded the facility's ability to further enrich uranium, as the specific speed required for that precise process was impacted. Other nation-states, namely Unit 8200 in Israel, have also been either blamed for the Stuxnet attack or have been implicated as possibly being tied to the malware's installation on Iranian target networks. Regardless of who specifically launched the attack, the results were undeniable. Physical systems, those that enriched uranium, were afflicted and were damaged. This caused a degradation in the Iranian nuclear program's efficiency and capability and did impact their ability to gain specific nuclear capabilities at the time.

However, this weapon did not simply stop at its intended target. Research following the attacks on the Natanz nuclear facility by Symantec indicated that over 100,000 unique **Internet Protocol** (**IP**) addresses had seen or been exposed to versions of the Stuxnet virus. Although Stuxnet was a weapon that was aimed at a very focused scope for its operations, it would not take long for that weapon to expand beyond the bounds of the Iranian networks. The methods and tactics that the weapon used to proliferate within the Iranian network, where most machines were running MS Windows software, meant that should that malware be exposed to vulnerable machines outside of those networks, it would replicate and move across the globe. Which was exactly what happened.

Over 40,000 other infections related to signatures of Stuxnet were noted "in the wild" up to three years after the Natanz attacks, and three different specific variants of the malware were found by researchers in countries as far away as Taiwan.

For the next seven years, different variants of the Stuxnet weapon were found in a variety of different organizations across the globe. Duqu, a different but closely technically-related version of Stuxnet, was discovered in 2011 in Budapest. Duqu had many of the very same technical components as the Stuxnet tool, but Duqu was more vectored to collect information, including keystrokes, rather than being built to destroy a system physically. Flame, another closely tied technical variant of Stuxnet, was discovered in 2012. Again, Flame contained identical portions of the Stuxnet code and protocols, but Flame was modified for collecting and recording voice and chat conversations, including Skype calls.

As late as 2017, Triton, yet another variant of Stuxnet's original tooling, was found lurking in systems far beyond Iranian nuclear networks. Triton was modified to disable safety systems in petrochemical plants that used variations of the same Siemens S7 PLC controllers. It was dubbed "the world's most murderous malware" by researchers. Triton's focus on disabling safety controls meant it could cause explosive control failures in chemical plants. While Stuxnet was most likely, and by all accounts, a US cyber weapon, its variants were not exclusive to the US or its allies. Follow-on research from the cyber firm FireEye attributed Triton to Russian organizations. Duqu was noted to likely have originated in the Middle East. And Flame still has no real specific point of origin, but some organization had to have manufactured it.

That first attack with a targeted well-built cyber weapon was the first strike in a covert war whose weaponry spilled outside of the target area. That weapon, Stuxnet, was the first purpose-built piece of nation state cyber weaponry that the world became aware of. And its use spawned variants and attack tools that are in use by cyber warfare operators far beyond the realm of its original intended area of operations.

Tit-for-Tat cyber warfare

Over the next few years, the Iranians would not simply sit idly by and take a position of non-response to the Stuxnet attacks. They quickly upped their cyber operations game and responded in kind. In 2012, Operation Cleaver, the Iranian response to Stuxnet, was launched. The targets for the operators of Cleaver included militaries, oil and gas, energy and utilities, transportation, airlines, airports, hospitals, telecommunications, technology, education, aerospace, **Defense Industrial Base (DIB)**, chemical companies, and governments. Other cyber-attacks had been launched in retaliation for the Stuxnet attacks, namely Shamoon and Operation Ababil. These attacks were targeted at the US banking systems and Saudi Arabian oil operations. Those attacks were significant but did not result in much other than a financial hit on the banks that were targeted and the oil facilities' abilities to ship oil.

Operation Cleaver was a direct response to the Stuxnet attack, but it was not entirely the same in its actions. Where Stuxnet was focused on causing physical damage in a relatively short timeframe on the Iranian nuclear centrifuges, Cleaver was more of a long-term ploy. Operation Cleaver was grander in scale in that it targeted essentially any "low-hanging fruit" that might contain intellectual property or data that could be used to gain an economic advantage in trading by the Iranians. Everything from the US Navy/Marine Corps Intranet, known as NMCI, critical infrastructure providers, and airline operations groups to educational organizations was hit.

The Iranian malware that was used showed that they had learned lessons in malware construction and design thanks to their post-attack analysis on the Stuxnet tools. The Operation Cleaver malware attacked systems in similar veins to Stuxnet. Cleaver malware would find a vulnerable target, conduct an exploit, worm deeper into the network, and then use command and control infrastructure to funnel data out of the compromised environment.

Just as Stuxnet had packaged its exploits and leveraged the network itself to find its ultimate target, so too did Cleaver. However, where Stuxnet was an elegant clandestine piece of malware, a digital scalpel, the tooling for Cleaver was an overt packaging of open exploits that hammered away at systems and did little to conceal its tracks, a sledgehammer. Ordinary cyber security providers were able to gather instances of Cleaver malware samples and find highly evident domains and sites that were openly registered to Iranian affiliated organizations. Many analysts, as well as the US and Allied government officials, noted after the Cleaver attacks that the reasons this malware campaign was not more subtle was that it was a show of force by the Iranians.

Pandora's box busts open

The latter half of the 2010s proved to be equally as formative for the future of cyber warfare as the earlier half of that decade. In this case, though, it would not be solely because of the back and forth between nation-states that cyber weapons were revealed; it would be due to rogue hacker groups aimed at causing chaos.

The Shadow Brokers came to the forefront of these operations in 2015 and 2016. The name Shadow Brokers was a reference to the popular video game at the time – *Mass Effect*. In that game, the Shadow Broker was said to be the head of an organization that trades in information, selling to the highest bidder. The Shadow Broker unit in cyberspace appeared to be highly competent at their chosen trade. The first leak that the Shadow Broker unit posted on the internet was one aimed directly at the US government, and specifically its cyber weapons creator, the NSA.

On August 13, 2016, the Shadow Brokers posted a Pastebin notice that stated that they had procured, via unknown means, access to specific tools that came from the Equation Group. The Equation Group is known to be either a part of, or directly related to, the Tailored Access Operations team at Ft Meade Maryland, that is, the base of operations for the NSA.

This is the unit that evolved out to the establishment of US Cyber Command in 2010 and is thought to be directly responsible for the design and deployment of Stuxnet. It is the digital weapons foundry for the US government. This Pastebin notice started with the following text:

"Equation Group Cyber Chase Weapons Auction – Invitation

- ---

!!! Attention government sponsors of cyber warfare and those who profit from it !!!!

How much you pay for enemies cyber weapons? Not malware you find in networks. Both sides, RAT+ LP, full state sponsor tool set? We find cyber weapons made by creators of stuxnet, duqu, flame. Kaspersky calls Equation Group. We follow Equation Group traffic. We find Equation Group source range. We hack Equation Group. We find many many Equation Group cyber weapons. You see pictures. We give you some Equation Group files free, you see. This is good proof no? You enjoy!!! You break many things. You find many intrusions. You write many words. But not all, we are auction the best files."

The posting follows up with the below:

"The Pastebin continues with instructions for obtaining the password to the encrypted auction file:

Auction Instructions

- --------------------

We auction best files to highest bidder. Auction files better than stuxnet. Auction files better than free files we already give you. The party which sends most bitcoins to address: `19BY2XCgbDe6WtTVbTyzM9eR3LYr6VitWK` before bidding stops is winner, we tell how to decrypt. Very important!!! When you send bitcoin you add additional output to transaction.

You add `OP_Return` output. In `Op_Return` output you put your (bidder) contact info. We suggest use bitmessage or I2P-bote email address. No other information will be disclosed by us publicly. Do not believe unsigned messages. We will contact winner with decryption instructions. Winner can do with files as they please, we not release files to public."

Following that posting on Pastebin in October 2017, the Shadow Brokers would again post that they had access to specific NSA-level tooling, again tools built by or used by the Equation Group.

Another posting by the Shadow Brokers emerged later that year, wherein access and screenshots for a variety of advanced exploitation tools were offered to whoever would contact the Shadow Brokers. The most impactful leak by the Shadow Brokers came in April of 2017 when they posted a tweet linked to their `@Shadowbrokers` account wherein there were links to codeword exploits. The most powerful of which was EternalBlue. That exploit directly resulted in over 200,000 machines being infected within the first two weeks of its posting online. Remnants of the EternalBlue exploit appeared in the WannaCry and NotPetya ransomware attacks that would follow, in which millions of machines would be affected and billions of dollars of loss would be incurred by organizations all over the world.

While the specific motivations behind the Shadow Brokers will never be known with much real specificity, the outcomes of their actions certainly became known. There has to date been no owner of the Shadow Broker leaks, probably due to the very real fear of reprisal by the US federal government. There were instances of individuals that the press noted who might be affiliated with those leaks. One of which was a former Booz Allen Hamilton contractor named Harold T. Martin who was thought to be a likely culprit, as he was found with over 50 terabytes of stolen NSA tooling and exploits during an FBI raid of his home, but those claims were never substantiated and the Shadow Brokers continued to post even after his apprehension. Edward Snowden stated on his Twitter feed that *"circumstantial evidence and conventional wisdom indicates Russian responsibility,"* but that was also never validated.

Regardless of who the Shadow Brokers were, Russian moles, disgruntled employees, nation state hackers, or political activists, the fact remains that those leaks were the equivalent of tactical government-designed weapons being offered freely to every man, woman, and child on the planet.

Conclusion

Although cyber warfare is currently limited to information networks and network-attached systems, it will drastically expand in the near future. Rather than decide between kinetic and non-kinetic effects, threat actors and cyber warriors will choose the effect that will best produce the desired outcome. Cyber-based effects will not be limited only to networks of computers and infrastructure; rather, they will encompass all electronic information processing systems across land, air, sea, space, and cyberspace domains. The future of cyber warfare is, unfortunately for the defender, not hindered or predicated by policy, technology, and threat. The leaks of major nation state-level exploits like BlueKeep and its variants, as well as the proliferation of force multipliers such as social media influence and bot tactics, will expedite and increase the variety and ferocity of future cyber-attacks.

New technology will have disproportionate effects, not only on the weapons used in cyberspace but also on the makeup of the domain itself. National policy on cyberspace dictates the objectives and rules of engagement for cyber capabilities as well as the organization and execution of operations, but those "rules" apply only to the nations and fighters that are willing to subscribe to them. There is no Geneva convention for cyberspace, and the establishment of those limits on defenders in truth only empowers those who don't play by the rules. Cyberspace is the only domain on the planet where a nation state such as North Korea or Iran can have the same devastating effect of impact as the most powerful nations on Earth. The use of the digital space has effectively leveled the playing field.

The digital world is where nations and organizations will continue to fight for the future. To own that "ground" and to take the initiative from the enemy is nothing new in the annals of espionage and warfare; it is simply a change in tooling and tactics that is necessitated by the evolution of where warfare will be fought that will continue to drive the New Cold War.

There is a hard truth for those of us caught in the middle of this no man's land between warring cyber superpowers and the hacker organizations of the world: we have built our systems and infrastructures to actually allow these attacks to succeed. Half a century of excessive speed of innovation and a reliance on a failed security paradigm will continue to enable these incursions and exploits to succeed.

In this chapter, we really dove into the history of this space in a very factual analysis of what brought us collectively to this arena. In the following chapter, we will discuss how the networks we have built and the foundational architecture of these infrastructures are flawed and will continue to fail.

References

1. Manners, D. (2016, October 21). *The Battle of the Beams*. Retrieved from electronicsweekly.com: `https://www.electronicsweekly.com/blogs/mannerisms/yarns/the-battle-of-the-beams-2016-10/`

2
The Perimeter Is Dead

For the past 30-plus years, the overarching plan to secure networks and digital infrastructure was one that was predicated on the concept of perimeter-based security. Most organizations across the globe subscribed to the concept and plan that if the walls were high enough and the outward boundaries of the network were hard enough, then the enemy would not be able to "get in." Entire global architectures have been built and deployed to leverage that concept and billions of dollars have been spent to engage in "defense in depth" and the "castle and moat" methodology of security. It has all been for naught.

The perimeter-based model of security has categorically failed to keep pace with the evolution of the internet, the proliferation of devices and accesses, and the explosion of cloud computing and an increasingly mobile and **Bring Your Own Device (BYOD)** workforce. There is no perimeter anymore. The moment a user can take home a laptop, log in from a home PC, or use a mobile device or app to access a component of the network, that defensible perimeter is essentially cut to pieces.

In this chapter, we will delve into the details that show how systems have been built to enable failure and data breaches:

- We will detail how the perimeter-based model of security is fundamentally flawed.

- We will discuss the limitations that the current technology places on infrastructure.

- We will analyze the proliferation of breaches and failure thanks to the interconnected nature of networks.

- We will provide insight into how enemy nations and adversaries exploit these failed architectures.

First, we'll consider a scenario that aptly demonstrates the death of the perimeter.

A scenario detailing holes in the model

Consider the following scenario. A user who works from home and has administrative rights on their machine (as most do, especially when it is their own personal device) allows their child to use that device because they need it for homework. The little tyke jumps on their parent's overly powerful, overly app-heavy, non-managed device and, instead of going to a safe homework site, they maneuver to what they thought was a seemingly innocuous site that they heard about at school.

This young user wants to see whatever this site has to offer, but in order to do that they must download a plugin on their parent's browser and an app that the site says they need to use the content on the site (remember the child can execute this operation because they have administrative privileges on this machine) – so they do.

Everything on the site works fine, no malware alerts are noted (because the malware they downloaded is new and has no known signature to trigger, and it is operating in non-specific memory space on the target machine), and the young user sees whatever they were interested in and jumps off their parent's machine and all is well. Or so they thought.

The now installed and fully operational malicious piece of software waits for the machine to go online again and with clandestine operations in the background, it downloads a keystroke logger and a follow-on malicious application that looks for VPN logins and credentials as well as administrative passwords and hashes.

The next workday, the actual business user fires up their work machine solely for the purposes of their work, and as they connect to the corporate network they introduce a direct pipeline, with full administrative privilege and control, for the now-installed malware to tunnel into their business infrastructure. Once the connection is made, the malware works to establish a beachhead into the network, and it can do this because that authenticated user has excessive privileges and is therefore an authenticated user. The program that is now maliciously moving within the network shares those same privileges.

The cross-connection between virtual LANs and network subnets and the usually weak authentications that are present on internal systems for users help to facilitate the now proliferating malware. Simply because they are inside the trusted perimeter zone, the network and its control apparatuses allow the malicious software to maneuver almost unimpeded.

This malicious software continues its tunneling into the network with the aim of finding the most valuable connected application, data resource, or critical asset it can locate. Then, with a low-and-slow data exfiltration protocol, it will extract information of value from the network towards the command and control for the malware operation. This extraction will be used for the purposes of extortion or sale, or to simply cause the system to lock up and become a victim of a ransomware exploitation that may follow.

If nothing of real value is found on the machine, its connections, or the network itself, the accesses and connections within that now compromised network will be resold on the underground or dark web to enable follow-on malicious actors to leverage that control point to enable their clandestine operations in the future. That network will at least become a jump host for criminal actions because of this compromise. No matter what, this is a failure that was not only helped but enabled by trusted zones within networks and a reliance on an outdated strategic implementation of perimeter-based security.

This scenario demonstrates that the security perimeter established by organizations or governments can be blown wide open simply because a user happened to take their device home with them. In the real world, organizations and governments have witnessed the consequences of this firsthand. In the next section, we'll look at a real example in which a company fell victim to what should have been a relatively contained ransomware infection.

A global perimeter falls

Another example of how the technical alignment of the perimeter-based model helps proliferate exploitation and is woefully ineffective at combatting current threat actions comes from an analysis of what happened to the shipping giant Maersk.

In 2017, a Ukrainian company with software used for accounting – the Linkos group – was operating as normal. Unbeknownst to the IT leaders and users at this company, the servers that were connected to hundreds of clients and responsible for updating their accounting software were the launching point for the initial proliferation of the NotPetya ransomware attack.

The Linkos group, which did nothing "wrong" other than be located in a country that was actively being targeted by the military wing of the cyber operations branch of the Russian government, had been the victim of months of covert exploitation conducted to gain a military advantage in the region.

The Russian cyber warfare group had cobbled together a first-of-its-kind piece of ransomware that was an amalgamation of the NSA tool EternalBlue, leaked in 2017, and the usually standard administrative password auditing tool Mimikatz, which has been in use since 2011.

The Russian cyber operations group combined these tools into a rapidly propagating tool solely for the purposes of locking down victim machines while spreading like wildfire throughout the network of the target. Excessive user privileges, combined with password reuse, simple passwords, and shared network resources, were the perfect breeding ground for this cyber weapon.

When directed, the malware (or in this case ransomware) launched. Within hours, the connections from the Linkos group servers to each and every connection that they supported for business operations would be afflicted, and thanks to the interconnected nature of those follow-on entities and networks, the attack would continue to propagate.

Microsoft had released a patch for the EternalBlue exploit earlier that year, but yet again the interconnected nature of the networks across the globally-connected internet, combined with failed business processes for managing updates and a lack of mandated patching protocols, helped to enable the flight path of NotPetya as it maneuvered towards Maersk. In other words, the very interconnected nature of those networks and the combination of shared technical aspects within the network, human, and business failures all combined to make a perfect breeding ground for this infection.

The proof of the use of NotPetya as a weapon, not an extortion tool, came as the victims realized that the ransom notice was a lie. The malicious software exploited the deepest parts of the infected machine, its master boot record: the very areas where every machine has its core operating system. All ransom payments were useless and did not resolve the issue; the machine was essentially now an overpriced paperweight.

The exploit did not even contain an actual decryption key that could be used; it was a weapon built solely for the purposes of degrading system usability by those that became infected, and Maersk was about to become part of that global group of victims.

The initial infection for Maersk came via common business practices, not especially technical ones. In a remote office for Maersk located in Odessa, Ukraine, an IT administrator had been tasked with installing business software M.E.Doc on one computer so that the accounting user could do their job. That software was sold and managed by the Linkos group, and the infection had all the ground it needed to activate.

Once the NotPetya worm entered the Maersk network, the ease with which the infection spread was shocking in its speed. In hours, the entirety of a billion-dollar network, with millions spent on security tooling and technology, fell like a house of cards in a stiff breeze to the power and focus of the malicious tools used by NotPetya.

Coupled with the misery of the infection was the realization by the Maersk IT staff that their practices for the command and control of that vast infrastructure had enabled a follow-on failure to respond to their Domain Controllers; following common industry best practices, the IT staff at Maersk had configured their worldwide Domain Controller configuration to essentially operate with a shared configuration model as they are the brain for all authentication across segments of the Windows enterprise. This, however, meant that the infection spread almost simultaneously to each interconnected Domain Controller, which helped to facilitate the blast radius of the attack and systematically "bricked" each of these critical pieces of Maersk's own internal command and control infrastructure.

It would only be because of a power outage prior to the attack in a remote Maersk office in Ghana that any of that infrastructure would survive. Were it not for that twist of fate, the likelihood that the company could have recovered from this attack would have been almost zero.

Almost every port terminal for the shipping giant would become infected and rendered useless, affecting logistics and shipping across the planet. Operators were forced to rely on paper spreadsheets, Gmail accounts, and personal mobile phones to keep the company above water. Thousands of machines and endpoints on the corporate network would become nothing more than bricks, and the worldwide network of Maersk's logistics providers, suppliers, truckers, and users would be hindered for weeks to come.

The total cost for Maersk alone was estimated to be roughly a quarter of a billion dollars or more, and that was before the costs of remediation and resolution were ultimately realized. In totality, the costs for Maersk are estimated to be close to a billion dollars (Greenberg, 2018). All because of one piece of software that needed to be installed for accounting on a system was connected to external customers and clients.

Across the planet, the costs were in the billions. Thousands of businesses, hospitals, and civilian organizations were affected. Patients and ambulances were turned away for treatment as hospitals succumbed to the infection. Even the US DoD networks were afflicted. If ever there was an indication that the globally adopted practices of the past have failed us, guaranteeing collective future failures and exponentially increasing the power of cyber weaponry, NotPetya is the perfect case study.

We've seen how a global giant, and other organizations across the world, suffered severe losses due to the failures of old practices. In the next section, we'll see how evenly the seemingly air-tight perimeter of a security-compliant organization failed due to the inadequacy of old practices.

Even compliant organizations' perimeters fail

The Equifax breach offers yet another case study in the dissolution and ineffective nature of the current state of security practices for enterprises. Even those that have spent millions on security and are fully aware of both the location of and the implications of their data security plans will fail epically when any instance of weakness is found in their perimeter-based security model.

Consider the technical and managerial aspects of the Equifax breach. The company had a large budget for their security team, all required and compliance mandated solutions were in place, and broad scope security monitoring and analytics were in place. And yet the entirety of the data repositories for the company, and more than 140 million Americans and over 800,000 UK citizens, was exploited over the course of a near year-long incursion.

The initial impetus for the infection occurred thanks to a vulnerability in the public-facing web server that was responsible for handling disputes in credit cases. This server was running a slightly outdated version of the Apache Struts framework, but a patch had been released for this item by the US CERT team within the same week that the initial exploitation occurred.

The attackers in this instance simply leveraged the exploit, which was publicly available, gained access, escalated their privileges, and then moved deeper into the network. This is an extremely common and well-known practice within exploitation operations, and one that was well-known to the security leaders and team at Equifax, yet it was successful, nonetheless.

Attackers then leveraged the credentials they had gained and escalated administrative control capabilities to establish accesses that would remain in the system for months. Equifax had firewalls and an intrusion monitoring and network analytics capability; however, thanks to an expired certificate, the system was not functioning optimally and the indicators that should have prompted remediation actions were never seen.

The certificate for this critical piece of monitoring had been expired for over 10 months and would not be fixed until long after the breach had been detected via manual means. What had initially begun with relatively localized access to a few limited servers had spread to more than 50 databases containing valuable personally identifiable information for hundreds of millions of people (Ng, 2018).

Added to the failure of monitoring and segmentation was the use of basic data governance practices. There was no multi-factor authentication configured for the administrators of the systems, and records indicated that a database containing unencrypted usernames and passwords was in use by administrators (Schwartz, 2018). Once discovered, this mismanaged and ill-advised administration tool rapidly empowered and expedited the attack on the company data stores.

Finally, the attackers were able to query the databases and data stores over 9,000 times during their exploitation operation (Government Accountability Office (GAO), 2018). This over-allowance on queries alone should have been more than enough to trigger an analysis of the activity, but thanks again to the certificate issue and the overly connected data infrastructure within the network, the activity was missed.

On the managerial side of this epic failure of security practices, it was noted that the leadership within the company tried to blame a single employee for the failures related to this breach (Brandom, 2017). While surely someone was responsible for the management of the devices used for patching and updates to software, the reality is that it was thanks to systemic technical failures, combined with a lack of realization that the system was literally built to allow exactly this type of malevolent action to occur, that was the reason for the breach.

Again, excessive privileges, bad segmentation, overly permissive accesses, and failed data security governance combined in a model that allowed movement within the perimeter were what ultimately doomed Equifax.

While the monetary and personal impacts of this massive failure are still to be seen, to date nearly every person in the US has had their credit information compromised and their ability to apply for credit has been impacted. Estimates are that 15 million UK citizens and tens of thousands of Canadian citizens were affected as well. The company, which is responsible for the credit rating information for almost half of the American population, now estimates its losses at $1.3 billion, and that does not include total costs for upgrades and changes to the corporate network.

As has been noted in the previous section, corporate organizations have been built to fail. Even with supposedly secure government organizations, this same paradigm exists. In the next section, we will detail how prevalent this approach of a failed model of security is in giant government organizations and discuss the impacts that have been seen thanks to the resulting breaches of those networks.

Governments' perimeters fail

Even governments can fall victim to the scourge of this failed approach to security. The US **Office of Personnel Management**, or **OPM**, is one of the most critical agencies within the US Federal system. This entity is basically responsible for housing the total collection of all human resource records for every person that is employed by the US Federal Government. This includes millions of current and past Federal employees' and military members' personal information, as well as the results and data for every security clearance investigation that is used by the DoD to validate access for its most secretive agencies and programs. One would think that with this type of data, and knowing the extreme value of this data, the agency would be one of the most secure within the DoD. Not so.

As with Equifax and Maersk, the OPM breach was architected from the start, decades ago in OPM's case, to be unprepared, and built to fail should an intrusion past the "high fences" of their perimeter ever occur. For OPM, this pinhole came in the form of a phishing email that contained a malicious PlugX remote access trojan that had been unknowingly introduced into the network.

Once the malicious attachment in the email was opened, the user had no knowledge of the nefarious activity that was occurring because the malware, which had been slightly modified in order to avoid anti-virus systems, bifurcated itself and began dropping malicious DLL files. Additionally, tooling was deployed, which included a follow-on binary file filled with explicit commands for the trojan to use.

As with every other exploitation scenario in the past, the malware did what any typical malware does and leveraged the users' accesses and the weak internal segmentation to tunnel further into the network until a more valuable target was found. In OPM's case, this was a "jumpbox" (Koerner, 2016), also known as a **PAM** tool or **privileged access management** tool for administrators. In lay terms, this is a machine that contains the administrative credentials for every user who can manage or control assets within the infrastructure.

A follow-on analysis and traceback of the likely original activator of that first malicious email attachment was traced to a third-party contractor that had been working as a system administrator on OPM's network. That provider's network had been targeted and breached at least a year before the follow-on incursion into OPM's network took place.

The threat actors had worked silently and diligently to cover their tracks, and had deleted log files and even worked to parse useful data files into small chunks that would evade detection by OPM's data exfiltration tooling. The patience and cunning that were used in the OPM breach allowed the attackers to make off with copies of some of the most critical and most focused data that is used by the federal government across the entirety of its many agencies.

In none of the cases we've discussed was there any use of a marvelous super tool or technology that had massively innovative technology powering it. In every instance of exploitation and hacking that has occurred over the last four decades, the reason that the systems failed was that they were entirely reliant on perimeter-based security tooling, technology, and planning, combined with failed or at best ineffective managerial practices.

It was due to lateral movement within the network, excessive user privileges, and a failure to be able to "see" what was taking place in those dark corners of the infrastructure that what should have been a nuisance became a failure of epic proportions. The perimeter-based model of cyber security has categorically failed in its most basic premise: to defend the borders of the infrastructure.

But there is a larger and even more confounding issue that will plague enterprises, small businesses, and even nations in the future. BYOD raises new challenges that open the doors wide for exploitation. In the next section, we'll discuss the implications of this.

Users, BYOD, and the obliteration of the perimeter

The power that is afforded to users, devices, and applications has exponentially increased over the last half-decade and with the proliferation of that power comes an ever-increasing multi-faceted patchwork of potential future failures for all infrastructures. Add the increasing complexity and reliance that the cloud offers and the problem of maintaining control and management of all those moving parts, which all exist by default outside of the boundaries of any perimeter, and things go from bad to worse at light speed.

In the past, it was a necessity for users to physically be present at their place of employment for them to have any connectivity or access to network systems, and in many cases, even computer technology. Over the last two decades, the reduction in cost of personal computing devices, and the power that those devices wield, has benefited the user population but has confounded infrastructure security. The need for enterprises and governments to embrace a culture that essentially lives in an increasingly mobile, geographically diverse, and transitory stream offers additional problems for those that are tasked with deciphering how to control those disparate work streams.

In most circles the **VPN**, or **virtual private network**, is the preferred technical method of securing remote access for those users that are on BYOD devices, in remote locations, or do not physically work in a corporate-controlled office or on a corporate machine. This solution has been available since the early 1990s, and while it can be beneficial in minimizing overt security misconfigurations, it is also known to facilitate attacks.

VPNs used by enterprises and commercial users are not much more than simple applications that leverage tunneling protocols to establish connectivity. This happens via a variety of methods. Most VPNs, corporate or commercial, use a specific protocol to transmit and encrypt data. Each protocol exchanged for VPN connections is the result of an agreed-upon set of rules for data transmission and encryption between the two endpoints. Many commercial VPN providers provide users with the option to choose from several different VPN protocols based on the users' security needs, while most assigned corporate or government-mandated solutions do not. The most common protocols for VPN are typically:

- Point-to-Point Tunneling Protocol (PPTP)
- Layer Two Tunneling Protocol (L2TP)
- Internet Protocol Security (IPSec)
- OpenVPN (SSL/TLS)

A VPN's primary function is to leverage encryption tooling and connection protocols to render data unreadable. This happens as plaintext data streams are encrypted and turned into unreadable ciphertext. Each VPN solution uses a specifically chosen algorithm combined with a cipher to encrypt and decrypt those data streams. Individual VPN protocols have their own strengths and weaknesses. The power of the protocol is based on the cryptography that is enabled via the algorithm.

Hacking into a VPN connection involves one of two tactics. A hacker can either break the encryption through known vulnerabilities or steal the key through unethical means. Cryptographic attacks are used by hackers and cryptoanalysts to recover plain text from their encrypted versions without the key.

However, breaking encryption is computationally demanding and time-consuming. It can take strong computers years to break encryption (although that time can be reduced substantially by using cloud computing or quantum computer technology). Instead, most attacks tend to involve stealing keys. Given that the math behind encryption is computationally complex (and quantum and cloud computing resources are often limited resources), stealing a key is a far easier task. The success of compromising a VPN solution comes from a combination of successful trickery, computing power, cheating, and social engineering.

All that is needed for a malicious actor to begin the exploitation of a VPN connection is a simple port scan against the target infrastructure. The majority of VPNs in use by enterprises and consumers give themselves away because of the ports they use for connectivity. A port scan against a target network discovers these following ports:

- For OpenVPN:
    - UDP ports 1194, 1197, 1198, 8080, 9201
    - TCP ports 502, 501, 443
    - L2TP uses: 1701
    - UDP ports 500, 1701, and 4500

- IKEv2 uses:
    - **UDP** ports **500**

- PPTP uses:
    - **TCP** ports **1723** or **Protocol 47** (GRE)

These scans immediately indicate to a threat actor that a VPN is present and will guide them to begin the work to obtain the keys in some manner. An even easier method for VPN exploitation that commonly occurs is simply to observe a targeted corporate user in a public place, such as a coffee shop, see that user activate and log in to their VPN, and then simply misdirect their attention and steal the actual physical machine while the VPN connection is still active.

In most cases, if the user is not logged off, or the machine locks, the connection remains live, and the malicious actor can leverage that resource at their leisure.

VPN providers can be targeted as well, such as the exploits against Avast and NordVPN in 2019. In those attacks the malicious actor was able to leverage temporary credentials, thanks to a vulnerability in systems within a temporary data center provider's remote management tool. That access provided the threat actors unfettered access within the data center connections to the servers that manage encrypted communications for those VPN providers.

During that exploitation phase, a **Transport Layer Security (TLS)** key was stolen, which could have allowed the follow-on exploitation of any of the company's 12 million mostly commercial users via cryptographic man-in-the-middle methods (Kan, 2019). However, how many of those commercial customers also have business-related interactions on those same devices, and share or reuse the same passwords for access to corporate resources?

Research from a variety of sources that have scanned and probed thousands of VPN providers note that:

- The majority of **Secure Sockets Layer (SSL)** VPNs still use the old SSLv3 protocol, which is more than two decades old and is no longer supported.

- Many SSL VPNs use an untrusted, unverified SSL certificate, which allows a possible man-in-the-middle attack.

- Insecure SHA-1 signatures are also prevalent.

- Almost 50% of SSL VPNs use insecure 1,024-bit keys for their RSA certificates. RSA key lengths below 2,048 are noted across the industry as being insecure because of their weaker cryptographic security.

- 1 in 10 SSL VPNs still rely on OpenSSL, and most of them are still vulnerable to the Heartbleed exploit, which is nearly half a decade old.

- Only about 5% of SSL VPNs are compliant with PCI requirements.

- Not a single VPN provider was found to be within the standards for NIST (the US government organization that provides standards and regulations for enterprises) guidelines.

Based on those statistics, it can be determined that there is a very high likelihood that most of the very tools many users, enterprises, and even governments rely on to allow BYOD and remote work to take place are basically fundamentally insecure.

Applications add to insecurity

When one realizes the flaws that VPN technology introduces to the enterprise perimeter security model, one can see there are certainly issues with that approach. Adding to that issue, but also closely coupled with remote work and the BYOD movement for the workforce, is the issue of application security. Applications are what everyone, everywhere, on every device, uses to interact with and access the tools they need to do their jobs and conduct tasks in their daily lives. These applications are in many cases built with a focus on speed to production in mind, not security. That fact means that many of those applications that are used are basically built to be insecure.

According to a study jointly conducted by the Ponemon Institute and IBM, more than 50% of enterprises have 0% of their security budget aimed specifically at application security (Ponemon Institute, 2016). Over 40% of enterprises do not scan the code that runs their applications for security issues prior to placing them in production, and roughly a third of enterprise applications that are in production have never been tested for known security flaws. According to a **Hewlett Packard Enterprises (HPE)** report from 2016, roughly 1 in 10 applications have hardcoded insecure passwords noted within their configuration (HPE, 2016). Lastly, almost half of all applications in production operate within enterprises that have admitted to having no vulnerability management program.

In other words, those organizations have openly admitted to research organizations that they have no plans for how to identify vulnerabilities within applications, and most do not have concrete plans for how to deal with the already insecure applications they have actively deployed.

So, the applications that are being used by users in their daily lives across enterprises, governments, and in personal consumer applications are almost all, at some level, insecure. This means that sooner or later a user will interact with or leverage an application that has an inherent flaw within that will lead to some form of compromise. That compromise can come in a variety of ways, from man-in-the-middle attacks thanks to **Transport Layer Security** (**TLS**) issues, binary handling issues, password security issues, or many other potential compromise actions, all of which will lead to further security issues that introduce flaws further into that perimeter-based security approach.

While applications are essentially being built with hardcoded flaws, there is a more overt issue that plagues security practitioners: the password. The next section will delve into the basic failures that are prevalent with this oldest model of authentication and secure access that man has used.

Authentication methods failed

The password: the single most prolific means of authentication for enterprises, users, and almost any system on the planet is the lynchpin of failed security in cyberspace. Almost everything uses a password at some stage. Basically, every application that is used, as well as every VPN, and even every machine on the planet uses a password for its means of authentication, as do administrative tools and internetwork shares and firewall systems. Everything, everywhere, has a password.

While that seems like a relatively simple and useful means of implementing security via authentication, passwords are only secure if they stay unknown to those who aren't the user of that password.

Over the past half-decade, almost every major instance of repository for usernames and passwords has been breached at one time or another. In 2019, an independent researcher released a list of over 700 million known breached emails and usernames that could be combined with over 20 million compromised passwords.

Those usernames and passwords came from breach postings related to Yahoo, Equifax, OMB, Target, Home Depot, and hundreds of other instances of breaches of usernames, passwords, and authentication-related information. The **Have I Been Pwnd** or **HIBP** service claims to have more than 8 billion total records available that are the result of more than 400 worldwide data breaches.

Thanks to all those compromised credentials, there is literally a nearly 100% certainty that each person on the planet has at least one compromised account. The fact that there are not 8 billion users on the internet, and there certainly aren't 8 billion users on any one corporate system, exponentially increases the likelihood of a multitude of those credentials being viable for an exploitation operation.

Using the tactic called credential stuffing, wherein a malicious actor simply uses a brute force attack on a target system to attempt to gain access via compromised credentials is exceptionally easy for threat actors. Many applications do not limit login attempts, or if they do, simple scripts can be used to wait for the timeout to pass, which allows threat actors to continually hammer away at a target asset until a valid set of credentials is found.

The criminal underground, as well as nation state threats, are known to possess vast troves of compromised password and username sets and have been observed "in the wild" repeatedly trying to gain access to systems via those simple means. In most cases, it is nothing more than a matter of time before some set of valid credentials is found.

Over a 17-month period, the security team at Akamai, which has security intelligence assets deployed globally, recently detected over 50 billion credential-stuffing attacks against a variety of targets (Constantin, 2019). Any one of those billions of attempts could have, and in some cases did, result in access to networks and infrastructures that maintain sensitive corporate or government data. One valid credential pair out of billions of attempts and an entire enterprise perimeter begins to crumble.

Consider also the typically abysmal construction of passwords by most users. In studies published as recently as 2019, two of the most prolific passwords in use globally were "password" and "123456." SplashData, an independent data research firm, conducted a study that noted the following as the worst to use, but those worst passwords have not changed in the same study conducted annually over a period of 4 years.

Rank	2018	2017	2016	2015
1	123456	123456	123456	123456
2	password	password	password	password
3	123456789	12345678	12345	12345678
4	12345678	qwerty	12345678	qwerty
5	12345	12345	football	12345
6	111111	123456789	qwerty	123456789
7	1234567	letmein	1234567890	football
8	sunshine	1234567	1234567	1234
9	qwerty	football	princess	1234567
10	iloveyou	iloveyou	1234	baseball
11	princess	admin	login	welcome
12	admin	welcome	welcome	1234567890
13	welcome	monkey	solo	abc123
14	666666	login	abc123	111111
15	acb123	abc123	admin	1qaz2wsx

So, while users are intimately aware of the power of the password, that is, the accesses that are afforded that point of control, they continue to use those same easy-to-guess, blatantly ignorant passwords in all manner of their daily lives.

Added to the failure of users to adequately design their passwords are those other instances of failed perimeter-based security practices, namely that everything revolves around the use of a password for access and control, and that in most small and mid-size organizations those terribly insecure passwords are not blacklisted from use. As noted, even an organization as large as Equifax had "admin" as a password on networked assets.

Even members of Congress and famous media personalities have been found to be using weak and insecure authentication methods and passwords. Representative Lance Gooden of Texas, who co-sponsored a bill titled "*Cybersecurity and Financial System Resilience Act of 2019*," was seen accessing his phone during a congressional committee hearing with the passphrase "7777777." Kanye West's phone passcode was seen to be "0000000" during a televised meeting with President Donald Trump. One would think that those high-profile individuals, especially one that is literally drafting legislation for cyber security in banking, would be focused and educated on using solid passwords and authentication methods, but obviously they aren't.

Logic would suggest that if any password would be impossible to crack and composed of intricate schemas to prevent the asset misuse, it would be in the US Minuteman Nuclear Weapons program. In a 2004 memo, Dr Bruce Blair, a former Minuteman weapons officer, stated that "the U.S. **Strategic Air Command** (SAC) once intentionally set the launch codes at all Minuteman nuclear missile silos in the U.S. to a series of eight zeroes."

In 1962, President Kennedy ordered his Secretary of Defense, Robert McNamara, to have a system called **PAL**, or **Permissive Action Link**, installed on all Minuteman nuclear weapons in the US arsenal. However, thanks to the sloth of the US Air Force in implementing those controls, and a general hatred within the US Air Forces leadership for McNamara, those changes took more than two decades to be deployed.

Dr Blair said in his memo that the standard operating procedure for US Minutemen officers was to be sure that "our launch checklist in fact instructed us, the firing crew, to double-check the locking panel in our underground launch bunker to ensure that no digits other than zero had been inadvertently dialed into the panel." In other words, the weapons team was told to make sure the "00000000" passcode was hardcoded into the sequence for the command and control of the 50 Minuteman nuclear missiles.

While this did not mean that it was any easier for an inadvertent launch to occur (there are many other checks that must be performed), it does mean that a very critical component of the launch sequence for the US strategic nuclear weapons was reliant on a simple 8-digit passcode comprised entirely of zeros.

While the anecdote on the Minuteman program is slightly tangential, the point is that even in an organization as strictly structured and disciplined as the US Air Force, password management is usually a woefully inept practice. If an organization with that much power and that much responsibility can ignore a best practice in password management for 20 years, what hope does the average enterprise or user stand?

IoT devices poke holes in any perimeter

Internet of Things (IoT) devices are now some of the most prolific network-enabled assets on the planet. Over 6 billion of these devices are known to be currently connected to the internet as of 2019. All these 6 billion devices are web-enabled, app-enabled, require passwords for authentication, and are usually developed and built in nations that are known to have adversarial ties to government hacking organizations. In other words, they are guaranteed to have some level of insecurity from the day they roll off the manufacturing floor. And most, if not almost all, enterprises have some form of an IoT device in their network somewhere.

Whether it's a smart TV, smart thermostat, wireless printer, internet-enabled camera, or some other device somewhere in an enterprise, it is a certainty that an IoT device exists in that infrastructure.

The use of proprietary wireless signals and protocols within IoT devices is the main avenue of compromise for hackers and threat actors. There is a multitude of possible IoT protocols in use by a variety of manufacturers. Listed here are just two of the major protocols and their associated vulnerabilities. The list of all the potential issues with these devices is too long for any one book:

- **ZigBee** – Sniffing for key exchanges allows man-in-the-middle attacks on encryption, and renders you vulnerable to a factory reset command, resulting in the device automatically connecting to any network that is available, which could be a malicious dummy network set up to collect unencrypted transmitting data (Zillner, 2015).
- **NFC** – With the appropriate know-how, NFC can be manipulated too: launch a browser to link to a malicious website, download malware, upload personal info, make unwanted calls, or even send SMS messages.

Even newly in use wireless-controlled lightbulbs have already been noted as leaking wireless network credentials outside the boundaries of their buildings. The very nature of the devices that are now in use, and the reasons they are in use, that is, to benefit the user and make some usually menial task easier and more remotely enabled, is also what helps them to be enablers of compromise. Ease of use, over-sharing, application accessibility, and hardcoded vulnerabilities introduce gaping holes into any network in which they exist. No perimeter with an IoT device installed should consider itself secure.

Unfortunately, regardless of how weak or hardened an IoT device may be, the users that touch those tools and operate on networks are almost always never built secure. In the next section, we will analyze the issues that surround basic user education, training, and practices that make security harder to manage and nearly impossible to maintain.

You can't fix stupid, or evil

In a perfect world, no human would ever touch a network. Machines would do everything and humans would simply benefit from those interactions. Machines operate logically and solely with a focus on function. They aren't easily tricked and are not typically open to influence via social means. But, for the time being, we don't live in that science fiction world where machines do everything for us. We still have users, and those users touch our networks, and their actions and issues introduce avenues of exploitation that can cripple what might have been a secure network. We must consider the following:

- The most secure network is the one that no human ever touches. The second that a human puts their fingers onto a keyboard, the threat of compromise via human means, social engineering, phishing, and other standard methods becomes a reality. While technology is relatively binary in nature, humans are not. We are open to influence, fear, folly, and stupidity. Where a machine will simply not open an email that clearly has indications that the email originates from suspicious origins or has suspect attachments, humans might click that email, knowing that it is possibly malicious in nature, because it has a super cute picture of a kitten.

- Currently in cyberspace the overarching method for securing the human relies heavily on training individuals to recognize possibly malicious actions or activities on their network and systems. This training is usually done by a combination of phishing and online teaching materials. While in many instances the use of these training modules does show a verifiable percentage of a reduction in clickthrough rates, it only takes one user and one click to introduce an exploit into a network. No matter how well trained the users are and no matter how current the material is, in most organizations there is usually a 3 to 5 percent continual click rate on follow-on exercises. While that seems small enough and very manageable, consider that in enterprises with 500,000 users, 3 percent is a substantial number of possible exploitation entry points.

- Humans are also fallible with respect to fear and intimidation in cyberspace. In 2019, the tactics of "sextortion" came onto the worldwide scene. This tactic is simple in nature but effective. During a sextortion event, an already compromised email address, one from any of the 400-plus mega breaches, is thrown into a list by a malicious actor. That actor then uses dummy, non-traceable email accounts and sends out hundreds, or possibly thousands, of emails to potential targets. Those emails consist of something similar to the following example:

Figure 1: Example of a "sextortion" email

Source: https://nakedsecurity.sophos.com/2019/03/13/final-warning-email-
have-they-really-hacked-your-webcam/

One of the most prolific of these campaigns is affiliated with an automated email-sending botnet called Phorpiex. Researchers at CheckPoint, a cyber security firm, have estimated this sextortion email-sending botnet to average about 30,000 emails per hour. Phorpiex uses an email spam botnet that continually downloads a database of email addresses from a command and control server of previously compromised assets.

Those databases used by Phorpiex include valid leaked passwords in combination with email addresses that help to sell the scam to the end recipient. Even those individuals that have no affiliation with pornography often pay the ransom notice as they genuinely believe that there is someone monitoring their infected machine or phone. The ransom is paid in Bitcoin, and thus there is no financial means to trace the originators of the attack.

However, in recent months this attack has begun to become more targeted and malicious as the same attackers are reselling the lists of those individuals who have paid the ransom to other nefarious actors. Those other threat groups are then retargeting those same individuals, but instead of asking for Bitcoin they are asking for usernames and passwords to specific systems. Essentially, they are leveraging the stress and the higher likelihood that those individuals who paid in the past have something to hide to extort them for access to networks. Should any of those targeted individuals be a high-level executive or a system administrator with higher privileges on a network, the compromise could be cataclysmic for that organization.

While there is a potential problem if an innocuous or innocent user happens to become infected, there is a much more malevolent issue associated with a human workforce: insider threats. Malicious insiders are those individuals who have a specific motivation or reason to exploit an infrastructure from the inside. These motivations come in a variety of possible vectors from monetary, to political, and even emotional, but the potential impact that stems from an insider can have impacts that are far more significant than that of an inadvertent user click.

When an insider makes the decision to conduct a malicious action against their network or infrastructure, they are already a validated user and usually have been provided with all the tools they need to be truly damaging. Most users have some level of administrative privilege, access to network shares, intellectual property, and the specific internals of that organization.

In many cases over the last decade, insiders have been able to maneuver unhindered within infrastructures, as they are not well monitored. Edward Snowden, Bradley (Chelsea) Manning, Jason Needham, Walter Liew, Robert Hanson, and many others all were able to gather valuable data from their employer's network and later wreak havoc on those systems. Even the NSA, with all of its technical prowess and monitoring, was unable to stop an employee from taking home highly classified information.

Nghia Hoang Pho of Ellicot City, Maryland, worked at the Tailored Access Operations unit within the NSA. Pho claimed during his trial that he was taking the files home to "work after hours and earn a promotion," but still he was able to steal (albeit unintentionally, he claims) the highly protected files because of the access and trust within the network that he was provided. It is thought that his home computer was the likely exfiltration point for the Shadow Brokers leaks of NSA-level tools.

Paige Thompson did not work for Capital One when she breached their systems. She was a former employee of a small business that had done previous work in Amazon cloud infrastructure services; her employer provided those services to Capital One. She was arrested in July 2019 for the breach at Capital One that affected as many as 100 million customers. The data she pilfered from Capital One had been stored on a vulnerable Amazon server, due to the fact that its protections were misconfigured by bank cloud security administrators.

Thompson acquired access to company computer login details, stolen from open Amazon servers, or S3 buckets as they are called. She then abused the control she had gained over those cloud machines to both steal data and use their excessive processing power to mine cryptocurrency.

Thompson was overt in the motivations and nature of her insider threat operations planning and execution. She posted on an AWS related Slack channel that she needed to "get information off her servers" and on Twitter she said *"I've basically strapped myself with a bomb vest, dropping capitol one dox and admitting it. I wanna distribute those buckets I think first"* (Merle 2019).

Thompson was a talented and highly technical engineer who had intricate knowledge of both hacking and exploitation, but her actual job with her employer was never to conduct exploitation operations. For her own, still mostly unknown reasons, she decided to manipulate vulnerabilities in AWS cloud systems that would impact a multitude of different organizations and potentially millions of users.

With all that we have covered in this chapter, there are a few key lessons that we should take away, lessons that have often been learned the hard way by organizations that have fallen victim to malicious attackers exploiting the era of the Fall of the Perimeter:

- Humans are one of the weakest links in the chain that is cyber security. We are easily tricked, open to influence, and fallible by our very nature.

- As infrastructures grow larger and ever more diverse with more devices, more access, and the speed of the cloud, humans will continue to be pivot points for failure in any system wherein they can access information.

- All the training and education in the world fails when one user clicks on a link that is malicious.

- No one specific control placed singularly on a user can hope to stop a malicious insider.

All that said, without truly specialized behavioral monitoring and strategically placed security controls, users will continue to be agents of failure for any network that ignores the power they wield and the damage they can inflict.

Conclusion

The perimeter-based security model is outdated and has unequivocally failed to secure businesses and enterprises across the planet. However, it is not because the basic concept of a secure edge is a failure. It is instead the proliferation of technology combined with the interconnected nature of current infrastructures that make this approach to security so ineffective. The very connectivity that is a boon for mankind, enabling business and everyday life, is its own worst enemy. A failure within one perimeter eventually will lead to a failure in many, and on and on it goes.

While the perimeter-based model of security has proven itself inefficient and a purveyor of failure, there are now issues far beyond those high walls that will afflict cyberspace for the coming decade. The time to understand what those items are and explore how they might be used for malevolent purposes is now, before they become problems that expand beyond the bounds of any control.

In the next chapter, we will move on from detailing the failures of perimeter-based security and discuss future issues that will affect security for governments and organizations. Also in this chapter, we will point out some of the new and more innovative attack types that will emerge in the near future.

References

1. Brandom, R. (2017, October 3). *Equifax CEO blames breach on a single person who failed to deploy patch*. Retrieved from theverge. com: https://www.theverge.com/2017/10/3/16410806/equifax-ceo-blame-breach-patch-congress-testimony

2. Constantin, L. (2019, October 30). *Credential stuffing explained: How to prevent, detect and defend against it*. Retrieved from csoonline. com: https://www.csoonline.com/article/3448558/credential-stuffing-explained-how-to-prevent-detect-and-defend-against-it.html?utm_source=twitter&utm_medium=social&utm_campaign=organic

3. Government Accountability Office (GAO). (2018, August 1). *Actions Taken by Equifax and Federal Agencies in Response to the 2017 Breach.* Retrieved from gao.gov: `https://www.gao.gov/assets/700/694158.pdf`

4. Greenberg, A. (2018, August 22). *The Untold Story of NotPetya, the Most Devastating Cyberattack in History.* Retrieved from wired.com: `https://www.wired.com/story/notpetya-cyberattack-ukraine-russia-code-crashed-the-world/`

5. HPE. (2016). *Cyber Risk Report.* New York: HPE.

6. Kan, M. (2019, October 21). *NordVPN, TorGuard Hit by Hacks Involving Insecure Servers.* Retrieved from pcmag.com: `https://www.pcmag.com/news/371439/nordvpn-torguard-hit-by-hacks-involving-insecure-servers`

7. Koerner, B. I. (2016, October 23). *Inside the Cyberattack that Shocked the US Government.* Retrieved from wired.com: `https://www.wired.com/2016/10/inside-cyberattack-shocked-us-government/`

8. Ng, A. (2018, September 7). *equifaxs-hack-one-year-later-a-look-back-at-how-it-happened-and-whats-changed.* Retrieved from CNET: `https://www.cnet.com/news/equifaxs-hack-one-year-later-a-look-back-at-how-it-happened-and-whats-changed/`

9. Ponemon Institute. (2016). *The State of Application Insecurity.* New York: Ponemon Institute.

10. Schwartz, M. J. (2018, September 11). *postmortem behind the equifax breach multiple failures.* Retrieved from www.bankinfosecurity.com: `https://www.bankinfosecurity.com/postmortem-behind-equifax-breach-multiple-failures-a-11480`

11. Zillner, T. (2015). *ZIGBEE exploited, the good the bad and the ugly.* las vegas: blackhat conference.

3
Emerging Tactics and Trends – What Is Coming?

As with anything else in technology, Moore's law applies. While Moore's law was about the number of transistors in integrated circuits doubling, in most technology circles this reference simply means that things get exponentially faster at a factor that doubles with each innovation. In cyber security this is just as true and, unfortunately, it is much more dangerous. Because of the nature and the speed with which technology and its many uses are evolving, and the never-ending consumer consumption of technology-related assets, the danger in this space also is only set to increase.

In this chapter, we will discuss some of the new and more innovative threat vectors that are known today. We will delve into the realities and truths around what AI is in this market space and vector in on how technologies related therein might be leveraged for malicious purposes.

A key takeaway from this chapter is an understanding of the facts on some of the most interesting and newest technologies that are on the open market and an awareness of how those assets might be leveraged for cyber warfare or attack purposes.

Other aspects of the cyber warfare sector will be covered as well, such as:

- Autonomous vehicle security issues
- Drone security and malevolent use cases

First, let's begin by discussing the changing focus of attackers in cyberspace, who have moved over time from large, high-reward targets, such as multi-national enterprises, to smaller victims that are much more open to attack.

Attacks move downstream

In the past few decades, attackers in cyberspace, be they nation-states or criminal organizations, were typically focused primarily on targeting the larger enterprises of the world. This was because of the "bang for their buck" that they were able to achieve as they often gained millions, or at least hundreds of thousands, of records when they managed to exploit a network of that magnitude. This was fine for the attacker, as they could basically continue to target one large enterprise after another, and there was almost always an easy way to gain access. Those opportunities have somewhat dried up thanks to the efforts and investments made by those large enterprises and governments. This means that those easy, large-yield targets are now more difficult to exploit, and so the adversary has now changed their strategy and tactics to aim their efforts toward other targets. In cyberspace, this means a move from large enterprise and government exploit attempts to one where small businesses are now, and in the future, the next best target.

Small businesses make great targets for exploitation operations. They are typically understaffed, overworked, their networks and infrastructures are misconfigured, and often they are negligent in their use of technology to avert cyber threat actions. Additionally, for the threat actors, both nation-state and otherwise, these targets are often connected to larger enterprises for the purposes of contracting or even technical support.

This gives the nefarious actor a means of access should they find a vulnerability or something that can be exploited on one of those unprotected networks. Yet again, the nature of the interconnected infrastructure that is in use lends itself to enabling exploitation, as a failure with one network becomes a failure with many.

According to the Verizon **Data Breach Investigations Report (DBIR)**, roughly 43% of breaches in 2019 involved small businesses (Verizon, 2019). Of that 43%, most attacks – nearly 60% – were the result of either phishing or the attackers using already-compromised credentials (Verizon, 2019). An interesting corollary to those data points is that an additional study on the ineffective nature of small businesses in cyber defense noted that 47% of the compromises they dealt with came from either negligent employees or contractors (Mansfield, 2019). This means that simply because of the way in which these small businesses operate, via a combination of remote workers and contractors, and their reliance on email and business applications that they do not develop or manage, those businesses are ideal targets for exploitation.

A phishing attempt or simple network intrusion with exploits or tactics that would not work on the larger, more well-architected enterprises is more likely to work when aimed at a smaller business or enterprise. This gives the attacker the same ultimate benefit, as they only need a way to gain access to their ultimate target, and because of the failures that are so rife in small businesses and the connections that they have to larger enterprises, the malicious actors still win in the end.

A multitude of studies have shown data that indicates the prevalence of mismanagement and, in many cases, woeful neglect of security tooling and systems in small businesses. In one study, it was noted that while most small businesses were concerned about cyber security attacks and their potential impacts on their future, over half of those same small businesses openly admitted to allocating 0 dollars in their budget for security (Mansfield, 2019).

When asked, most small business leaders simply didn't think they are actual targets for hackers or nation state exploitation operations, as said leaders didn't think that they possessed any data that was of value to those nefarious entities. This is in spite of the fact that statistics reveal that, of those same businesses:

- 68% store email addresses
- 64% store phone numbers
- 54% store billing addresses

All of which either are or contain **Personally Identifiable Information (PII)** and would be considered valuable data by threat actors (Crane, 2019).

Additional data points collated from a variety of source material offer other insights into just how bad this problem is for those small businesses:

- Less than half report regularly upgrading software solutions
- Only a third of small businesses say they monitor business credit reports
- Only 2 out of 10 encrypt databases

For the next decade, the likely targets of opportunity for entry into larger networks will not be large enterprise networks, as they are in many cases well defended and usually at least monitored. Small businesses will be the preferred points of entry into those bigger networks, and it will be because of the way in which those small businesses conduct their typical operations, combined with the connections that exist within digital businesses of all sizes, that those exploits will succeed.

As the malicious actors and cyber warfare agents across the globe move their attacks downstream to easier, more vulnerable targets, they will also have to adapt their methods of exploitation. The variety of technologies that the average human has access to today provides the avenues from which those attacks will likely emerge. It is necessary to understand the failure points and intricacies that make those technologies vulnerable to have any hope of being better prepared.

Autonomous vehicles…Bad data, bad day

One of the newest innovations gaining in global adoption is the self-driving vehicle. Over the last few years, the autonomous vehicle has come to be a much broader global phenomenon than just that of the self-driving car. There are now autonomous tractors, helicopters, taxis, and boats – there is all manner of self-driving or self-navigating vehicles in use in almost every viable use case on the planet.

As more vehicles are made to "think" for themselves and are enhanced to further eliminate human errors and expedite movement, the likelihood that something will go awry is considered a certainty. Even organizations as large as the US Navy and the US Army have tested and fielded autonomous vehicle systems. Should a sensor or faulty input be acted upon by a weapons system, causing real physical damage as part of that attack cycle, it is possible that something very bad may happen. As those systems are further networked together and interconnected, the possibility of an exploit or manipulation of the logic that makes those systems function becomes more real as well. The day that a fatality is attributed to an autonomous system's action may not be far away.

As vehicles have become functionalized beyond their traditional purpose as a means of transport, the on-board software requirements have risen exponentially. A modern autonomous vehicle may have approximately over a hundred million lines of code directing the effective operation of up to 70 electronic control units.

To put that number into perspective, the Windows Vista operating system has about 40 million lines of code. However, that simpler operating system also has 905 known vulnerabilities listed in the **National Vulnerability Database** (**NVD**) and was exploited in the widescale WannaCry and NotPeyta ransomware cyber-attacks in 2017 (Barry Sheehan F. M., 2019).

Therefore, it is very realistic to expect that the same, if not larger, types of attacks can be leveraged against autonomous vehicles, and because of the more complex requirements within the operating system, more exploits are even more likely.

Autonomous vehicles are not much more than a few thousand pounds of metal with hundreds of sensors built into that apparatus. These vehicles use data and inputs from LIDAR, lasers, radar, cameras, and ultrasonic sensors (Jianhao Liu, 2018). In airborne or waterborne autonomous vehicles, other sensors are often present, such as altitude and depth sensors as well as a variety of others.

Those sensors typically have direct control input to the most critical of drive accessories on those vehicles. Usually, this consists of the throttle, steering, and braking systems. Obviously, those critical control systems are integral to the safe operation of those vehicles, and if any one of them is either modified or fed faulty input data, the results could be catastrophic for the operator of the vehicle or those that are in its vicinity.

Tesla's cars are probably the most well-known autonomously operated vehicles on the planet at this time. A Tesla requires inputs from a variety of data points and sensors spread out across the vehicle. In total, the vehicle has over 30 sensors just to help it drive on its own. With that many sensors, most users think that the car is basically crashproof. However, this has proven to be untrue repeatedly.

In 2016, a Tesla made flawed autonomous driving decisions based on its analysis of a tractor trailer ahead of the car. Thanks to the vehicle's logic making an incorrect decision, the car barreled into the tractor trailer, killing the driver. Again, in 2018, a Tesla running on autopilot made a faulty driving decision based on its analysis of a fire truck parked at an angle in the road in front of the vehicle. This time, the vehicle judged the distance incorrectly and increased its speed until it slammed into the fire truck.

It has been noted in follow-on investigations by the National Transportation Safety Board, or NTSB, that the reason for these types of crashes with the Tesla is because the car does not do well with vehicles that suddenly stop in the road in front of the car. This is for a few rather specific reasons, such as:

1. Radar is better at tracking moving objects than those that are stopped (which is problematic as stops often occur suddenly in traffic situations).

2. Radar sees stalled vehicles, but because the radar system only has a rough idea of where the radar signal returns are coming from, it can be confused. It gets returns from everything else on the road at the same time – guardrails, signs, bridges, road debris, and more – all of which are stationary on the Earth. When it gets a radar return from a stopped vehicle, the vehicle can have trouble distinguishing a dynamic input from other dynamic and stationary inputs. The vehicle can't stop every time it receives an input that is possibly indicative of an object in the road. If that were the case, it would stop every 6 inches for every pebble or stick on the road. The logic in the "brain" of the vehicle must be more decisive and discerning.

3. In a special case, where a truck or vehicle was tilted in its road position, it is possible that the radar signal returning from that object back to the Tesla's sensors would be weaker than usual because of the angle of offset. This could cause an incorrect decision to occur.

4. Cameras on the car are there to see the road and the objects on it. The car's computer vision is constantly trying to recognize and differentiate those items from others as it drives down the road. Those cameras also function more optimally if those objects are moving as well. The way that the cameras work is partially by learning from large numbers of tagged pictures of cars and trucks that are fed into its visual data backend. Those cameras might have a problem recognizing a vehicle, especially at night or in rain or fog, because the image data stores may not have an image that correlates to that specific situation or vehicle.

5. Some autonomous cars do not use a stereo camera (or binocular vision). These types of cameras are better at distance views and should be better able to identify a stopped vehicle with more time for a response action. Tesla is not known to use stereo cameras.

Many autonomous vehicles now rely on ultrasonic sensors for proximity alarms and alerts. Those sensors are vulnerable to jamming and exploitation. The way that those sensors work is that they emit an ultrasonic frequency – sometimes a pulse, other times a steady wave – outward into space. As that sound wave bounces off objects, it reverberates back to the sensor. A calculation is performed by the logic internal to the vehicle and decisions are made. This seems like a relatively foolproof method of determining the distance from an object, but if any of those processes are interrupted or corrupted, this process goes awry.

Attacks on ultrasonic components or processes can be achieved with something as simple as jamming the signal or even just spoofing a faulty reverberation back to the sensor. Researchers have shown that injecting specific tones in the 40 to 50 kilohertz range is enough to cause a denial of service and essentially blind the sensor (Jianhao Liu, 2018). In their research, the team found that this attack worked on 8 different models, including models from Ford, Volkswagen, Audi, and others. The researchers were even able to modify the pulse return at those frequencies to distort the minimum and maximum feedback data points to the sensor. This could cause a vehicle that is relying on those inputs to either stop too far away or not stop in time, based on the inputs it receives.

Another vulnerable sensor in autonomous vehicle applications is the **millimeter wave radar**, or **MWR**. The purpose of the MWR is like that of acoustic sensors, but MWR sensors are much better at the long-range sensing of objects, at up to 300 meters in many instances. MWR sensors do this by emitting a pulse of electromagnetic energy that bounces off objects in the distance. This occurs thanks to modulation in amplitude that is achieved by the sensor.

These sensors typically operate in one of two frequency bands: either at 24 gigahertz, or in the 77 gigahertz range (Barry Sheehan F. M., 2019). It has been discovered by hackers that by injecting electromagnetic energy at the same frequency but with slightly higher power settings, these sensors can be tricked into reading faulty data. MWR is usually the main sensor used by autonomous vehicles for automatic cruise control and lane-change sensing. Were one of these sensors to receive faulty data inputs, the car would either sense an object that is not there and slam on the brakes, or it might accelerate into the vehicle in front of it.

A final attack type on autonomous vehicles focuses on their camera systems. Autonomous vehicles rely heavily on image input and analysis to make decisions as they navigate. A simple "hack" of those camera systems requires only a well-aimed laser. During the Blackhat conference in Las Vegas in 2018, a team of white hat hackers used a common laser pointer aimed directly at the lens for a common camera that is used in autonomous vehicles and blinded the vehicle. Although the vehicle still thought it was "seeing" the road in front of it, in truth it was blinded, and the sensing system could not make heads nor tails of the images presented to it. The vehicle was confused and blinded but continued to maneuver down the road – a dangerous gambit for sure.

Autonomous vehicles are a boon for humanity, no doubt about it. But those vehicles are not much more than a combination of sensors feeding a computer that is coordinating huge amounts of data all while rocketing down the road, or across the water, or through the air, at significant speed. Should any infidelities in those data inputs occur, something will go wrong in the calculations and that vehicle can quickly become a destructive force.

While autonomous vehicles with their security issues are still somewhat restricted in their adoption, the general consensus is that we must collectively be working to make those systems more secure. Drones, on the other hand, are already everywhere and in use in nearly every industry one can think of. The rush to push drones into production, however, introduced a variety of security issues and design flaws that have left them open to exploitation and uses far beyond their originally intended purposes.

Drones...Death from above

Drones are everywhere now. They deliver packages, resupply submarines, and can even deploy medical equipment in an emergency. They are used to map out pipelines, find holes in roofs, and they travel the railways measuring intricate variations in the configurations of steel rails for safety purposes. The applications for these flying computers are limitless.

While the potential use cases of drones are many, so too are the potential threats they represent. Drones are not much more than flying minicomputers. They are composed of systems that enable flight, autonomously or manually, and have intricate control software and capabilities. Military-grade drones are a different story as they have their own internal power plants and are often built to be more resistant to common attack vectors. However, even those drones designed and built with military applications in mind have been compromised in several notable instances.

In December of 2011, an American RQ-170 Sentinel **unmanned aerial vehicle (UAV)** was captured by Iranian forces near the city Kashmar, a northern city in Iran. While there was no real way to prove exactly how the drone was brought down, news coverage and expert analysis of the wreckage indicated that no damage indicative of anti-aircraft or missile impact was visible. Therefore, it was plausible that the Iranian cyber warfare division had in fact been the group who had exploited the drone into crashing. The Iranian government announced that the UAV was brought down by its cyber warfare unit, which had managed to exploit the aircraft's control and navigations systems and safely land it. While the US officials argued that this was not possible or likely, 2 years later, Iranian officials released footage they claimed came from that RQ-170 stealth drone. That footage showed the drone coming in for a controlled landing at the Kandahar base.

In July of 2018, the research firm Recorded Future had interactions with a vendor on a dark web marketplace who claimed to be selling detailed schematics and documents on the US Air Force Reaper Drone.

Through relatively benign open source methods, the hacker said he had obtained access to a computer of an Air Force Captain who was stationed at Creech Air Force Base in Nevada. The hacker also claimed that he then stole Reaper maintenance course books and a list of airmen assigned to controlling the drone. Those specific documents are not highly classified, but they could be used to assess technical capabilities and weaknesses in one of the most technologically advanced drones that is active in covert and combat missions across the globe.

As far back as 2009, hackers were able to access drone feeds from highly specialized drones that were covering the war in Iraq (Macaskill, 2009). For less than one hundred dollars' worth of expense, hackers were able to intercept drone feed video from CIA observation drones in near-real time. The software used was built by a Russian developer and was titled Skygrabber. The setup required nothing but a PC, a satellite dish, a satellite modem, and the Russian Skygrabber software. Because of the terrain issues in those operational locales, namely Iraq and Afghanistan, the CIA drones often lost line-of-sight communications with their controllers.

To avoid this loss of communication, the drones would then switch to satellite-based communications for guidance and control. But for some unknown reason, those satellite communications were not encrypted, and the data feeds transiting that communication medium were open to interception to anyone who could find the proper frequency (Gaylord, 2009). It would not be until a follow-on special force's operation where an insurgent's laptop was collected, over a year later, the hacked drone feeds were discovered. During that time this flaw in the drone communication system allowed insurgents and terrorists to change their tactics and plot their moves based on the drone's video feed. Due to a flaw in planning combined with vulnerable technologies and run-of-the-mill open source hacking, one of the planet's most powerful nation's primary tools for reconnaissance was exploited for less than the cost of a new computer.

Between October 2014 and February 2015, 17 nuclear plants were flown over in France. Commercial drones have invaded the protected air space over the US Capitol building and have crashed on the White House lawn.

Fortunately, those stories had harmless endings. Commercial drones are just devices that are equipped with autonomous features such as altitude stabilization, take-off, and landing. These drones can also obey remote orders to accomplish various tasks such as mapping, surveillance, and search or tracking operations. The usability and computers that command these devices are what make them so vulnerable to exploitation.

Commercial drones are just as insecure as the military kind, often even more so. Security is not a priority consideration during the development process; in most cases, it is an afterthought at best. A variety of instances provide evidence of this. In commercial drones, exploitation is most done via attacks on the controller WiFi or its wireless systems. WiFi is the common interface for most commercial drones that are present on the market. It functions as an interface between the controller and the medium, wherein the data and video are exchanged with the drone and the ground. The most prolific drones in the commercial space are Parrot's Bebeop and the DJI Mavic drone, both of which rely almost entirely on WiFi communications. This means that if the attacker is familiar with common wireless hacking or exploitation techniques, they have an easy target in the drone itself. In other words, because these drones are basically flying computers with constant WiFi connections, they are just as exploitable as any normal computer that is using wireless protocols. However, a drone can become a physically moving and possibly kinetically employed weapon if that communication were to be overtaken and the drone's command and control were modified for purposes outside of its original intent.

Take, for instance, an attack on the AR Drone 2.0, one of the most prolific commercial drones on the market. When powered on, the AR Drone 2.0 basically becomes its own wireless **access point (AP)**. This AP is then connected to by the operator via a smartphone. That new AP is easily identifiable as ardrone_2 followed by a random number that the computer generates. In its default configuration, it offers no encryption or authentication and is open to exploitation if it has power.

Using a USB WiFi card and a small antenna, it is easy to demonstrate an attack on this common drone. The steps to demonstrate a simple attack are as follows:

1. Power on the drone
2. Fly it for 5 to 10 seconds
3. The new AP ardone_(something) will show up as an available AP
4. Remote to the new AP network via a terminal on a computer (the default gateway is `192.168.1.1`; telnet is commonly open and requires no authentication depending on the model)
5. Explore the filesystem via common commands

That's it!

While there is not much in that specific example of what could possibly be done against that drone, one can imagine the possibilities. Everything from forcing the drone to land, changing its GPS location, or any other manner of command is potentially possible. Adding to the issues with a singular drone being overtaken and surreptitiously commanded would be to use a drone against other drones to conduct malicious operations.

In 2013, researcher Samy Kamkar demonstrated Skyjack. Skyjack is an open source contribution that could be used to build a drone capable of autonomously hacking other drones in flight. What Mr. Kamkar's GitHub states is that with his code base and a few hardware add-ons, one can build a "drone engineered to autonomously seek out, hack, and wirelessly take full control over any other drones within wireless or flying distance, creating an army of zombie drones under your control" (Kamkar, 2017).

His Skyjack drone simply detects the WiFi signal transmitted by a target drone. It then injects specific protocol WiFi packets into the target's connection. This series of WiFi injections will de-authenticate or disconnect the drone from its actual controller.

Then the target drone will seek to reconnect and because the Skyjack drone has a stronger connection and wireless signal. The target drone will then authenticate itself to the Skyjack drone. Once connected, the Skyjack drone can then send commands to the hijacked drone. This can all be done from the ground, or by using a normal Linux box and Kamkar's code connected to the drone in flight (Kamkar, 2017).

Kamkar's attack scenario also uses an open source WiFi tool, Aircrack-ng, to help find target drones at an extended range. Those drones are found by looking for specific MAC addresses that are registered to Parrot, the company that makes the small drones. The range of the Skyjack drones is limited only by the range of the WiFi card, but it is possible to extend that coverage with a powerful WiFi adapter called the Alfa AWUS036H, which can be procured from any reseller, such as Amazon.com. This adapter produces 1000mW of power and extends the range coverage of the attack drone exponentially.

Using that publicly available drone exploitation tooling could allow a malicious user to continually target and exploit drones as they are in operation. With enough of those drones under malevolent command, the possibilities of an attack are very real. A swarm of hacked drones could be used to fly in front of an oncoming airliner, or could simply be used to crash into a stadium of attendees in order to cause chaos and death.

Beyond exploitation specifically, drones are now being used as weapons of choice by terrorist organizations in the Middle East. ISIS is well documented as using technology for both propaganda and kinetic purposes. ISIS has made extensive use of drones, for offensive, defensive, and intelligence collection purposes. Additionally, ISIS used its drones' video collection capabilities to document attacks by suicide bombers in order to disseminate media propaganda to YouTube, Facebook, Twitter, and other outlets.

In October of 2018, an Israeli Special Forces unit raided an ISIS safehouse in the Idlib region of Syria. Inside of that facility, several Mavic DJI drones were found (The MEIR AMIT Intelligence and Information Center, 2018).

One of the first documented uses of a drone for offensive kinetic purposes was discovered in 2016, when an **improvised explosive device (IED)** was attached to a small quadcopter drone. That drone strike killed two Kurdish soldiers (Ware, 2019).

In 2017, ISIS was found to be operating armed drones over Mosul to combat local Iraqi Army forces. Those attacks were filmed by other ISIS drones in the area and their footage was used for propaganda purposes.

Figure 1: An IED (boxed in red) is filmed being dropped from an ISIS drone on an Iraqi army vehicle in the west Mosul neighborhood of Al-Maamoun (the photo was released by ISIS's Nineveh Province on a filesharing website, February 25, 2017)

Other examples of kinetic physical attacks are readily available. In early 2018, a Syrian rebel group sent a coordinated swarm of over a dozen modified drones to simultaneously attack a small Russian outpost. In August of that same year, there was an assassination attempt aimed at Venezuela's Nicolas Maduro using IED drones. Most recently, Iran deployed a larger explosives-laden drone against Saudi oil facilities, causing millions of dollars of damage and significant revenue losses.

The use of drones for these purposes shows the power that they can have, should they be used for malicious or nefarious purposes. It is not hard to imagine a scenario wherein a hacked drone could be overtaken, landed, fitted with a small bag of volatile fluids (for example, the components for napalm), and then launched toward a facility or public event. No ignition source would be needed for such a mixture, and upon crashing at high speed it would ignite and cause death and harm to those in the immediate vicinity. This could, of course, be made substantially worse if a group of drones were used and coordinated to conduct the same type of attack on a chosen target.

Conventional military groups are also deciphering how to use small drone technology to conduct kinetic strike attacks. The Russian version of the US **Defense Advanced Research Projects Agency (DARPA)**, the Advanced Research Foundation, has been noted as testing and researching this topic. Their version, tentatively dubbed Flock-93, is a drone swarm composed of essentially 100 small drones, each fitted with 5.5-pound explosive warheads (Atherton, 2019).

The aim of this swarm of drones is for it to be launched and commanded by conventional infantry forces that would direct the swarm toward a target within a range of roughly 90 miles. These small drones carry a minimal radar cross signature and would likely be missed or misidentified by radar defenses as birds. Upon reaching their target area, the drones would descend in a coordinated formation to destroy their target. Each individual drone would have the capability to lead the swarm should a lead drone be destroyed or rendered unusable. Interestingly, the Russian developers of this project claim that their thoughts for the swarm were inspired by the terrorist use of drones in the battlefields of Syria and Iraq.

The US military is also developing this type of capability. In a recent demonstration, DARPA showed a coordinated drone swarm conducting a systematic tactical analysis of a combat area and then cordoning off the resulting threat area (Peters, 2019).

This demonstration was focused on reconnaissance and mapping a threat area to help ground forces find a target, but it could just as easily be used to conduct a tactical strike. All that would be needed would be to fit the drones with weapons systems. The US Army, in conjunction with DARPA, has a dedicated project called **offensive swarm-enabled tactics (OFFSET)** devoted solely to figuring out how a drone swarm of up to 250 drones could be used by small units in combat areas to substantially increase the unit's effectiveness.

Drones are one of the most potentially revolutionary technologies that are present in the market. But as with any other technology, when those assets are used for purposes beyond their original intention, things go awry. Drone technology will result in benefits for humanity, but there is also very real evidence that shows that for every potential benefit, there are also possible negative applications of these flying computers.

Singular attacks by drones or autonomous vehicles or any exploitation vector, for that matter, are old tactics. Threat actors and enemy nation-states now seek to combine their attack tools and techniques to greater impact their targets. By "packaging" their attack capabilities, threat actors can now inflict more sophisticated and damaging outcomes.

Threat actors combine tactics to optimize attack effectiveness

As a point of note, in a strict sense, there is no such thing as AI – *yet*, that is. There are very functional, focused, specific applications of mathematics combined with powerful computing backend infrastructures, but there is no true AI as of today. That term is one that is more a result of marketing spin and misunderstanding on the part of the general non-computer science population, based on movies and overhyped capabilities that simply do not exist. That being said, it does not mean that there are not a variety of very applicable uses for machine learning and powerful computational mathematics that can be leveraged for nefarious purposes.

Just as there have been massive innovations in areas such as self-driving cars, biometrics, data use, and a myriad of other applications, there are also innovations of a malicious nature in those same spaces. The AI space is no different. Innovation and exponential capability gains for the benefit of man from AI-related systems can just as easily be manipulated for malicious purposes.

The main benefits of most AI systems in use today (and that term is used loosely more for familiarity's sake, not as a statement that there is actual AI on the market) are most beneficial when they are aimed at automating repetitive manual tasks. In the cyber security industry, AI systems are typically used to help analysts in security operations centers sift through vast troves of alerts. Those AI tools are focused, math-backed applications specifically built to make human analysts better at their job. Those tools are made to make the analysts faster at finding a key point of data that might be related to a compromise or threat action within a system, and in some instances even to remediate an issue should one be found. Those tools or systems are enhancing the human's ability to act on specific determined data when a specific indicator is found that warrants a response.

Another prevalent type of AI in cyberspace is vectored at the identification of malware. Companies like Cylance have grown to billions of dollars in revenue with their applications of math-based malware identification. While there is plenty of marketing hype around this capability, what is taking place is the malware identification engine is analyzing specific indicators of a technical nature that malware has, or it might be triangulating domain and open source threat information against possible malware data, or it might be looking at past examples of malware indications and making an educated guess. Those are the main defensive applications related to AI (machine learning or ML) that are in use in the cyber security market today. With only slight modifications of those approaches, malicious actors and nation-states can weaponize those tools and approaches.

Offensive use of AI tooling can benefit malicious actors and nefarious campaigns. Social networks, especially Twitter and Facebook with their volume of access to extensive personal data, bot-friendly APIs, user-related syntax, and prevalence of easily modified and shortened links, are the great arenas for spreading machine-generated malicious content.

In the days immediately following Donald Trump's election in 2016, Russian-affiliated operators launched targeted Twitter campaigns aimed directly at the US **Department of Defense (DoD)** employees. Each of those tweets was aimed specifically at exploiting the interests and personal views or opinions of those targets. Mainly, they contained inflammatory messaging meant to incite a response from the reader that could further foment discourse on social media platforms. Even third- and fourth-link family members were targeted with the links in the tweets. This was conducted at a magnitude of over 10,000 tweets in a compressed time frame, vastly larger and much more effective than the previous manual "troll farm" attacks that the Russians had attempted in the past. Because of the specialization in the tweets and the specificity of their targeting, the malicious links within those tweets operated at a 70% click rate (Bosetta, 2018). Many of those clicks resulted in follow-on compromises of government-related networks and ransomware infections that would plague DoD-related employees for months to come.

The question herein becomes this: why would tweets be so effective and result in actual exploits against targets that were familiar with the social engineering tactics that enemy nation-states use? DoD employees are regularly trained to be aware of exactly this type of threat activity, and in many cases, they share that knowledge with their families. So why would these particular actions result in a more effective campaign by the Russian operators? The reason why this series of weaponized tweets succeeded where past exploit operations had failed because of a well-planned combination of timing, tactics, and foresight by the enemy nation state.

Thanks to the explosive spread and use of social media platforms such as Twitter, Facebook, Instagram, LinkedIn, and others, and the multitude of data breaches that have spilled users' personal information across the web, the need for malicious actors to conduct internal discovery and mapping of potential human targets has been nullified. In the past, in order to discover specific personal data or a user's persona-related information that might be of use, a hacker or nation state had to actively exploit a target network. Then that malicious actor would have to extract the pertinent information and build a profile for the future intended ultimate target. That required a lot of work and a lot of access and was often labor-intensive for the operators. All that information is now publicly available. And in many cases, there is much more data available openly on those public spaces than was ever stored within a corporate or government system. Everything from home addresses, drivers' licenses, medical records and information, pictures, biometric data, and all manner of data needed to build an effective targeting profile are easy to obtain for those who know how to look.

Data collection for the purposes of targeting is made even easier thanks to the availability and access afforded to developers and users via the **application programming interfaces** (**APIs**) of most social media sites. A simple search to find a tool on GitHub that helps with scraping LinkedIn's API for data that would be of value yields a ready-built code set that can be downloaded by anyone.

`https://github.com/linkedtales/scrapedin` works on the 2019 version of LinkedIn.com and can be downloaded and configured by anyone with a basic level of knowledge of API use. Other tools and frameworks such as Recon-NG and a variety of tools within the Kali Linux VM series are all built for web scraping and gathering intelligence via social media platforms. Using those tools or highly specialized ones that function similarly will bring in a collection of data that can help with targeting for spear phishing and social media exploitation.

The data collected during that reconnaissance phase can be combined with tailored AI (ML) applications to generate very realistic online personas, complete with picture profiles. Using that approach, a threat actor could simply go to `https://thispersondoesnotexist.com/` and use the ML engine to generate a realistic profile picture for a person that does not exist on this planet. That picture is combined with a specialized and targeted online persona that shares similar likes, dislikes, and other related online profile information to form a weaponized profile.

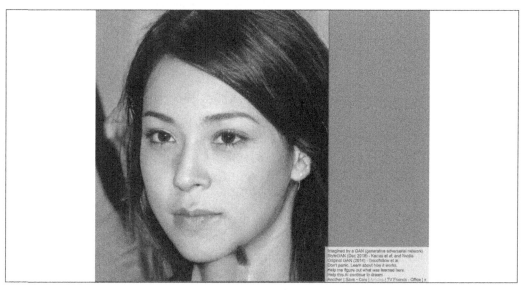

Figure 2: A user profile picture generated by the author from www.thispersondoesnotexist.com

Social media profiles with pictures that profess to share similar interests and work histories to those of the target are exponentially more likely to be interacted with than those without. Social profiles that have more followers (500 is the magic number on LinkedIn.com) and related connections are also much more likely to be interacted with when they share a file or send a message (Bosetta, 2018). Again, this too can be automated and enhanced with the use of specialized AI (ML) tooling. All the connections and followers can be bots or fake users. As well as the hit-or-miss real-world user connections, numbers bolster the veracity of the profile.

Additionally, as one targeted profile begins to "work" or land end user interactions, the method that helped make those connections realistic and that resulted in the successful attack can be further automated in a cycle of attack automation.

AI and its impact on the world is still being deciphered. It is a new medium and one that many experts think we are not collectively ready for. In opposition to that, the threat that an old medium can bring to bear continues to evolve. Ransomware is not really much more than a manipulation and weaponizing from the days of computer viruses, but it is now one of the most significant threat tactics that is present on the planet.

Ransomware goes mobile

Security experts have been warning the industry and the public for years that smartphones are the next big target that is due for a major cyberattack. Much like how attacks on PCs became commonplace back in the 1990s, in the coming decade, mobile phones are the next most likely target. They are generally unprotected by antivirus software, usually unmanaged, excessively powerful, and contain massive amounts of valuable information. Targeted phishing combined with ransomware as a means of exploiting the target is the most likely combination of threat tactics that will be employed.

Indications that this scenario will play out in this manner have already emerged. In the summer of 2014, a large number of user's mobile devices, iPads, and iPhones, located in Australia and the UK, reported that they had been subject to a mobile device attack that held their Apple devices and accounts hostage until they paid a $100 ransom.

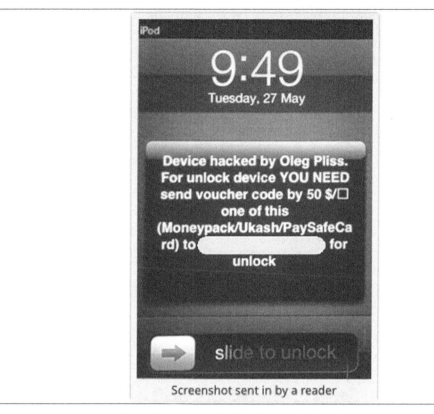

Figure 3: A screenshot of the iPhone ransomware message

Android phones have also already been targeted in a similar fashion. Scarepackage emerged on the scene in the late summer of 2014. This Android-specific ransomware exploit infected users via fake apps on the Android store. Those apps appeared to be Adobe Flash applications that were disguised as antivirus apps that enticed the user to download them to "secure" their Android device.

Victims of the scam would then receive the following message:

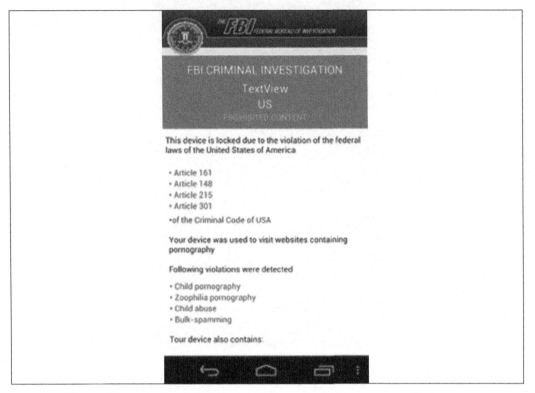

Figure 4: "You are guilty of child porn, child abuse, zoophilia or sending out bulk spam.
You are a criminal. The Federal Bureau of Investigation has locked you out of your phone and the
only way to regain access to all your data is to pay us."

The device would remain locked and did not allow the user to navigate away from that screen, even if the phone was restarted. The only way for a user to regain control of their device was to pay several hundred dollars in a MoneyPak voucher.

Another Android ransomware strain was discovered in the fall of 2014. This version, dubbed Android.Locker.38 by researchers, did not just lock the device once, it locked the device twice. The attack spread by using social engineering. It did this by disguising itself as a system update for Android users' phones' operating systems. When the user downloaded the app, the app would ask for administrative rights to the user's phone operating system.

The malicious app would then be installed with those high privileges. A message was then sent to a remote server that the infection was successful so that the cyber criminals would be prompted to continue their actions.

The threat actor would then install a feature on the infected phone that was actually a second lock function. This feature would activate when the user tried to remove the first ransomware infection on the phone. The second command to lock the device was sent through the criminal command and control server and through SMS text. That second stage of the attack would put the phone into a standby screen (screen lock) mode and then show a second fake warning that all files would be erased if the user did not pay the ransom. When the user tries to use their phone to make a choice to avoid that warning, the ransomware would then activate the lock screen again. Following that, the malicious software would also launch a feature that would require the user to enter their password to disengage the lock screen. Regardless of the user's actions, the ransomware would enable its own function and sets its own administrator password on the phone: "12345." By doing this, the threat actors ensured that the infected phone or tablet would remain locked until the ransom was paid.

There are other versions of mobile device ransomware that have shown up on the market. LockerPin is a particularly nasty type of ransomware for mobile devices, which, after installation, resets the device PIN of a phone. This is done to lock the user completely out of the device and ransoms the access to the device itself, not just the data on the device. The ransomware then requires 500 dollars to unlock the phone and issue a new PIN. However, because the PIN is being reset randomly by the malicious software, there is no way for anyone to actually know what the new PIN will be. The device is essentially "bricked." Even when the ransom is paid, the attackers might not give the user back the PIN or access to the device.

This particular ransomware is spread via a pornographic website that prompts the user to download an app called Porn Droid in order to have full access to the content. The only way to regain access to the device is to do a full factory reset to the locked device, which removes all currently installed data and applications.

Contrary to the majority of ransomware, this variant does not really deliver on its promise to fix the "bricked" device if a ransom is paid. This ransomware simply locks the user out of the devices in the hopes that the infected user will pay the ransom, while the ransomware has no plans, or capability, to remediate the issue. The LockerPin attack is downloaded and installed from third-party websites, warez forums, and torrents. Those sites operate outside of the Google Play Store.

Part of the reason for the success of these new mobile-specific attacks is due to the rapid proliferation of mobile applications masquerading as consumer applications in app stores. According to the Mobile Threat Landscape report by RiskIQ, the number of blacklisted apps rose by nearly 20% in early 2019. Research suggests that the main reason for this is because of the variety of non-specific application stores and the growth of mobile application developers in the industry. Similarly, that same group of researchers noted that about 25% of the over 4 million apps that were downloaded in a single quarter were known malicious apps that had been on industry blacklists. The growth and use of third-party app stores and the focus of threat groups on targeting mobile devices are indicative of the fact that threat actors and APT groups will manipulate those easier targets and continue to innovate in and around mobile devices and app stores.

DDoS reaches weapons-grade refinement

Denial of service (DoS) attacks, or **distributed denial of service (DDoS)** attacks, are not new to the realm of cyber security. DDoS attacks have been active in the cyber security realm since 1999, when a computer at the University of Minnesota was attacked by a group of roughly 100 machines that were infected with a piece of malware known as *Trin00* (MIT Technology Review, 2019). That bit of malicious code caused those disparate machines, all running on separate networks, to coordinate sending large amounts of packetized data traffic toward that university endpoint, resulting in a network crash.

It took university administrators a few days to get the systems and the university network back online – not exactly an end-of-days attack, but it would be an early indicator of what was to come. In the months that followed that attack, cyber-criminal operators and nation-states took on that attack strategy and began to leverage openly available machines to generate massive packetized data streams and aim that barrage of electrons at targets of their choosing. Over the decades since then, DDoS attacks have become a 2 billion-dollar-a-year industry on the cyber underground (MIT Technology Review, 2019). Hackers and threat groups sell their DDoS tools and services to nefarious agents and users that extort victim sites for exorbitant sums of money.

That 1999 attack involved roughly 100 computers, a laughable number by today's weaponized DDoS standard. In the Mirai botnet, DDoS attacks involving hundreds of thousands of machines operating in nearly every country on the planet sent such a volume of data to targets that entire national-level subnets were affected. In some instances, the Mirai botnet DDoS attack exceeded 1 terabyte per second, or TPS size (Cloudflare, 2017). Mirai, however, took a slightly different tactic to gain its efficacy and power. Mirai did not rely on host computers and typical endpoints to spread its coverage and elevate its traffic-generating capacity. It instead used **Internet of Things (IoT)** devices like cameras, routers, air quality monitors, vending machines, and even traffic signals to escalate its capability to generate packets. Mirai was so well versed at finding open ports and vulnerable IoT devices that by the end of its first day in operation, the bot army was growing by a factor of 2 every 80 minutes (USENIX, 2017).

Mirai is probably the most directly applicable reference of the coming state of DDoS weapons in that it was a purpose-built self-propagating worm combined with a targeted attack capability. The botnet was composed of two different modules: first, a replication module, and second, an attack module. The replication module functioned by randomly scanning the internet, probing for devices that were communicating on standard IoT-based ports, specifically ports 23 and 2323.

The replication module then would infect the machines, not by some malevolent type of engineered malware, but by simply guessing one of a combination of 64 possible standard usernames and passwords. Luckily for the makers of Mirai, hundreds of thousands of IoT devices, mainly routers and IP-enabled cameras, had been installed at client sites and no one had ever changed the factory administrator usernames and passwords. So, by simply brute-force guessing, and because those IoT devices did not limit failed attempts, sooner or later the combination would be correct, and the device would grant the attacker administrative access.

Next would be the attack module. After access had been obtained by the replication module, the worm would take command of the IoT asset, reach back to the command and control server of the botnet, and install an executable that contained the attack capabilities. Mirai's attack module was elegant enough to obfuscate the running process by following the attack modules' installation with a string of random text, and by deleting the previously downloaded binary (USENIX, 2017). To establish full control and optimal attack capability on the IoT device, the attack module would also shut off other processes that were competing for compute resources on the device.

Once installation and configuration were complete, Mirai was ready to conduct DDoS attacks across the globe. In one instance, researchers saw that the Mirai botnet attempted over 15,000 attacks during its time in operation (Cloudflare, 2017). Targets ranged from politics-related service providers in Poland, to the website Krebs on Security in the United States, to a variety of gaming companies. Everything from Amazon.com to Minecraft and Netflix was affected as the attackers used Mirai's ability to generate packets to bring unprepared internet providers to their knees.

The spread and power of the DDoS attacks that Mirai was able to inflict took the security industry totally by surprise. The use of Mirai as a focused weapon that was sold by members of underground criminal forums was also a first for a weapon of this magnitude. Moreover, identification of the actors behind the attacks was made difficult, as almost anyone could have launched the attack once the attack code was leaked.

Anyone with Bitcoin and knowledge of the TOR network could gain access to the Mirai infrastructure and launch attacks against targets of their choosing. There have been a few arrests related to this particular attack, but there has never been a real answer as to who created this weapon. The only thing that stopped this global threat was a singular researcher, a 20-something-year-old self-described "malware nerd," who managed to derail the propagation of the attack by interrupting its use of vital connections as it crawled across the globe.

Mirai was essentially commoditized DDoS weaponry that had exploited basic failed security practices to build a juggernaut for packetized attacks. The ease of use and massive impact that this type of attack exhibited made it a next-generation attack weapon that was custom built for underground and criminal threat activity.

Conclusion

Time is not on the side of the defender in cyberspace. Threat actors are not limited by laws or compliance requirements; they have no bounds on the ways in which they might operate and innovate to beat the good guys. For them, everything and everyone is a potential asset for exploitation. The longer that enterprises and governments wait to update their defenses and embrace new optimal infrastructures and tactics to combat these coming threats, the worse things will get. Adversaries at both the nation state level and in cyber-criminal groups are just as innovative, in some cases more so, than defenders. Each new device, user, account, or technology that is offered to the market becomes an additional weapon that can be used for malicious purposes.

In the next chapter, we'll focus upon one of the emerging trends that we mentioned in this chapter. We'll take a look at the potential for threat actors to utilize social media in order to influence opinion in order to achieve certain ends.

References

1. Atherton, K. D. (2019, November 5). *Flock 93 is Russias Dream of a 100 strong drone swarm for war*. Retrieved from c4isrnet.com: `https://www.c4isrnet.com/unmanned/2019/11/05/flock-93-is-russias-dream-of-a-100-strong-drone-swarm-for-war/`

2. Barry Sheehan, F. M. (2019, June). *Connected and autonomous vehicles: A cyber-risk classification framework*. Retrieved from sciencedirect.com: `https://www.sciencedirect.com/science/article/pii/S096585641830555X`

3. Barry Sheehan, F. M. (2019). *Connected and autonomous vehicles: A cyber-risk classification framework*. Chicago: ScienceDirect.

4. Bosetta, M. (2018). *The Weaponization of Social Media: Spear Phishing and Cyber Attacks on Democracy*. New York: jstor.org.

5. Cloudflare. (2017, December 14). *Inside Mirai the Infamous IoT Botnet a Retrospective Analysis*. Retrieved from cloudflare.com: `https://blog.cloudflare.com/inside-mirai-the-infamous-iot-botnet-a-retrospective-analysis/`

6. Gaylord, C. (2009, December 17). *Skygrabber is Hacking Military Drones too Easy*. Retrieved from csmonitor.com: `https://www.csmonitor.com/Technology/Horizons/2009/1217/SkyGrabber-Is-hacking-military-drones-too-easy`

7. Jianhao Liu, C. Y. (2018). *Can You Trust Autonomous Vehicles: Contactless Attacks against Sensors of Self-Driving Vehicles*. Tokyo: pacsec.jp.

8. Kamkar, S. (2017, November 21). `skyjack`. Retrieved from github.com: `www.github.com/samyk/skyjack`

9. Macaskill, E. (2009). *Skygrabber American Drones Hacked*. Washington DC: theguardian.com.

10. Mansfield, M. (2019, August 22). *Cyber Security Statistics Small Business*. Retrieved from smallbiztrends.com: `https://smallbiztrends.com/2017/01/cyber-security-statistics-small-business.html`

11. MIT Technology Review. (2019, April 18). *The First DDoS Attack Was 20 years Ago. This is What We've Learned.* Retrieved from technologyreview.com: `https://www.technologyreview.com/s/613331/the-first-ddos-attack-was-20-years-ago-this-is-what-weve-learned-since/`

12. Peters, J. (2019, August 9). *DARPA drones robots swarm military test.* Retrieved from theverge.com: `https://www.theverge.com/2019/8/9/20799148/darpa-drones-robots-swarm-military-test`

13. The MEIR AMIT Intelligence and Information Center. (2018). *ISIS's use of drones in Syria and Iraq and the threat of using them overseas to carry out terrorist attacks.* Jerusalem: `www.terrorism-info.org.il`.

14. USENIX. (2017). *Understanding the Mirai Botnet.* Vancouver: USENIX.

15. Ware, J. (2019, September 24). *Terrorist groups, artificial intelligence, and killer drones.* Retrieved from warontherocks.com: `https://warontherocks.com/2019/09/terrorist-groups-artificial-intelligence-and-killer-drones/`

4

Influence Attacks – Using Social Media Platforms for Malicious Purposes

The power of influence has now moved well beyond just getting folks to like a picture on Instagram or a cooking show on YouTube. Influence can now be weaponized and used to manipulate a narrative that could have national implications. The nation state attackers of the world are aware of this and are actively engaged in leveraging these seemingly innocuous social engagement systems as part of their attack strategy.

In this chapter, we will discuss some of the lesser known methods of influence attacks that are active today. In this analysis, we will detail some very real attacks that have already taken place and provide examples of the impact that these approaches can have on the populace:

- What has changed within the cyber warfare landscape as part of the evolution of attack vectors using social media platforms.

- What has already happened to show the power that influence attacks can have on targeted populations.

- How this will be used by nation state attackers in the future.

First, let's begin by providing an insight into what the state of this space is in the current cyber context.

The new cyber onslaught

For decades, analysts in the defense and intelligence communities have warned leaders and lawmakers of the risks of a potential cyber Pearl Harbor scenario. Recently, the focus in this space has been on numerous attacks where large-scale kinetic strikes took place at critical infrastructure components, shutting the nation's electric grid down, or that disrupted the very fabric of American society. These were common yet pervasive themes that permeated the news cycle. The fear of a widespread cyber-based attack lingered about the media as more and more exploits and data breaches became common occurrences. Most of the American populace did not understand the technical details of how, or why, these attacks continued unabated. Experts noted that the enemies of the United States were actively targeting vulnerable power generation stations, financial markets, transportation networks, academic institutions, and communications systems as part of this new type of warfare.

While those attacks were certainly noteworthy and were indicative of the future state of cyber warfare, they were the sledgehammer that was being struck against the anvil of cyber infrastructure. Those attacks were a neverending onslaught, but they were nonetheless only successful when the adversary found a flaw or weak point in those architected systems. Here, victory was possible and did occur, but the effort and technological requirements that were needed to bring about those victories were extensive. In contrast to these sledgehammer attacks, 2016 saw the most elegant and surgical attack of the 2010s. This attack took the form of the so-called *influence attacks* that occurred during the 2016 US election.

In these attacks, US adversaries sought to control and exploit the ability of a social media-based trend to influence the populace and affect American interests, discredit public and private groups and institutions, and spread domestic strife at lightning speed.

Those attacks exhibit a relatively new and increasingly dangerous means of weaponizing social media and leveraging influence to further propagate these attacks.

Cyber combat is changing

The ability to command and manipulate trends and influences in social media requires few technical resources and minimal ability. Nation state and non-state actors and cyber threat groups can access streams of online data that is readily available within social media to discover points of influence of networked users within a target environment or nation. This means that now, instead of being forced to work to attack the military, infrastructure, or potentially better defended assets, cyber threat groups can now target the general population of a society.

By doing this, they can inflict specific influence on that target group's beliefs, thoughts, and even behaviors. Because of the interconnected nature of users and the public within social media platforms, the ability to spread disinformation and fear is exponentially increased, literally at the speed of a "like."

The evolution of social media into a tool of cyber warfare is not surprising. According to Douhet's analysis of the command of airspace as a key capability in warfare (Douhet, 1942), "technology must adapt itself to the needs of war, and not the needs of technology." Social media technology evolved because of the information-age warfare actions that were taking place around 2006 with the dawn of Web 2.0. This was the catalyst that removed the "control" that only large corporate entities had over content generation and messaging and opened up the internet to all users. This dispersion of control and the new allowance that enabled users anywhere to create content instead of just consuming online material was the pivotal point at which social media and shared content began to function as tools of propaganda and warfare.

Mankind's own inherent need for connectivity and our social nature has basically helped to facilitate the current state of massive online virtual networking. Traditional forms of media have acquiesced in this war of attrition between old print media, and the new digital space has given way to a tailorable, manipulative form of communication. Nation state and cyber adversaries have moved quickly to find ways to exploit the openness of the internet and the constant drum beat of the new age internet media explosion. A variety of organizations have become extremely adept at leveraging specific tools and techniques that employ social media and online networking as tools to spread propaganda.

#Hashtag or ammunition?

A very applicable and interesting example of how the simple targeted use of social media can be leveraged by a nation state actor is in the form of the *#DraftOurDaughters* hashtag trend during the 2016 presidential election. The premise for the creation of the hashtag was somewhat bounded in truth. The Hillary Clinton campaign had a very early iteration of a possible social media campaign wherein they were working to champion a potential Clinton campaign initiative that would advocate for women of the appropriate age to register for the US Selective Service Program. The potential social media campaign never actually came to pass. It was abandoned quickly as it was thought to be too divisive.

However, within the pseudo-underground channels of 4Chan, the narrative that hackers had compromised the Clinton campaign server, which hosted their working campaign messages, was spread (Lacapria, 2016). Affiliated users and groups that were known to be in direct opposition of the Clinton for President campaign had cobbled together realistic looking tweets and imagery that would be used to manipulate the narrative around this issue.

Stronger Together #17 Anonymous (ID: [illegible]) 10/28/16(Fri)10:04:02 No.94894741 ▶ >>94895018 >>94895023 >>94895092 >>94895126 >>94895281 >>94895396 >>94895466 >>94895558 >>94895622 >>94895736 >>94896178 >>94896282 >>94896495 >>94896775 >>94896825 >>94807360 >>94897693 >>94898717 >>94898822 >>94900794

KILLARY MAKING INFOGRAPHICs
IF YOU ARE PLANNING ON MAKING MEMES READ THESE AND STICK TO THE FORMAT
KEEP THIS GOING TIL THE 8TH

>---------DOWNLOAD OFFICIAL FONT--------- from her campaign if making new meme's

https://a.hrc.onl/secretary/fonts/SharpUnity-Extrabold.ttf

>---------OFFICIAL HILLARY CAMPAIGN COLOURS --------- and Tips from a Brit:

#E4002B - red, used only for important highlights (hashtags, bold words) [90% opacity]

#00B7E9 - light blue, used for the main statements [75% opacity]

#000033 - dark blue - used for information or sentences [80% opacity]

>Avoid using too much text and always use the bold font. Usually increasing the contrast and slightly decreasing the brightness will help your background image stand out.

INCLUDE RUSSIA IN INFOGRAPHIC
INCLUDE THE IMWITHHERLOGO
INCLUDE THE ENLISTING WEBSITE
INCLUDE "Paid for by Hillary for America"

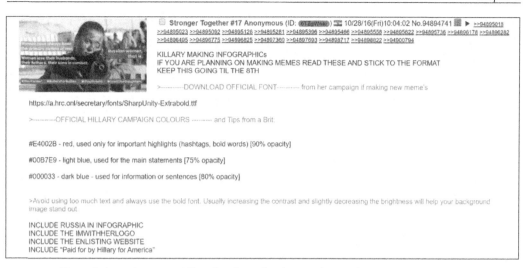

Figure 1: A user's post on 4Chan detailing what fonts, colors, and images to use to target Twitter and meme postings for the Clinton campaign

FONTS AND COLOR INFO HERE

Fonts:

https://a.hrc.onl/secretary/fonts/SharpUnity-Book.ttf

https://a.hrc.onl/secretary/fonts/SharpUnity-BookItalic.ttf

https://a.hrc.onl/secretary/fonts/SharpUnity-Semibold.ttf

https://a.hrc.onl/secretary/fonts/SharpUnity-SemiboldItalic.ttf

https://a.hrc.onl/secretary/fonts/SharpUnity-Extrabold.ttf

https://a.hrc.onl/secretary/fonts/SharpUnity-ExtraboldItalic.ttf

Colors:

E4002B - red, used only for important highlights (hashtags, bold words) [90% opacity]

00B7E9 - light blue, used for the main statements [75% opacity]

000033 - dark blue - used for information or sentences [80% opacity]

Figure 2: Users on Reddit posting the correct Clinton Campaign fonts and color scheme

The opposition groups used the specific texts, images, content, and fonts selectively chosen by the actual Clinton campaign for other social media management endeavors to add validity to their postings.

The opposition groups used the same images, fonts, and content from the real campaign and then pillaged them via the use of Google searches and Google Image analysis. Following the postings by that opposition group, there were instances of follow-on social media campaigns spread by a threat group thought to be affiliated with a known Russian social media troll group.

Around the same time that the 4Chan opposition group campaign started sharing their fake Clinton message on women in the Selective Service, the narrative from the troll group began posting their further augmented version of those sanctioned tweets in October 2016. The Twitter account `"@alishabae69"` was created in that same month and soon began posting content only related to this singular #DraftOurDaughters hashtag. The Twitter avatar for that particular account was correlated with an image of a woman named Alena Ushkova. However, the online account name for that Twitter user was Alisha Arsenault, which was a somewhat more "Americanized" name.

Figure 3: An example tweet of a user that "flipped" their vote based on a fake image and associated hashtag

A deeper analysis noted that the photograph affiliated with that avatar and the user was first noted 2 years before the Twitter account came online. A 2014 instance of that name and account were found based on Google searches. Logic suggests that the user of that account is likely to be a person not from the United States and is evidence of the likely operational involvement of a Russian-affiliated organization as part of this disinformation campaign.

Pages that include matching images

Alena Ushkova (Алёна Ушкова) | Pin by @settimamas | m18+ Alena ...
https://www.pinterest.com/pin/474215035735827826/ ▾
236 × 346 - Alena Ushkova (**Алёна Ушкова**) | Photography: ФОТОГРАФ СПБ YouLaAngel Photographer | #SimplySexy #Sexy #BlackAndWhite #Photography #Lingerie ...

Alena Ushkova (Алёна Ушкова) | Pin by @settimamas | m18+ Alena ...
https://www.pinterest.com/pin/474215035735634070/
681 × 999 - Alena Ushkova (**Алёна Ушкова**) | Photography: ФОТОГРАФ СПБ YouLaAngel Photographer | #SimplySexy #Sexy #BlackAndWhite #Photography #Lingerie ...

Alena Ushkova (Алёна Ушкова) | #Bikini | Pin by @settimamas | m18+ ...
https://www.pinterest.com/pin/474215035735634054/ ▾
236 × 346 - Alena Ushkova (**Алёна Ушкова**) | #Bikini | Pin by @settimamas | See more about LUSH and Bikinis.

Alena Ushkova (Алёна Ушкова) | Pin by @settimamas | m18+ Alena ...
https://www.pinterest.com/pin/474215035735633968/
236 × 346 - Model: **Алёна Ушкова** (Alena Ushkova) | Photographer: Andres Sivtsov .... Alena Ushkova (**Алёна Ушкова**) | #SimplySexy #Sexy #Photography | Pin by @ ...

Figure 4: "Alena Ushkova" avatar affiliations with the "alishabae69" Twitter account

Those postings also led to the creation of other follow-on hashtags such as the #dieforher, #enlistforher, #fightforher, and even #AbortForHer Twitter campaigns. Each of those modifications of the original Twitter hashtag was used by 4Chan, Reddit, and Facebook groups to sew seeds of discontent around Clinton's actual campaign messaging. Within days of the launch of the #DraftOurDaughters hashtag, the generated images and postings were trending on social media and had spread to Instagram.

On Instagram, a Russian-affiliated account tagged with the name "AngryEagle" posted hundreds of images and led to the trending of new hashtags such as the #imwithher and #strongertogether Instagram hashtags and even the #AbortForHer hashtag.

One of the more blatant images can be seen here:

Figure 5: A trending hashtag from "AngryEagle" on Instagram

The truth behind these postings is that none of them were ever actually sanctioned or approved, or even tied to the actual Clinton campaign. At no time during her campaign did Hillary Clinton ever endorse any of these messages, nor did she or her staff ever post any of these memes or images to any of her verified Twitter, Instagram, or other social media accounts.

In the past, Mrs. Clinton had voted for a bill that was both approved and had specific language within it that advocated for the inclusion of women in combat roles, but only in the case of a national emergency. And that bill, the "Draft America's Daughters Act of 2016," was later changed, and those provisions were dropped. So while candidate Clinton had in fact supported the bill and the general idea that women should be part of the Selective Service registry, she was not an advocate for women in combat, and certainly was not espousing a view that anyone should abort their child to serve in the armed forces.

Yet, because the memes, images, and postings all carried the same coordinated colors and images, and appeared to be affiliated with Mrs. Clinton's past voting record and her online presence, the postings were accepted as real by many. Her actual position on the matter was stated by her as such:

> *"I am on record as supporting the all-volunteer military, which I think at this time does serve our country well. And I am very committed to supporting and really lifting up the men and women in uniform and their families."*

Candidate Clinton was not, in fact, championing this particular initiative. She had simply voted for the measure, which would eventually be modified, but the narrative was already spun and her campaign was now affiliated to that issue.

The real "gasoline-on-the-fire" moment took place when high profile supporters of the Trump campaign began reposting and revising those bogus messages. In some instances, hundreds of thousands of shares, likes, and reposts occurred in minutes thanks to those influencer postings and followings. This led to the hashtags going viral and becoming a trend (averaging over 1,000 impressions per hour (Lacapria, 2016)) that was able to influence users on a variety of social media platforms.

Figure 6: Twitter tracking showing the viral spread of the #DraftOurDaughters hashtag

In the weeks that followed there was even a recut and modified version of an ad for feminine hygiene products that was posted to further the narrative of the Clinton campaign's desire for drafting women into the military. That narrative was pushed with a subtle combination of online video campaigns, social media propagation, and the follow-on media tie-ins that followed. In those instances, teams of either automated bots or human click farms were used by the adversary to "beat" the algorithm and push the story further into visibility. The more likes, the more looks, and the more the story grows along with the adoption of whatever message is part of that campaign.

Additionally, a video on the same YouTube channel that was reposted and reshared claimed to have comments from the Clinton campaign saying, "I want the Iranians to know that if I'm the president, we will attack Iran" (Mackey, 2016).

Figure 7: The follow-up video for the #DraftOurDaughters campaign that claimed to have comments from candidate Clinton

During this disinformation campaign, often, a single account would send tweets appearing to ally with both supporters and opponents of the Clinton candidacy. Each tweet would employ that same hashtag in order to induce a trend and help spread its virality, mainly by the increase in numbers of conversations and postings; these are the things that increase an item's views online.

Many of the tweets also included other currently trending topics to maximize views across several trends at the same time. Those images inspired more and more users to interact with the hashtag, based on the political leanings and personal beliefs of the user. But thanks to the ways in which social media works online, each discussion, argument, conversation, or reshare kept the trend going and increased its views and virality. This resulted in the trend around this hashtag spreading to a worldwide audience within hours. All of this regardless of the truth behind the events, and with no measure of fact behind the content.

While this one singular instance of a twisted narrative thanks to Twitter and social media is not the fail point in the totality of the Clinton campaign, nor was it solely responsible for Donald Trump being elected, it is worth noting the impact that this type of attack had. The fact that the tweets and social media actions were as viral as they were, combined with the constantly evolving attacks by validated users and opposition groups in the space at the time, made the campaign respond.

In having to do that, the Clinton campaign had to take time away from what should have been focused on online activities and social media engagements to counter this skewed narrative. In doing so, this meant that the campaign was not focused on winning campaign initiatives and was engaged in literally countering false news and narratives. This activity, combined with the delicate touch that is required for such controversial topics as women in the military and abortion, dragged the campaign managers far away from their intended topic areas.

Each tweet or Instagram posting was one that required a counter and forced the Clinton campaign to be constantly engaged in a game of cat and mouse on social media outlets and in the media.

Lastly, this hashtag trend proved the approach was a viable one that could impact the campaign's presence and actions, and that nation states (Russia in this instance) could reach out across international boundaries and influence the outcome of a democratic election in an adversary nation.

While it is possible to conduct these operations in a one-off manual approach, it is much easier to push the influencers that already have millions of dedicated followers to propagate the narrative. Using those already installed user groups and influencer individuals to help foment a narrative is a valid method for threat actors to vastly expand their spin. One like or comment from the right person and the story can go viral in seconds.

Influencing the influencers

Singular tweets and postings are not scalable and will not reach a wide-enough audience to influence any action or outcome. In order to gain virality and appear as if the message is worthy of further views and, ultimately, promote the narrative, it is necessary to have an influencer push the narrative into the public view.

The goal of any troll or Twitter operation is ultimately to get the message retweeted or reposted by an influencer with a massive following. Once that occurs, this is when the message will attain widespread dispersion and the message's veracity will increase.

In 2017, the US House Intelligence Committee publicly released the Twitter handles of over 2,700 handles that were directly tied to the **Intelligence Research Agency (IRA)**, a Russian intelligence agency-linked firm. Within those names and handles were hundreds of viral Twitter accounts that had directly targeted over 3,000 global news agencies and had been noted as directly influencing more than 40 celebrities, all with millions of followers (Popken, 2017).

Those same news outlets had, at one time or another, inadvertently published articles that contained embedded tweets by confirmed Kremlin-linked troll accounts in that list in more than 11,000 articles during the 2016 election.

A sample of some of the names of the influencer Twitter and Instagram handles that were found to be influenced by those operations is listed here (Popken, 2017):

President of the United States, Donald J. Trump (@realdonaldtrump)

Richard Spencer (@RichardBSpencer)

Roger J. Stone Jr. (@RogerJStoneJr)

Former US UN Ambassador Samantha Power (@AmbPower44)

David Duke (@DrDavidDuke)

Sen. John Coryn, (R-TX) (@JohnCornyn)

Kellyanne Conway (@KellyannePolls)

Trump's digital media advisor Brad Parscale (@parscale)

Former Trump White House communications director Anthony Scaramucci (@Scaramucci)

Former White House press secretary Sean Spicer (@seanspicer)

Sen. Ted Cruz (R-TX) (@tedcruz)

FOX News host Sean Hannity (@seanhannity)

Ann Coulter (@AnnCoulter)

MSNBC host Chris Hayes (@chrislhayes)

TV and radio host Laura Ingraham (@IngrahamAngle)

CNN anchor Jake Tapper (@jaketapper)

Fox Business Network host Lou Dobbs (@LouDobbs)

Sarah Silverman (@SarahKSilverman)

The Daily Show host Trevor Noah (@Trevornoah)

James Woods (@realjameswoods)

CEO of Twitter Jack Dorsey (@jack)

Those retweets and postings did not in all instances make the links or material go immediately viral, but simply having celebrities and highly visible political figures and news outlets share or reference the material was often enough to promote the message. Even if those highly visible accounts were noted as countering or disparaging a particular message, the damage had already been done as that interaction would be enough to get "eyes on" the message. Simply by engaging with that post or message was enough to provide it with validity and credence and would likely get more users talking with or interacting with that post.

One of the most prolific Russian-affiliated accounts that was active during the 2016 election was the Twitter account "@TEN_GOP." This handle gained over 130 million followers while posing as the official Twitter account of the Tennessee Republican Party. Even after the fake account was shut down and blocked by Twitter administrators, the self-described "backup" account for that group, "@10_GOP," collected over 40 million followers. This account was retweeted and had its postings shared by Donald Trump Jr., Ann Coulter, and even President Trump:

Donald J. Trump ✓
@realDonaldTrump

So nice, thank you!

Tennessee @10_gop

En réponse à @realDonaldTrump

We love you, Mr. President!

19:33 - 19 sept. 2017

Figure 8: Donald Trump's response to a bot that was actively targeting him for responses

Donald Trump Jr. @DonaldJTrumpJr

RT @TEN_GOP: BREAKING: Massive riots happening now in Sweden. Stockholm in flames. Trump was right again!
https://t.co/ZQa9Res2tu https://t...

Tue Feb 21 19:46:55 +0000 2017 DELETED   VIA POLITITWEET.ORG

Figure 9: Donald Trump Jr. reposting manipulated headlines that would further a questionable story

Ann Coulter @AnnCoulter

RT @TEN_GOP: .@AnnCoulter: "If Hillary wins, she will amnesty 30+ million illegal aliens and Republicans will never win an election again."...

Tue Oct 11 04:38:29 +0000 2016 DELETED   VIA POLITITWEET.ORG

Figure 10: Popular influencer Ann Coulter falling for the same bogus posting group posts

Again, it is not necessarily a reflection on the individual person's political leanings, but the fact that celebrities or influencers with millions of followers has reposted or retweeted an article that comes from a troll factory tied to a Russian intelligence agency is clearly a problem.

Interestingly, the algorithms within social media platforms are built specifically to counter fake news, at least on a cursory level. There is some degree of fact-checking and intelligence applied to posts and images in order to keep blatantly false items from gaining public prominence, but when an influencer likes or retweets an article or posting, this beats that algorithm.

Twitter has specific controls within its code base to stop unadjudicated or fake bot-based content from automatically retweeting a topic. However, when an influencer or famous person shares or retweets a piece of content and their followers then engage, it becomes a piece of organic content and starts getting ranked higher than any other photo or post that comes from another Twitter account.

When a celebrity retweets a bot or fake news, whether intentionally or not, the algorithm will then basically act as if that item is an item of importance. Therefore, the system will then inadvertently create a trend and then prioritize it on Facebook or Twitter. Because the algorithm does that it is basically the same thing as the company legitimizing that information or news by default.

Because those social media platforms are, in reality, businesses that profit from advertising, it makes sense for the system to promote stories and postings that gain looks and views. In doing that and by making the influencer action a default promotion caveat to the algorithm, it is a means for the malicious users and propaganda-spreading agents to get their message to the masses.

Nation states and nefarious user groups have become extremely adept at using these platforms as a method to share their messages on a massive scale. Simply by targeting the right influencers and users and by ensuring that they leverage the correct publicly available imagery, colors, and fonts is a force multiplier for malevolent actions. Social media platforms are the newest forms of collaboration and data sharing that have almost limitless influence and impact across social circles. By leveraging these assets, adversary groups and nation states can have the same impact on fundamental institutions and national initiatives as can be had with major ransomware attacks or targeted exploitations.

Combatting influence is difficult; not impossible, but difficult. It requires the defensive team to have a plan for action and that the leadership be ready to be open about their position or a mistake if one has been made. No action is worse than a less-than-optimal response. Stock prices and political campaigns have been afflicted by these sorts of attacks; they are not just digital harassment. There is a real-world impact. Tools exist that can help an organization have a more vectored response plan and a capability to know what is active online and is related to their position in that space, but that capability requires a focus on innovation in order to leverage these tools correctly.

Conclusion

In this chapter, we pointed out how powerful influence can be and provided some insight into the actions that take place as these attacks are activated. But in most cases, as noted in the previous section, these past attacks were at least based on actual humans and "real" personas.

What happens when not only the narrative is fake, but so is the person or persona that is involved? And what happens if that attack is coupled with an AI-related approach? How big and how bad can things get when AI comes into the equation? We will explore these questions in the next chapter.

References

1. Anthony Nadler, M. C. (n.d.). *Weaponizing the Digital Influence Machine: The Political Perils of Online Ad Tech*. Retrieved from apo. org.au: https://apo.org.au/sites/default/files/resource-files/2018/10/apo-nid197676-1225751.pdf

2. Douhet, G. (1942). *Command of the Air*. Retrieved from airforcemag.com: http://www.airforcemag.com/MagazineArchive/Documents/2013/April%202013/0413keeperfull.pdf

3. Lacapria, K. (2016, October 28). *Hillary Clinton and #DraftOurDaughters*. Retrieved from snopes.com: https://www.snopes.com/fact-check/hillary-clinton-and-draftourdaughters/

4. Mackey, R. (2016, November 7). *Troll the Vote: Trump supporters spread disinformation with fake Clinton ads*. Retrieved from theintercept.com: https://theintercept.com/liveblogs/trumpdown/troll-vote-trump-supporters-spread-disinformation-fake-clinton-ads/

5. Popken, B. (2017, November 4). *Russian Trolls Duped Global Media and Nearly 40 Celebrities*. Retrieved from nbcnews.com: https://www.nbcnews.com/tech/social-media/trump-other-politicians-celebs-shared-boosted-russian-troll-tweets-n817036

6. Prier, J. (2017, June). *DTIC.mil*. Retrieved from Defense Technical Information Center: https://apps.dtic.mil/dtic/tr/fulltext/u2/1039253.pdf

7. UsHadrons. (2017, October 14). *#DraftOurDaughters: A Russian and American PSYOP. Fraud and the impersonation of a presidential campaign*. Retrieved from medium.com: `https://medium.com/@ushadrons/this-space-is-a-repository-for-memes-and-tweets-from-the-hashtag-draftourdaughters-7c28875c573d`

5
DeepFakes and AI/ML in Cyber Security

In this chapter, we will bring to light some of the newer innovations in the industry that surround **artificial intelligence (AI)** and **machine learning (ML)** uses that are applicable in cyber security and potentially cyber warfare. While time could be spent specifically detailing exactly how to build and deploy your own AI/ML-based DeepFakes, that is not what this chapter is about. In all honesty, that is a dangerous gambit. These tools and techniques have broad implications and could impact the fabric of truth around a variety of important topic areas. Instead of specific "how to" sections, we will discuss:

- What are DeepFakes and where are they being noted today?
- How can AI/ML be used in these applications to weaponize facts, video, sound, and even biometrics?
- What broad impacts are possible thanks to these innovations and their coupling to massively powerful cloud computing resources?

First, let's begin by providing some history and an overview of what these tools are and some of the possible implications that can be seen from their use.

From big screen to smartphone –
the dawn of DeepFakes

Video and audio technologies have exponentially increased in capability over the last decade. The demand for more realistic, diverse, and fantastic content – both for movies and music – has forced the industry around this space to push current technical boundaries. It was less than 30 years ago when dinosaurs showed up on the screen in the *Jurassic Park* movie and audiences were exposed to the first realistic animations that were made possible using computer technology.

That earliest instance of very real-looking, but totally unreal, imagery shocked the world. At that time, the technology needed to produce that quality of imagery was limited only to the big screen and was both cost-prohibitive and technologically unattainable by all but the wealthiest production studios. That is no longer the case. Because of the rapid advances in the technology behind digital imagery and voice, and the advent of freely available ML tooling, it is now possible for anyone, anywhere, to produce extremely realistic content with the only technical requirements being an image and the internet.

The dawn of the DeepFake era is now.

Defining DeepFakes

In its most basic terms, a DeepFake is simply the combination of deep learning and a fake video. At the basic level, these "videos" are produced by taking in enough imagery, be it other footage or simply pictures of a target, and then using applied deep learning algorithms to stich the images together into a believable piece of content. With enough available media, it is very possible to create a near-Hollywood quality video of any person saying or doing anything. This ability tailors itself well to disinformation and fake news campaigns and, if paired with social media attack vectors, can exponentially increase the threat that is posed by this type of attack.

In yet another twist on the old paradigm of "no good deed goes unpunished," the technologies that have been the precursor for DeepFakes came from the very tools that have been used to create the content that we all enjoy today. Tools like Adobe Photoshop and other video editing software are now so powerful and easy to use that anyone with a bit of time and a decent quality video card can craft literally anything they can imagine. Many of the DeepFake videos that are common online are typically created by sending an algorithm many different submissions of images of a singular person's face. The algorithm will then "train" itself based on that specific face's intricacies. Everything is mapped, measured, and recreated by the algorithm before it is ultimately compounded and then swapped into the final target video. That process may take hours or possibly days, even with access to expensive hardware. This can take even longer if the creator is restricted to only using run-of-the-mill consumer-grade video and audio programs and processing hardware.

This approach is limited mainly by the way in which the algorithms function to create that ultimate output video, a method involving **General Adversarial Networks (GANs)**.

GANs power DeepFakes

In most ML algorithms of the past, the overarching methodology was to use a discriminative approach. The way that those ML applications work is that they seek to basically prove something is not what it claims to be. In a simple use case, consider a spam email. For a discriminative approach to work, the algorithm seeks to show that an email is not a valid email because of the contents within the email. In other words, using a sample of what is a known good bit of content, obviously at a large scale, the algorithm uses that known good content to judge subsequent submissions.

Unless a certain threshold is met, the algorithm works using that available data to prove that what was newly submitted is not a "good" email; it is spam. This works well mainly for this application because in this use case, most spam emails are relatively formulaic and typically are easily detected.

There are clear giveaways that the email does not contain "good" content. This is a vast oversimplification, but it makes the basic point. This particular ML algorithm works because it has somewhat simple "boundaries" of input data and a clearer intended output.

In the past, this type of ML algorithm was tried in early DeepFake videos, but it would not suffice as video content is not usually formulaic and there is not a known "good" corpus from which to pull. Video content, and audio for that matter, can basically be anything from anyone, anywhere, at any fidelity, so there is no real constant baseline from which to draw clear definitions regarding what is "good." This is where the GAN algorithm approaches come in.

Using GAN approaches allows for a much more fluid type of input to be offered to the system for processing, which works well for video and audio content generation. While, in a discriminative approach, the aim is to disprove something is not what it says it is, for a GAN, the aim is to use the available data or inputs and try to "make it fit." The fundamental way that a GAN works is different as well. In a GAN, two different neural networks are working competitively with one another to process the data or inputs. One neural network, the *generator*, generates new data instances. The other, the *discriminator*, measures and evaluates that data, in this use case, video or audio content, for authenticity. The discriminator neural network decides whether each instance of data that it reviews belongs to the actual training dataset, and this process continues repeatedly until the analysis is complete. In a GAN, the generator tries to create random fake, or synthetic outputs (like images or video snippets of a human face, for example), while the discriminator conversely works to try to tell these apart from real outputs that it knows are correct (say, a database of driver license photos). As those two neural networks work to "outsmart" each other, they in turn perform their individual tasks better and better because they are trying to "win" this game of trickery. Ultimately, the resulting data or output winds up being a generator network that produces realistic images or videos:

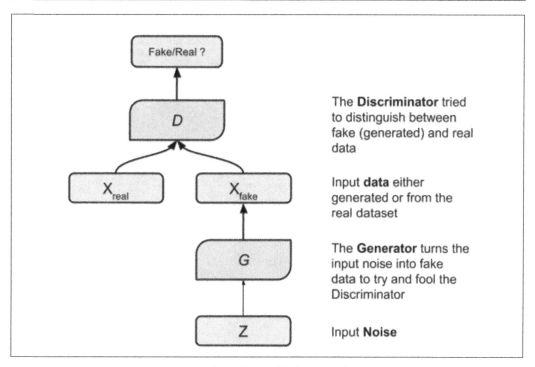

Figure 1: A simple graphic detailing a GAN

The possibility of using this approach for generating totally fake images, videos, and audio content is very new to the tech world. It was just in 2020 when a group of researchers at Nvidia, the graphics card company, proposed an experiment and framework to see just how good their approach could be if applied in this manner. Using the Nvidia researchers' methods, the team was able to generate extremely realistic, high-fidelity images of human faces from persons that have never existed on this planet. Interestingly, the team found that their method of modifying the input noise level for their GAN increased the fidelity of the output rather than decrease it. This happened because the ML they leveraged was paired with their Nvidia graphics' processing capability, which helped to increase the system's output over time. In other words, they found that the better the horsepower applied to the engine, the better the imagery or output got (Tero Karras, 2019).

The following image demonstrates some outputs from Nvidia's GAN:

Figure 2: High-fidelity images of humans that do not exist created by Nvidia's GAN

In follow-on research from this endeavor, the team at Nvidia was even able to show that with their tooling and approach, their GAN was capable of even producing transitory images of those fake human faces. The system was so good at producing quality fake imagery that the outputs were modified, by the GAN itself, and the images were made to either show age in the human faces or were modified with different features (Tero Karras, 2019):

Figure 3: GAN imagery that shows the changes from age,
or simply modifications of facial features of non-human entities

A GAN is currently the "best" method of using an applied ML solution set to the generation of imagery (as we've seen) or audio content (as we'll cover in a later section) that is present on the market. Using more powerful graphics processing tooling, as in the Nvidia experiment, helps to increase the quality and fidelity of the outputs, and, should the approach or tooling be moved into an applied cloud-based service, such as on a AWS Deep Learning system or Microsoft Azure cloud, then logic would suggest that the increases in those outputs would scale in parallel.

It is not all perfection, however. GAN approaches and tooling is still generally restricted by the amount of processing power that a user can leverage as they try and build their DeepFake imagery or audio. Even the extremely skilled team at Nvidia noted that it took them over a week to accurately tune their model and required the use of eight different Nvidia Tesla GPUs to make their system fully operational.

For common users without these powerful tools, unless they happened to own an extremely powerful home PC, often, the output of inadequate imagery processing can result in strange or even comical outputs:

Figure 4: A DeepFake image of a frog wherein there were insufficient sample images and a lack of processing power applied

Because of the power of this type of approach and the reasonable accuracy that is provided (assuming sufficient samples and sufficient processing power), the use of this type of approach will likely be the most widely used solution for the near future. There are already a variety of examples of this approach and the tooling being applied that are notable on the internet, as shown here:

Figure 5: The Jordan Peele/President Obama DeepFake YouTube video

And here:

Figure 6: Bill Hader DeepFake video sample images

The majority of what has been related to the use of GANs and DeepFake methods to date has mainly been for comedic purposes or for generalized humor. But as with other technologies explored thus far in this book, including malware, exploits, networks, and IoT devices, it is only a matter of time before these same solutions and tools are applied to nefarious ends. In the future, possibly during the next election cycle, it is highly likely and probable that a DeepFake video of a candidate will be augmented and used for some malicious purpose. Imagine the implications and chaos that might occur if a realistic and plausible video emerged during the election cycle that showed a leading candidate conducting compromising actions, or simply touting an overt message of hate aimed at one political group. The outcome could literally be literal riots and may have profound impacts on democratic processes.

There are other applications of this type of ML for the purposes of circumventing or impacting security practices and protocols, such as using GAN solutions to avoid or trick biometric solutions. We'll discuss some of these applications in the following section.

Applied DeepFakes, AKA DeepMastersPrints

One of the most prolific types of security authentication in the market today is that of biometric security, specifically, fingerprint biometrics. This application of biometrically-enabled authentication can be found on nearly every smartphone on the planet. Only recently, that is, in the last 18 months, has the use of the human face become another avenue for biometric authentication. The widespread use and adoption of fingerprint biometrics can be seen as an almost unhackable means of verifying a user's identity, but that is not always the case.

Fake digital fingerprints can be created by AI engines that are capable of fooling fingerprint scanners on smartphones and other devices that use this form of authentication. Smartphones from Apple and Samsung use biometric fingerprint technology to allow users to easily unlock their devices instead of entering a passcode. In enterprise systems, there are instances of fingerprints being used for physical access to restricted areas of operation, and on a variety of computing devices, such as laptops and PCs, fingerprints are used for authentication and access. Banks and hospitals have followed this trend and, in trying to add some of the convenience that smartphone users tout, are increasingly allowing customers to access their checking accounts using their biometric authentication means, typically in the form of fingerprints.

Those seemingly unhackable biometrics, however, are possibly compromised. There have been instances of hackers and researchers exploiting biometric authentication with nothing more than clear tape and a good camera, but that method has been negated as time has progressed and authentication tools have improved. In the newer, more complex methods of exploiting biometrics, researchers have shown that ML-based applications using neural network approaches are well suited to beating biometrics. The method that is employed in this approach is known as **MasterPrinting**.

The concept behind the use of a MasterPrint approach is basically focused on using a partial fingerprint image from any user and combining that with neural network ML tooling to try and brute force the authentication mechanism. In the same basic fashion that a brute-force password attack takes, where a piece of a password or hash is known, a MasterPrinting approach hammers at the image until a match is found, or until a sufficient sample works that defeats the authentication system.

In the work conducted by the researchers on this approach, they found that it was inconsequential whether or not they had entire fingerprint images available to test, nor did it matter if only partial fingerprints were used. This happened because the authentication systems that employ fingerprint biometrics are designed to have certain error rates built in and often only used a small percentage of the available print map (usually, 150 x 150 pixels (Ross, 2017)) to decide if the supplied image is valid or not. This very small sampling area of the image and the intrinsic logic within the authentication mechanism leads the biometric authentication system to have a fundamental flaw. So, if a sufficient image is supplied with either the correct singular imagery of a print, or if a piece of a print is submitted that is within the bounds of the parameters of the acceptable error rate for the authentication solution, access will be granted:

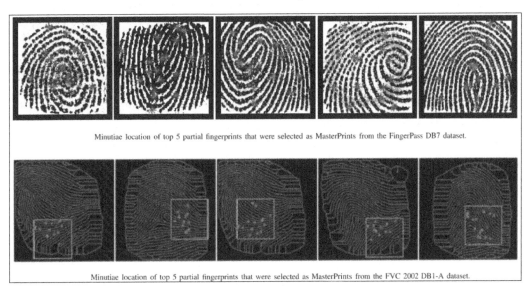

Minutiae location of top 5 partial fingerprints that were selected as MasterPrints from the FingerPass DB7 dataset.

Minutiae location of top 5 partial fingerprints that were selected as MasterPrints from the FVC 2002 DB1-A dataset.

Figure 7: Images of full and partial fingerprints used for biometric authentication subversion in MasterPrinting (Ross, 2017)

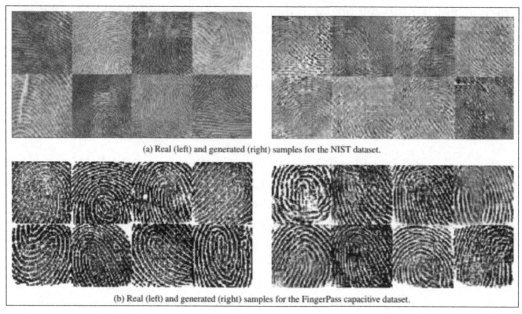

(a) Real (left) and generated (right) samples for the NIST dataset.

(b) Real (left) and generated (right) samples for the FingerPass capacitive dataset.

Figure 8: Real fingerprint images on the left and fake MasterPrint images on the right

By using neural network ML and cloud-based processing, the ability to beat this type of authentication can be increased and expanded. As explained in the section on generating DeepFake images and video, GANs are well-vectored to be applied to this type of activity. Using a GAN combined with a repository of fingerprint images that can easily be accessed via a Google search, a malicious actor with a basic understanding of ML could build out a MasterPrint image repository. Those images could then be leveraged via printing, 3D printing, or copying to be used for attempting to subvert biometric authentication means. While obviously there is a requirement for some form of physical proximity for these types of exploits to operate, the fact that something as personal and potentially useful as biometric fingerprints being "hacked" is certainly a concern.

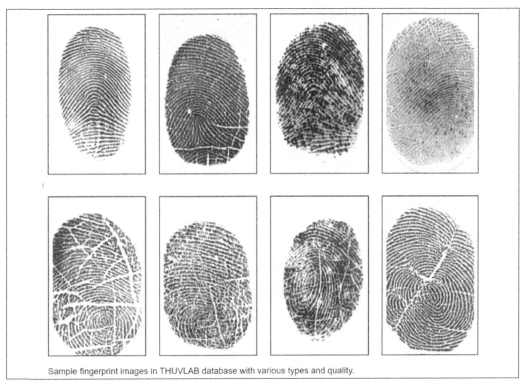

Sample fingerprint images in THUVLAB database with various types and quality.

Figure 9: A sampling of actual fingerprint images available via Google search

In the next section, we'll look at how DeepFake can be applied not only to images, but also to sound. It is even possible to generate fake, yet realistic, human voices.

Hacking voice using ML, AKA DeepVoice

As with the examples of imagery for video and fingerprints, ML applications are also suited to manipulate voice content and even to generate realistic fake voices from nothing. The original impetus for most voice generation and cloning was supposed to be for voice commands and voice assistant technology applications.

Because humans typically prefer to feel that they are interacting with other humans, retailers have spent significant time and money building out realistic human voice assistants and online support solutions. Those bots and fake human voices are composed of either real past human recordings that have been strung together to reproduce realistic human voice outputs, or they are built using ML backend systems that literally generate human voices out of thin air.

When Siri, Alexa, or our GPS use voice generation, it is usually quickly obvious that it is a bot or non-human speaking to the user. This is because virtually every legacy text-to-speech system on the market is built on a prerecorded set of words, phrases, and utterances (usually recorded from voice actors). Those bits and pieces of prior speech are then strung together in a Frankenstein-like fashion to produce complete words and sentences. The result is a vocal delivery that often sounds distinctly uninspiring, robotic, and, at times, comical. This common approach to voice synthesis means that users are usually listening to the same prerecorded, monotonous voice over and over again. No matter what the application, it is usually the same variant of the cobbled together pieces of that narrative. However, this outdated approach is now being improved significantly thanks to the use of ML applications.

A relatively new-to-market solution that shows the improvements in this old approach, which can be made with focused ML modifications, is from a company called Lyrebird. Lyrebird has developed an ML-powered voice-imitation algorithm that mimics any person's voice, realistically. This tool can also read text in any chosen voice while also using a predefined emotion or intonation to help improve the believability of the voice. Thanks to the power of the algorithm and the increased accuracy that the backend ML provides, Lyrebird can perform this function after analyzing only a few dozen seconds of prerecorded audio from the target voice.

The way Lyrebird does this is made possible using artificial neural networks, like the same neural networks that are used in video augmentation and DeepFakes.

These neural networks function by using the algorithm to learn to recognize patterns in a target person's speech, and then reproduce those patterns during simulated speech.

Lyrebird trains its model for the neural network on a huge dataset with thousands of speakers. Then, when a new speaker target is needed, the Lyrebird system compresses that voice dataset into digitally usable data points that constitute a small key value that contains the target voice "DNA." That first sample output has not been perfected. The resulting samples still exhibit flawed digital artifacts, clarity problems, and other inadequacies. As more samples are processed and the model learns what the correct output should look like, the system gets better at imitating the subtle changes in speech patterns for the target. As this improvement continues, even changes in intonation, inflection, and emotion become discernible. Unlike older systems that do not rely on neural networks or ML-based approaches, Lyrebird's solution requires fewer samples per target to produce a simulated voice. This system is so good at this process that it can even work in real time.

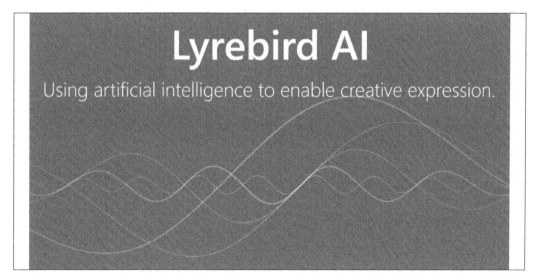

Figure 10: The Lyrebird home page

There are also open source **Text-To-Speech** (TTS) solutions that use neural networks and ML. Google released it's own TTS toolset to GitHub recently. It is called Google Voice Builder and is found at the following URL:

```
https://github.com/google/voice-builder
```

According to Google's abstract on their release of this tool to the public, they claim that "We (Google) describe an opensource text-to-speech voice building tool that focuses on simplicity, flexibility, and collaboration. Our tool allows anyone with basic computer skills to run voice training experiments and listen to the resulting synthesized voice. We hope that this tool will reduce the barrier for creating new voices and accelerate TTS research, by making experimentation faster and interdisciplinary collaboration easier. We believe that our tool can help improve TTS research, especially for low-resourced languages, where more experimentations are often needed to get the most out of the limited data." While this seems like a noble mission, and their tool is supposed to be used to benefit researchers and those that need improved TTS tooling, it can be postulated that malevolent uses of this toolset could have a significant impact on a target's perceived truth or veracity.

There are a wide variety of possible tools that can be gathered from GitHub or via a targeted Google search that could be used for faking a human voice. The use of ML backends to increase the accuracy and the speed with which these DeepVoice samples are produced shows the power that can be applied to these applications.

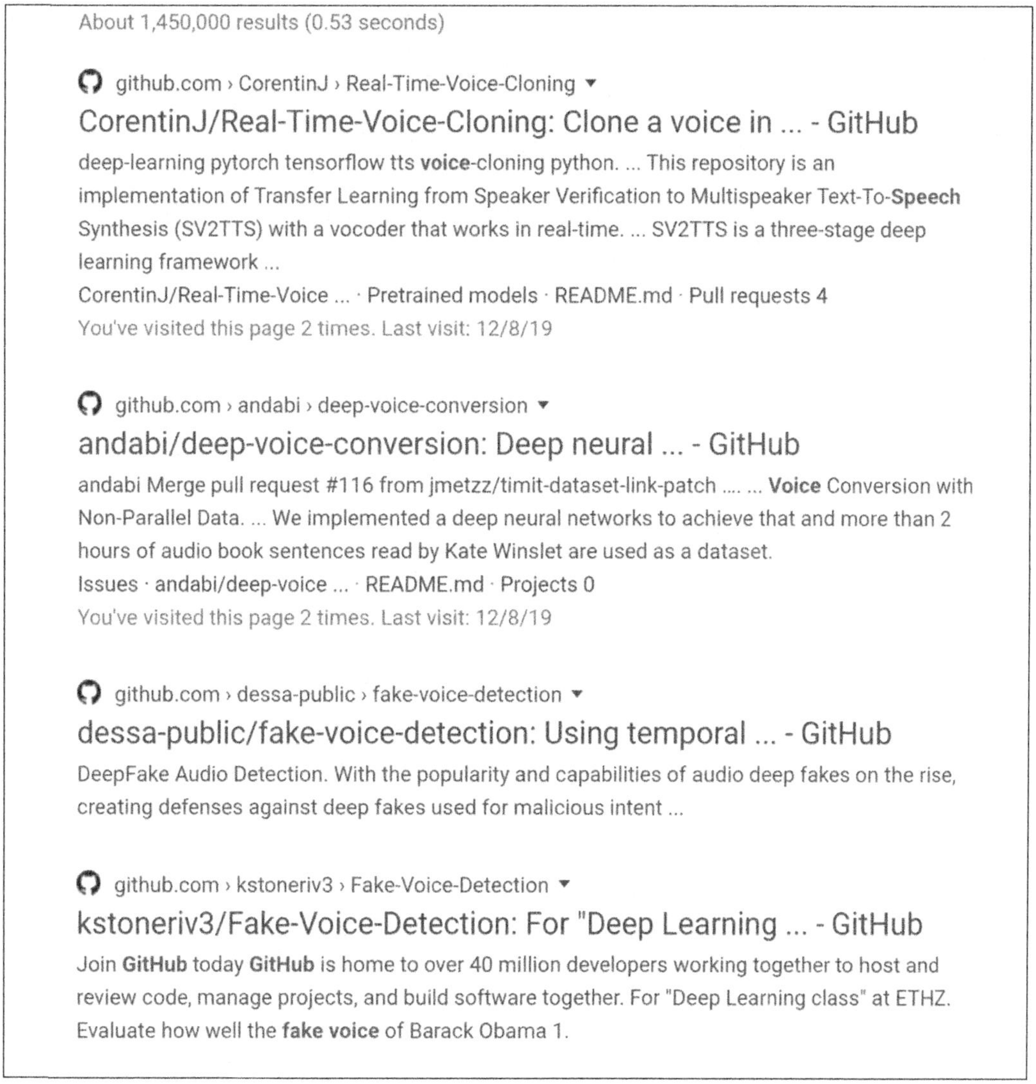

About 1,450,000 results (0.53 seconds)

github.com › CorentinJ › Real-Time-Voice-Cloning ▼

CorentinJ/Real-Time-Voice-Cloning: Clone a voice in ... - GitHub

deep-learning pytorch tensorflow tts **voice**-cloning python. ... This repository is an implementation of Transfer Learning from Speaker Verification to Multispeaker Text-To-**Speech** Synthesis (SV2TTS) with a vocoder that works in real-time. ... SV2TTS is a three-stage deep learning framework ...

CorentinJ/Real-Time-Voice ... · Pretrained models · README.md · Pull requests 4

You've visited this page 2 times. Last visit: 12/8/19

github.com › andabi › deep-voice-conversion ▼

andabi/deep-voice-conversion: Deep neural ... - GitHub

andabi Merge pull request #116 from jmetzz/timit-dataset-link-patch .... **Voice** Conversion with Non-Parallel Data. ... We implemented a deep neural networks to achieve that and more than 2 hours of audio book sentences read by Kate Winslet are used as a dataset.

Issues · andabi/deep-voice ... · README.md · Projects 0

You've visited this page 2 times. Last visit: 12/8/19

github.com › dessa-public › fake-voice-detection ▼

dessa-public/fake-voice-detection: Using temporal ... - GitHub

DeepFake Audio Detection. With the popularity and capabilities of audio deep fakes on the rise, creating defenses against deep fakes used for malicious intent ...

github.com › kstoneriv3 › Fake-Voice-Detection ▼

kstoneriv3/Fake-Voice-Detection: For "Deep Learning ... - GitHub

Join **GitHub** today **GitHub** is home to over 40 million developers working together to host and review code, manage projects, and build software together. For "Deep Learning class" at ETHZ. Evaluate how well the **fake voice** of Barack Obama 1.

Figure 11: A simple Google search shows the varieties of tools that are available for voice impersonation

As these tools continue to proliferate, and more and more digital interaction takes place via voice interactions, there will be more possibilities for malicious actors to try and leverage these actions for nefarious means. There have already been examples of this occurring. In one case, an executive assistant at a UK-based firm was tricked by hackers into transferring more than 200,000 dollars to a bogus account because they "heard their CEO tell them to" on the phone (Damiani, 2019).

According to this account, the fake voice used even carried subtle intricacies of the fake CEO's German accent and the "melody" of his voice. Additionally, in this example, the malicious actor called the company using the AI-based fake CEO's voice three times. It wasn't until the third call that the assistant finally put it together that something was amiss, and it was not due to the fake voice; it was because the caller continued to ask for changes to the transfer. This indicates that the voice was so realistic that the malicious actor was able to trick the assistant repeatedly.

It is highly likely that this type of attack will continue as the tactics employed are easily achieved by the malicious actor, and there is little chance of the threat actor being caught. Using DeepVoice techniques to evade detection and to trick or socially engineer targets is only one potential application of this method. Another would be to use a DeepVoice approach to broadcast a realistic message in a target's voice on a hacked Twitter, YouTube, or podcast account to broadcast a fake message to a mass audience. Imagine a podcast on a known channel where a celebrity or thought leader espouses a message of hate. Or imagine a scenario where a fake learning message or market analysis is spoken by a fake DeepVoice system to influence purchasing or acquisitions in a business vertical. It would be very easy to effectively leverage these types of attacks to promote a false message, confuse the populace, or influence a business decision. And any of these could have significant outcomes.

ReadFakes

Aside from video and audio content, there is only one additional medium that provides information and daily – if not hourly – data to the world at large: text. We read the news, we read blogs, and we all gather our preferred information from sources that produce and generate textual information. This information can come in a variety of formats, but it is the largest amount of information that is available to the masses. If we accept that truth, then we also must accept that it is possible for a sufficiently powerful and well-tuned ML system to generate textual information that could be used for malicious purposes and disinformation campaigns.

Machines are now just as adept at generating textual information and data as humans are. In some cases, machines have been proven to produce text that is as poetic and narrative as that of Shakespeare. One researcher, Andrej Karpathy, used a relatively small sampling of past literature attributed to William Shakespeare to generate totally fake textual output that is passable for this literary master. Using only 4.4 megabytes of previous text data and processing it through an algorithm built for text generation, using a recursive neural network backend, the researcher needed to wait only a few hours for the system to return the following samples of "Fakespeare":

```
PANDARUS:
Alas, I think he shall be come approached and the day
When little srain would be attain'd into being never fed,
And who is but a chain and subjects of his death,
I should not sleep.


Second Senator:
They are away this miseries, produced upon my soul,
Breaking and strongly should be buried, when I perish
The earth and thoughts of many states.


DUKE VINCENTIO:
Well, your wit is in the care of side and that.
```

```
Second Lord:
They would be ruled after this chamber, and
my fair nues begun out of the fact, to be conveyed,
Whose noble souls I'll have the heart of the wars.


Clown:
Come, sir, I will make did behold your worship.


VIOLA:
I'll drink it.
```

Fakespeare text generated by a recurrent neural network

While some of the sentences are not grammatically correct, and most do not make sense, it still shows that the approach is functional and may even hold up to cursory scrutiny. In this case, the model has not had enough time, training, or a large enough dataset to accurately learn the meaning of words. But also consider:

- This model is character-based. When the training started, the model did not know how to spell an English word, nor did the model or system understand that words were even a unit of text. It basically "figured that out" as it worked to produce text.
- The structure of the output resembles a play, which Shakespeare is obviously famous for. Just as with a play, each block of text begins with a speaker name, in all capital letters, as shown in the provided dataset.

All of this took place autonomously. The system was not specifically trained to do any of this. The neural network did what it was built to do, and the applied algorithm helped to guide the production of semi-acceptable Shakespeare. Should a user seek to improve the speed or accuracy of these types of applications, they could leverage cloud-based processing and applications such as Tensor Flow, or SageMaker on AWS, to bolster their text-generation capabilities.

Using that scale and speed, the malicious actor could then work to generate very realistic text that mimics an author for a variety of potentially negative outputs. Fake blogs, reports, papers, or literally any other variance of text could be generated, some even in real time, that could then be posted to try and manipulate an opinion or a user's position on a topic.

There are instances of fake Twitter bots being built using autonomous text generation as a means of spreading messages that aren't totally "correct." An example of an open source tool that is built for this type of application is `https://github.com/minimaxir/tweet-generator`.

While it is doubtful that the author of this code base ever intended for their tool to be used for malicious purposes, the fact is that the tool could be applied in this very manner. Observing the demonstration of the code functioning on the GitHub page even shows that the tool can generate false tweets and post that content to a target account. This is a prime example of how the use of a neural network-powered application or tool can be leveraged for ulterior motives. It would not be difficult to use this solution set as a code base and take over an easily compromised Twitter account from any number of celebrities or influencers, or potentially a news organization, and allow the system to generate bogus content.

Breaking news may mean breaking bad

In the world of news and media, the winner in that space is whoever gets the article out fastest. The speed to market for news and media-related content is now capable of moving at a speed that has never been seen in the past. A news story or article can literally go from a note on a Twitter feed to a full production news item in hours. While speed is a good thing for sharing information in as close to real time as possible, it is problematic in that speed is often the enemy of fact-checking and true analysis of the full veracity of a newsworthy item.

That speed to delivery is often increased by news producers and outlets using automated solutions to help them ingest more news from more sources at the greatest speed possible. The majority of the applications and code bases that work to enable the automated ingestion of news articles and feeds work via RSS polling, or an API-based interaction. RSS is nothing more than a web feed for users and applications to access updates to websites in a computer-readable format. Those feeds allow a user to keep track of many different websites in a single news aggregator. WordPress has relatively simple capabilities to pull news from a variety of sources via RSS polling, as do sites like *Feedly* and the *Google News* application. While these are useful tools, often, they pull from a variety of sites across the internet that are vulnerable to attacks and potentially modification of the relatively simple HTML code that is responsible for handling the posting of those news articles.

Should a compromise of the backend of any of those sites take place, a malicious actor could surreptitiously post fake news items or articles, which could then be automatically ingested into the news feeds on those aggregator sites. Because those sites are not fact-checking their sources, they simply post articles. This means that whatever was posted on a feeder site will work its way up the chain to a final news source. If no human takes the time to trawl back through that chain of information and verify what is actually being posted, it is very likely that an article of fake information can be considered as a newsworthy item. Couple that process with the need for speed to production of news outlets and providers and the possibility of this augmentation of the truth becomes more and more real.

The way that we humans interact with news articles and media content is problematic in the context of the speed to ingestion issue as well. Human beings typically check their phones roughly 1,500 times a week, an average of 3 hours per day. We look at our email on our phones an average of 30 times per hour, and our average attention span has reduced from 12 seconds in the early 2000s to less than 8 according to research in 2015 (Spangler, 2019).

The continual onslaught of data that we ingest and the variety of sources from which we gather our news articles combined with the lack of our own attention spans to actually pay attention to the content within a posting make us ripe for potentially relying on faulty news or inputs.

If a human has an attention span of less than 8 seconds and news items are constantly coming at us from our phones, online news, emails, texts, tweets, videos, and a variety of other streaming sources, it is realistic to assume that if any false narrative is introduced that is not wildly absurd, we would simply read it and move on to the next item. But once that item has been read and either overtly or covertly inserted into our collective consciousness, the damage has already been done. The more news sources and the different areas and technologies from which we derive our truth both increase the volume and velocity, this could lead to more and more fake news items sliding into the news cycle and impacting a user's or group's understanding of what is the truth.

When data and AI "studies" go awry

In doing the research for this book, it became clearly evident that there is a fine line that must be walked between providing some insights into the particulars of AI/ML applications and the potential nefarious use cases. The aim of doing research is never to "teach" anyone how to do something that is potentially malevolent, but there is a necessity for the researcher to provide real-world instances and use cases around these items that help to solidify the collective understanding of those that seek this type of information. And in that spirit of sharing the information and adding clarity to this space, I present the following points of research. Please know that the researcher finds even the basis for the study that follows abhorrent and thinks that even the consideration of such a study as being perverse and wrong.

Our brain is an exceptional reader of the human face. In most cases, our ability to determine a wide variety of subtle indicators of what a person is thinking or feeling is amazing. The average person instinctively knows the difference between a real smile and a fake one, or if a person has rage hiding behind their eyes. Lies are given away by coy smiles, and joy is seen in the curve of the mouth. However, humanity is also now moving beyond the bounds of just what our own eyes can see. We are inventing technologies that analyze faces as well as, or better than, we can. For those machines, the face is a just a database, that is, a bank of data points composed of muscles, scars, and imperceptible changes that collectively speak to what a human is feeling, and even who they are.

Facial recognition technology is being deployed in airports and public spaces around the globe. In most cases, it is supposedly only being used to match camera footage against government provided credentials. In China the use of this technology is ever-present. It is used there to conduct social observations and is part of a social compliance ranking effort. It is also employed in mundane tasks like identifying jaywalkers, helping with menu suggestions at fast food places, and stopping thieves in public places.

In 2017, a study was published in the *Journal of Personality and Social Psychology*, that took the creepy "big brother" potential of AI/ML into a further realm. In that study, the designed facial recognition software was touted to be able to correctly identify an individual's sexuality based on an analysis of photos associated with that user. In that study, the researchers culled tens of thousands of photos from online dating sites and used a custom ML model to extract users' facial characteristics. The model looked for dynamic data points, like eye makeup and hair color, and static ones, like nose or jaw shape. Those data points were then fed into a second, more specific model built specifically by the researchers. That follow-on model classified users by what the machine determined was their sexuality based on the photo analysis. To "calibrate" their model, when the system was shown two photos, one of a gay man and one of a straight man, the system could accurately determine which photo contained an image of the heterosexual individual and which one as homosexual about 81 percent of the time. For women, its accuracy dropped to 71 percent.

Non-identified human viewers fared worse in the early stages of the study, before the model was improved. In those analyses, the system only correctly picked the homosexual photo for males 61 percent of the time and the photo of the homosexual woman 54 percent of the time (Wang, 2018).

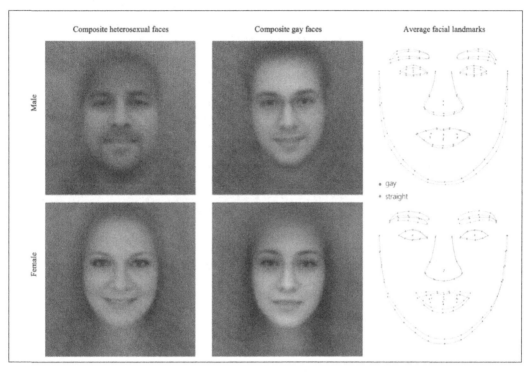

Figure 12: An image from the study showing the analysis of the ML model and its output determining the sexual affiliation of the user based on their photo

While the implications of that study are evident and the reasons behind it in the first place are not clear, the point is that this is a use case of an AI/ML model that is built by academics for research purposes wherein there are clear potential societal impacts. The actual conduct of the study was found to be conducted in a less than optimal matter and was ultimately retracted from publication, but nevertheless, the "cat was out of the bag." That singular study resulted in responses from the LGBT community and was referenced as a "tool to help identify" homosexual individuals by right-wing groups in the United States.

This study and its resulting influence on the issues that surround sexual identity would continue to bubble up for the next 2 years and was even noted as an influence for TV shows like Netflix's *Black Mirror*.

While, luckily, this was an academic study that had no real malevolent intention behind it, ill thought-through as it might have been, imagine if the datasets had been larger and more diverse, or if the team that built the application and model were focused on an effort to identify and eradicate a group of people based solely on a "guestimate" that a machine made from a photo. If datasets like the vast breached datasets from OPM, Facebook, Equifax, and online dating sites like Dolly Madison were used to try and build more detailed and intricate models to classify and identify groups of users for malevolent purposes, this scenario could go from bad to worse in a matter of days. In nation states where the population is constantly under surveillance, these types of tangential and possibly malicious applications of AI/ML can be a slippery slope toward weaponized applications. To date, there has been no specific instance of such an application being used to justify a kinetic physical action, but with extremism and prejudice never far below the surface of online interactivity, the potential is certainly there.

Conclusion

Using DeepFake videos and the other "deep" approaches, malicious actors aim to manipulate the truth or sway a target group or user into taking an action outside the bounds of their normal activity or thinking. The more accurate and realistic a fake appears to be, the more likely it is to be accepted as "truth." With the spread and scale that is offered via online means, and in combination with social media avenues to help spread the disinformation, almost any message could be shared and placed into the target audience's decision-making process.

Nation states and threat actors are intimately aware of this capability and the power that resides therein. It is a guarantee that in the very near future, the use of these types of approaches to "hacking reality" will take place.

It is no longer necessary for a government threat actor to use a piece of malware or targeted technical exploit to achieve an impact on a potential target. Now, by simply twisting the narrative and spreading doubt and inconsistencies around a topic or persona, an adversary can achieve their desired outcome without breaching a single security measure.

There are means and methods to better defend organizations from these types of attacks, but this is no easy task. This space moves extremely quickly and, thanks to the availability and power that AI and automation offer, things can go from bad to worse in seconds. Knowledge, a running inventory, and a planned response to fake items are a must. AI can beat AI, but the crux of the response remains on humans.

References

1. Damiani, J. (2019, September 3). *A Voice Deepfake Was Used To Scam A CEO Out Of $243,000*. Retrieved from Forbes.com: `https://www.forbes.com/sites/jessedamiani/2019/09/03/a-voice-deepfake-was-used-to-scam-a-ceo-out-of-243000/#3e159da32241`

2. Karpathy, A. (2015, May 21). *The Unreasonable Effectiveness of Recurrent Neural Networks*. Retrieved from github.io: `http://karpathy.github.io/2015/05/21/rnn-effectiveness/`

3. Ross, A. R. (2017, September 9). *MasterPrint: Exploring the Vulnerability of Partial Fingerprint-Based Authentication Systems*. Retrieved from cse.msu.edu: `http://www.cse.msu.edu/~rossarun/pubs/RoyMemonRossMasterPrint_TIFS2017.pdf`

4. Spangler, T. (2019, November 14). *Are Americans Addicted to Smartphones? U.S. Consumers Check Their Phones 52 Times Daily, Study Finds*. Retrieved from Variety.com: `https://variety.com/2018/digital/news/smartphone-addiction-study-check-phones-52-times-daily-1203028454/`

5. Tero Karras, S. L. (2019, March 29). *A Style-Based Generator Architecture for Generative Adversarial Networks*. Retrieved from arxiv.org: `https://arxiv.org/pdf/1812.04948.pdf`

6

Advanced Campaigns
in Cyber Warfare

"First attack the enemy's strategy, then his alliance, next his army, and last his cities."

– *Sun Tzu, The Art of War*

Warfare has fundamentally changed over the last decade. In the past, it was necessary for an enemy nation, adversary, or insurgent to physically bring weapons to bear during combat. It was a requirement for warfare to be engaged, in that lead had to be sent toward the end target; rounds had to be fired somewhere for combat effectiveness to take place. That requirement is no longer a necessity. In the world of digital warfare and cyber operations, the only weapons that need to be employed are bits and bytes.

The ammunition in the new era of warfare is one that is ethereal and does not necessitate the logistics issues that often restrict and limit conventional warfare and weaponry. This new weaponry moves at the speed of light, is available to every human on the planet, and can be as surgical as a scalpel or as devastating as a nuclear bomb.

Cyber warfare is the new standard in global combat and will impact nations and organizations of all sizes over the coming decade.

The goal in any combat engagement is to overpower the enemy and degrade their ability to function at both the strategic and tactical levels. Historically, the power in warfare was levied only by the nations that could spend the necessary cash to finance their arsenal. Cyber operations and the explosion of digital capabilities, along with the spillage of nation state-level cyber weaponry, has removed the need for vast expenses for any organization to bring the fight to the enemy. Every nation and, in truth, every user on the planet now has access to a variety of exponentially powerful weaponry that can be aimed at any target of their choosing, at any time.

In this chapter, we will discuss and analyze the events and scenarios that indicate what the future state of cyber weaponry and tactics will bring in the coming decade:

- We will detail what a coordinated cyber-attack campaign comprises
- We will discuss the reality of the impact that cyber weapons can have on infrastructure
- We will analyze the weaponry that is currently available and discuss how malicious actors at a variety of levels might combine those assets into a powerful campaign

First, we will analyze a few past offensive cyber warfare campaigns and discuss the impacts that those activities had on target systems and infrastructures.

Cyber warfare campaigns

Warfare operations are not typically singular events. Nor are they usually composed of one-off engagements between adversaries. In nearly every instance throughout history, when opponents engaged one another in combat, the actual fighting was the culmination of a long series of interactions and provocations. In cyber warfare, this is often even more true.

Consider that in cyber warfare campaigns it is often more imperative that the adversaries spend exponentially more time analyzing, researching, and planning or plotting their actions compared to performing those actions. Often, this comes in the form of a series of reconnaissance actions that start with network and technical asset discovery and mapping. Typically, this is not much more than Nmap scanning or using vulnerability mapping tools to begin to plot the follow-on actions on a target. That activity is most often followed by building, modifying, or constructing the specific technical aspects of the attack campaign, in other words, sharpening the sword to be used. Then, finally, the use of the detailed technical data, combined with vectored and carefully chosen weaponry, is launched against the enemy target. This might be in the form of malware, a drone strike, a **Distributed Denial of Service (DDoS)**, or any other variety of potentially damaging technical attacks, using cyberspace and the connectivity of the global internet as the vehicle for the attack delivery.

In an effort to detail some of the diverse attack campaigns that have taken place just in the year 2019, let's analyze the actions and tactics that were employed by nation states that are active in cyber warfare and whose actions are publicly available. Additionally, let's attempt to categorize the overall goal of the campaign associated with each attack to provide clarity on what the focus of the attack actions truly might have been.

For the purposes of this analysis, we categorize the perceived outcome of the cyber attack as part of a larger campaign goal. Of course, were any group of cyber security threat researchers or analysts to be asked to categorize a variety of attacks in this space, each one would surely have their own particular views and logic. However, for the purposes of this book, these are this author's general points based on years of experience and exposure to these activities.

In the author's opinion, these attacks can be categorized in this manner:

- **Nation State Industrial Espionage Campaign** – a campaign whose focus is mainly to either disrupt or degrade an asset with criticality for some aspect of a target nation's collective infrastructure.

- **Nation State Disinformation and Election Interference** – a coordinated effort from an adversary with the goal of either disrupting a democratic process or to impact the credibility and veracity of public officials or offices that are pivotal to the target nation's prosperity or survivability.

- **Nation State Espionage and Intelligence Collection** – a series of actions, or a singular operation, where the focused outcome is one vectored for the collection of data or intelligence that will benefit the attacker at some future date.

- **False Flag Operation** – a campaign by an adversary nation state or its intelligence apparatus aimed at placing attribution on an alternate entity or nation.

- **Nation State IP Theft** – a focused specific campaign launched by an enemy nation state singularly related to the theft of critical intellectual property or proprietary intelligence assets that will provide the collector with a potential economic advantage.

Let's get into a few of the major cases:

Indian Nuclear Plant campaign

October 2019. India announced that North Korean malware designed for data extraction had been identified in the networks of a nuclear power plant (**Nation State Industrial Espionage and Intelligence Collection**).

In this example, India confirmed that its newest nuclear power plant was the victim of a cyber attack likely emanating from North Korea. This hack took aim at the country's most critical sectors as it related to cyber espionage. The Kudankulam nuclear power plant was exploited using malware designed for data extraction linked to the Lazarus Group. The Lazarus Group is known to be affiliated with North Korean-backed nation state threat actor groups. The **Nuclear Power Corporation of India Limited (NPCIL)** confirmed that malware had been identified within the systems of the infrastructure.

NPCIL operates 22 commercial nuclear power reactors in the nation with a capacity of 6,780 MW, according to the corporation. And each of those other reactors and their affiliated control systems and networks are connected to the Kudankulam power plant network. Researchers affiliated via *VirusTotal*, a threat research tool, posted a note on the related data dump on Twitter:

Figure 1: The Twitter post referencing VirusTotal tied to the nuclear plant infection

The attack on the nuclear plant was tied to malware identified as DTrack. DTrack was also used in 2016 to infiltrate Indian financial systems and steal the data of millions of Indian citizens. In those instances, the DTrack virus targeted Hitachi Payment Services, a private operator running ATMs and point-of-sale devices across the country. DTrack is primarily an espionage and reconnaissance tool that is used for gathering data about infected systems. DTrack can log keystrokes, scan connected networks, and monitor active processes on infected computers. So the most likely goal here was not to exploit and impact the actual nuclear power plant; instead, it was to gain access to the infrastructure in order to dive deeper into the network and use follow-on back doors as future avenues for intelligence collection.

Chinese manufacturing campaign

October 2019. Chinese hackers engaged in a multiyear campaign between 2010 and 2015 to acquire intellectual property from foreign companies to support the development of the Chinese C919 airliner (**Nation State IP Theft and Intelligence Collection Operations**).

The goal of that hacking operation was the acquisition of specific intellectual property to help China's aviation industry. Specifically, to enable Comac, a Chinese state-owned aerospace manufacturer, to design and build its own airliner, the C919 airplane, in order to compete with industry rivals like Airbus and Boeing. Ultimately, the threat actors' mission was to steal manufacturing plans and requirements so that those vital components of the airliner could be manufactured within China. Researchers at the security company CrowdStrike issued intelligence reports that stated that the **Ministry of State Security (MSS)** in China had tasked the Jiangsu Bureau (MSS JSSD) to conduct those attacks:

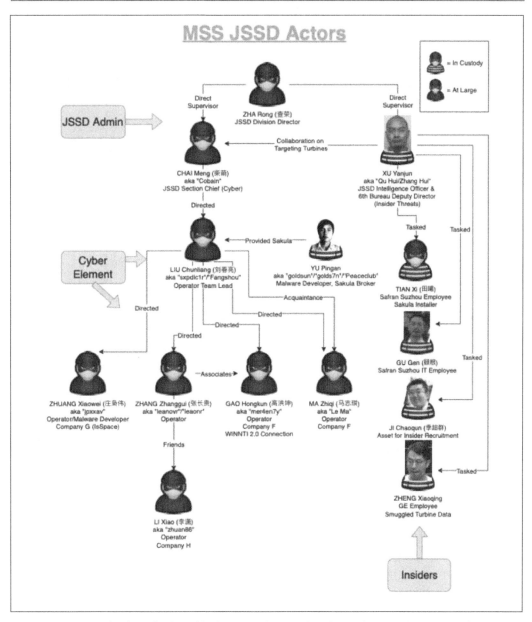

Figure 2: A graphic from the CrowdStrike report showing the relations between the agents in the case

In this case, the Chinese threat actors did not solely aim to exploit any one competing airline manufacturer. Instead, they targeted companies that were suppliers of C919 parts like Ametek, Honeywell, Safran, Capstone Turbine, GE, and others. In most cases, the Chinese threat actors were noted using custom malware. The malware, named Sakula, was developed by a legitimate security researcher named Yu Pingan, but this legitimate security tool was perverted and used for this operation by nation state actors. The final outcome of this operation was basically a "forced technology transfer," at a national level. By targeting and breaching business partners and then systematically stealing their intellectual property, Chinese companies were able to manufacture competing products in less time at substantially lower prices.

The US and Libya election interference campaign

July 2019. Libya arrested two men who were accused of working with a Russian troll farm to influence the elections in several African countries and were affiliated with US election interference operations (**Nation State Disinformation and Election Interference**).

In October 2019, Libyan police arrested two men accused of working for a Russian troll farm that was noted as trying to use social media and online forums to influence elections in African countries. The police found laptops and memory sticks that showed that the two men likely worked for a hacker team identified as Fabrika Trollei, which was literally the Russian translation for "troll factory." The group specialized in influencing elections via social media and other online outlets. Fabrika Trollei was previously assigned to a group of media and political influence teams that were connected to the Russian oligarch Yevgeny Prigozhin:

Figure 3: Yevgeny Prigozhin with Russian President Vladmir Putin

Prigozhin was also included in accusations from the US DoD for funding and organizing interference operations in the 2016 US presidential election. Hundreds of fake accounts were created by the "factory" in social networks, like Facebook, Instagram, and others, to promote fake "opinion leaders." Mainly, this was done to support political radicals and promote the most radical opinions of the disenfranchised population in the target area. Fabrika was adept at creating communities for controversial topics around the election. Topics such as migration, racism and violence, religion, and others were hot areas for disinformation:

Figure 4: An image of the building where the troll factory is said to operate

In addition to these cases, *Appendix* sums up a number of cyber incidents that occurred throughout the year 2019. The following table sums up the category that these attacks fall under, and there is a clear trend toward nation state espionage and intelligence collection:

Nation State Industrial Espionage Campaign	Nation State Disinformation and Election Interference	Nation State Espionage and Intelligence Collection	False Flag Operation	Nation State IP Theft
9	10	37	3	10

What should be the takeaway from the preceding brief analysis of the major cyber warfare related activities from 2019? Mainly, that there are ever-increasing instances of nation state activities that are mostly related to either intelligence collection or meddling in democratic processes. Why is this worth noting? Well, because this increase in activities that are not bound by the limitations of delivering a specific technical exploit on a target but are more related to the "soft" skills that can be leveraged by nation state operations groups to impact an adversary. Even 2 years ago, the overt instances of attacks aimed at a country's democratic processes or elected officials were not seen in the space. This also lends credence to the new standard of nation state cyber warfare actions that do not require actual exploitation to take place.

To better understand how this "sharpening of the axe" plays into nation state attack campaigns, in the next section, we will discuss the use of false flags as part of those activities.

False flags corrupt campaign attribution in cyberspace

In any other area of warfare, there is typically a somewhat systematic series of escalations that occur as a conflict emerges. Most experts in the field refer to this activity as "climbing the escalation ladder."

Usually, this is predicated on a series of ever-increasing actions by adversaries and enemies that engage in a back-and-forth tit-for-tat campaign of actions. Typical stages in this series are as follows:

- Pre-crisis, diplomatic maneuvering, gesturing
- Military signaling, testing, and displaying of weapons and capabilities
- Selective mobilization of forces, further displays of capabilities (saber-rattling)
- Covert actions against the adversary (intelligence collection and/or clandestine activities)
- Pre-positioning of assets
- Limited escalation of engagement
- Selective strikes
- Full engagement (war)

While there can, of course, be a variety of differing "ladders" in this space, the point is that there is generally a formulaic progression when one looks at conventional warfare actions. This includes conflict engagement all the way from low-level insurgencies onward into full-on nuclear warfare engagements. There is a "process" to war, and the campaigns behind planned actions against the enemy are part of that process. In cyberspace, however, this "ladder" falls apart.

Mapping campaigns to matrices

The very nature of the conflict environment – the digital battlefield – throws the formula for warfare, and thus the applicability of the ladder of escalation, out of the proverbial window.

The closest "mapping" that exists that is useful for detailing the "phases" of an attack escalation in cyber warfare would be to leverage either the Cyber Kill Chain model from Lockheed Martin or the MITRE ATT&CK framework.

In the following image, we reference the Lockheed Cyber Kill Chain model, which is applicable to this concept of an attack escalation ladder:

Figure 5: The stages of the Lockheed Cyber Kill Chain model

The MITRE ATT&CK framework is slightly more detailed and specific in its mapping. This framework is detailed in the following tables, although, for brevity and practicality, the framework cannot be represented in its entirety:

Initial Access	Execution	Persistence	Privilege Escalation	Defense Evasion	Credential Access
Drive-by Compromise	AppleScript	.bash_profile and .bashrc	Access Token Manipulation	Access Token Manipulation	Account Manipulation
Exploit Public-Facing Application	CMSTP	Accessibility Features	Accessibility Features	Binary Padding	Bash History
Hardware Additions	Command-Line Interface	AppCert DLLs	AppCert DLLs	BITS Jobs	Brute Force

Replication Through Removable Media	Control Panel Items	AppInit DLLs	AppInit DLLs	Bypass User Account Control	Credential Dumping
Spearphishing Attachment	Dynamic Data Exchange	Application Shimming	Application Shimming	Clear Command History	Credentials in Files
Spearphishing Link	Execution through API	Authentication Package	Bypass User Account Control	CMSTP	Credentials in Registry
Spearphishing via Service	Execution through Module Load	BITS Jobs	DLL Search Order Hijacking	Code Signing	Exploitation for Credential Access
Supply Chain Compromise	Exploitation for Client Execution	Bootkit	Dylib Hijacking	Component Firmware	Forced Authentication
Trusted Relationship	Graphical User Interface	Browser Extensions	Exploitation for Privilege Escalation	Component Object Model Hijacking	Hooking

The following are the five further categories within the framework:

Discovery 19 items	Lateral Movement 17 items	Collection 13 items	Exfiltration 9 items	Command and Control 21 items
Account Discovery	AppleScript	Audio Capture	Automated Exfiltration	Commonly Used Port
Application Window Discovery	Application Deployment Software	Automated Collection	Data Compressed	Communication Through Removable Media
Browser Bookmark Discovery	Distributed Component Object Model	Clipboard Data	Data Encrypted	Connection Proxy

File and Directory Discovery	Exploitation of Remote Services	Data from Information Repositories	Data Transfer Size Limits	Custom Command and Control Protocol
Network Service Scanning	Logon Scripts	Data from Local System	Exfiltration Over Alternative Protocol	Custom Cryptographic Protocol
Network Share Discovery	Pass the Hash	Data from Network Shared Drive	Exfiltration Over Command and Control Channel	Data Encoding
Password Policy Discovery	Pass the Ticket	Data from Removable Media	Exfiltration Over Other Network Medium	Data Obfuscation
Peripheral Device Discovery	Remote Desktop Protocol	Data Staged	Exfiltration Over Physical Medium	Domain Fronting
Permission Groups Discovery	Remote File Copy	Email Collection	Scheduled Transfer	Fallback Channels
Process Discovery	Remote Services	Input Capture		Multi-hop Proxy

These matrices for attack types and tactics are commonly considered across the cyber security industry as the gold standard for what an attack life cycle is made up of. For a full account of the entire framework, please refer to the MITRE ATT&CK website (`https://attack.mitre.org/`). While this is essentially true, the point to take away is that in breaking down the past instances of what an attack is built upon, one can see that there is a means of systematic escalating steps in each instance.

Those campaign building blocks, however, are all reliant on one another to ultimately culminate in a successful exploitation outcome. For the defender, luckily, this means that if any one point in that campaign attack ladder or cycle is interrupted, then the whole process can be impacted. For the attacker, that means that they must be successful in each step in the process or they will be required to continually reengage and modify their approach, which is often time- and cost-prohibitive. But this is mostly only applicable in past instantiations of exploitation life cycles, where a specific technical exploit was to be leveraged to exploit a target.

In the new and future attack campaign approaches, the change in tactics from one of technical exploitation to one of human, social, brand, and external attacks combined with the addition of false flag operations in cyber warfare throws the legitimacy of a structured attack map on its head.

False flag operations are not new to warfare. They have been a part of attack campaigns ever since the first caveman threw a rock at another caveman and pointed to his innocent neighbor. This has evolved into the digital combat space as more "hackback," where an organization attempts to digitally target via exploitation their perceived aggressor, grown as one nation state continually attacks another. The Russian APT groups are some of the best in using false flags and misdirection in cyber warfare campaigns to redirect potential attribution to other adversaries.

The Turla APT group, also known as *Waterbug* or *VENOMOUS BEAR*, depending on the attribution method, is most likely and widely suspected to be a Russia-based, government-affiliated group of hackers. The Turla group uses a variety of tools and techniques to target government, military, technology, energy, and commercial organizations primarily for the purposes of intelligence collection. The Turla group is commonly associated via their use of specific technical tools that are variants of the Neuron and Nautilus exploitation toolsets.

Their tools are designed to exploit older Windows Vista, XP, and Windows 7 platforms. Mainly, they are focused on targeting mail servers and web servers of their targets. Their attacks and campaigns are used to maintain persistent network access to allow their operatives to compromise networks for the purposes of intelligence collection that benefit their upper echelon leadership in the Russian government.

A technical analysis revealed that Turla operatives make use of the Snake rootkit. The Snake rootkit is a tool used by this group that allows them to maintain access to target networks to steal sensitive data over a longer period. Additionally, this toolset is used to act as a gateway for internal network operations and is used to conduct onward attacks against other organizations, and even other hacker groups and adversary nation state actor groups. Turla will infect multiple systems within the target network and deploy a diverse range of tools to ensure that they retain a foothold in a victim's system even after the initial infection vector has been mitigated.

While those tactics and technical aspects are used by cyber security defenders in conjunction with the MITRE ATT&CK matrix or the Cyber Kill Chain model to associate technical aspects of the Turla group, the tools that that the group uses are in truth Iranian APT hacker tools. The Turla group managed to exploit Iranian hacker infrastructure, belonging to the hacker group OilRig, sometime in 2017 or 2018. OilRig was noted as having targeted American infrastructure and vulnerable commercial assets in 2017 and 2016.

This Iranian group had managed to use the same tools the Russian Turla group would later be associated with, in order to gain access to hundreds of targets across both adversary governments and commercial entities.

Threat groups avoid attribution intentionally

To show just how difficult, and honestly flawed, the application of those mappings and matrices can be, all one has to do is consider the twisted journey of how Turla wound up using OilRig tooling as part of their operations.

Before we talk about Turla, we should try to understand the nature of OilRig. Cyber security defensive firms have categorized OilRig as no less than three separate and different hacking groups, each with different names. According to Dell SecureWorks, Dell names the OilRig group Cobalt Gypsy. CrowdStrike calls the same group using the same tooling Twisted Kitten, and meanwhile IronNet names the group Poison Frog. And follow-on categorizations from the same security providers even categorize the group as Helix Kitten. And those are just for the actual mapping of this one threat group when mapped into likely Iranian APT activities. Due to the lack of any real global standardization, and no existing binding agreement between security firms, combined with the already complex nature of the field, it is extremely hard to identify threats back to their source and thus accurately attribute blame with regard to hostile cyber activities.

Once the Russian Turla group managed to hack into the infrastructure that the Iranians had been using to conduct their operations and pilfered their tools and toolkits, any potential mapping of those campaigns or follow-on campaigns was effectively compromised or, in some cases, totally invalidated. Follow-on attacks by the same Russian Turla group have added to this false flag narrative and further nullify the ability of campaign mapping.

Modifying command and control for confusion

Follow-on analysis of a variety of attacks showed that Turla accessed and used the **Command and Control (C2)** infrastructure of Iranian APTs to deploy their own tools to victims. Part of the confusion around classifying the campaigns of the Turla actors stemmed from when they accessed "Poison Frog" C2 panels, another Iranian tool.

The exfiltration of data from Iranian APT infrastructure to other infrastructure associated with the Russian Turla group has also taken place. That data exfiltration from the Iranian infrastructure by Turla actors included directory listings and files, along with keylogger output containing operational activity from the Iranian actors, as well as connections to Iranian C2 domains.

That access gave Turla actors insight into the **tactics, techniques, and procedures (TTPs)** of the Iranian APT actors affiliated with OilRig. Some of that information included lists of active victims and credentials that would allow Turla actors to gain access to OilRig targets, and would provide Turla actors with the code they would need to build future versions of tools such as Neuron.

Naming the beast

Consider that following the exploit by the Turla group on the OilRig Iranian hacker infrastructure, the Turla group used those tools and infrastructures in Ukraine.

In one instance, a group calling itself Cyber Berkut hacked Ukraine's Central Election Commission. "Berkut" is Ukrainian for "eagle" and is also the name of a police force that supported the pro-Russian regime in the Ukrainian revolution and killed more than 100 protestors. Those Cyber Berkut hackers compromised a web server and email system that was then used to spread political messages via the Ukrainian commission's website. The Russian group further added to confusion and difficulty in attribution by using the disguise of acting as activists that were accusing the Ukrainian government of corruption. The Russian hackers later planted an image on the commission's web server that appeared to show fake voting results from the Ukrainian election.

In other instances of Russian false flag operations that confound and invalidate cyber warfare campaign attribution and mapping, hackers calling themselves Cyber Caliphate, targeted the French television station *TV5Monde* in 2015. Those Russian hackers posted a jihadi message on the French TV website. This misdirection by the Russian hacker team led to speculation that it was an ISIS hacker group that was responsible for the attack. It would not be until months later that the French intelligence agency, ANSSI, ultimately attributed the attack to the Russian GRU. In 2016, CrowdStrike identified the Russian GRU as the agency behind a US-targeted hacking operation.

In this instance, it was the hacking of the Democratic National Committee, and later Hillary Clinton's presidential campaign. In that series of attacks, it was later, much later, discovered that the attackers were affiliated with the FancyBear Russian hacker group.

Sometimes it doesn't add up

More recent actions by Russian APT groups also show their ability to confound and confuse a defender's ability to decipher their involvement in activities in cyber warfare arenas. In February 2018, members of a Russian GRU hacker group succeeded in an attack on the IT systems of the PyeongChang Winter Olympics. This was thought to be in response to the doping ban of Russian athletes. However, after the attack, researchers discovered snippets of code and other pieces of past attack techniques that matched previous tools used by Russian hackers, but they also contained items from North Korean and Chinese state-sponsored hackers.

The Olympic Destroyer attribution was solved much later when correlated with a phishing document used to plant the malware to a collection of other malicious files that had been used in previous Russian GRU-related attacks. Many of those earlier targets were typical victims of Russian hacking, like Ukrainian government agencies and activists. Further analysis led to more associated indicators of past GRU activities. Some of those indicators included domains previously used in the C2 servers of those used by the same Russian hackers who had breached two US states' boards of elections 3 years ago.

Chaos is the goal

The Turla incident highlights that even when there is a clear and present indicator of what would have indicated clear lines of action to known threat actors, using false flag tactics help to veil those ultimately responsible. In the case of the Russian hacker teams, they used stolen adversary nation state tools and tactics to conceal their actions and derail the attribution of their campaign for an extended period.

Because of the specific technical actions and items involved, the immediate categorization of the activity is usually associated with Iranian hackers, not Russian groups. The takeaway in this section is mostly to detail that there is not really a "good" way to commonly categorize attack campaigns in cyber warfare. When the very nature of the activity is to attempt to remain covert and undetected, then it is guaranteed that the actors behind the attacks will work to circumvent detection. Combining that reality with the notes around the broader engagement of every nation state and every hacker group on the planet being guided and mandated by their respective governments to attack one another and to leverage compromised assets to cover their tracks, steal other hacking tools, and confuse attribution, and the ability to pigeonhole a campaign becomes increasingly difficult.

Cyber attack campaigns for the coming decade

As noted in the previous examples, it is altogether difficult, if not nearly impossible, to categorize cyber attacks with broad strokes. In the past three decades, however, cyber attacks from nation states and APT-related groups were at least somewhat bound by the necessity of finding a vulnerability, crafting an exploit, and conducting the operation; that is, they were bound by the paradigms associated with legacy cyber attacks. But in the coming decade, those restrictions aren't nearly as limiting, as cyber attacks from these entities move outside the bounds of the need for that life cycle to be complete. In the digitally-connected and technology-enabled world we find ourselves in, there is no longer a requirement for an attacker to follow that chain of events. The proliferation of technology, combined with the explosion of social media and leaks of extremely advanced exploitation techniques and tools, helps threat actors operate outside of past boundaries like network infrastructure, domains, or even legal restrictions.

The attack campaign process is now shortened in terms of time-to-action and is enhanced in terms of the likelihood of success. The more technology that is available and the more our collective lifestyles are anchored to that technology, combined with the ever-increasing spread of constant connectivity, help attack campaigns move faster and be delivered with more impact.

While there is still the need for those legacy types of attacks to continue to engage in nation state espionage and intelligence collection activities, the new focus of future attack campaigns in cyber warfare will be targeted more broadly and will focus on regional, or, in many cases, national-level manipulation of narratives to sew discord and strife around topics of collective interest.

These influence attacks will be composed of tactics that are similar to older methods, like phishing and exploit deployment, but where past campaigns focused on exploiting a technical target for an outcome, these new campaigns will focus on the use of influence and influencers. The added benefit of powerful algorithms and increased computing resources will help nation state actor campaigns grow and spread.

Hoaxing

An example of the newer methods of narrative manipulation can be found by observing the tactics and techniques around the #SyriaHoax campaign.

The background to this campaign is interesting for sure. On April 4, 2017, Syrian fighter jets dropped chemical munitions on the Syrian town of Khan Al Shekhoun, injuring over 200 people and killing nearly 100 others. Victims of the attack experienced symptoms including redness of the eyes, foaming from the mouth, constricted pupils, blue facial skin and lips, severe shortness of breath, and asphyxiation.

It was noted by the UN and western news outlets as one of the worst chemical attacks in modern history. The attack sparked a Twitter storm that revolved around two competing narratives. One, represented by the #SyrianGasAttack hashtag, supported the narrative that has since become international consensus. That consensus states that Syrian president Bashar al Assad was responsible for ordering the use of a nerve agent against his own people. The other, fake narrative was represented on Twitter by the #SyriaHoax hashtag. This counter narrative was set up by the Russian and Syrian governments in order to quell the international pressure on those that were engaged in the actual conflict in the affected region. This false narrative claimed that the gas attack was either a hoax perpetrated by a US airstrike on a Syrian chemical plant, or was the result of an aid group, the White Helmets, targeting civilians in the area (Brian Ross, 2017):

Figure 6: An article from RT.com spreading the narrative that the Syrian Civilian Rescue Unit, the White Helmets, are using chemical weapons being posted to target and counter the stories from news articles about the Assad regime's actions. RT.com is a Russian international television network, funded by the Russian government

While international consensus was basically unanimous that the Syrian President was responsible for the gas attacks, what was troubling was the twist that came as the #SyriaHoax hashtag spread across the internet. This false narrative spread at a much higher rate than the truth or even the news stories that spoke to the specific facts of the attack. Not only did the false narrative spread quickly but it also reached more people across a greater area of influence than its more truthful counterpart. Numerically, the fake narrative was the recipient of over 40,000 interactions over the same time period as compared to just over 3,600 interactions. All of that occurred in just over a 72-hour period. Literally, a 10x factor of interaction and visibility for a fake story that was aimed at covering the tracks of the actual perpetrators of the attack versus a narrative based on facts that assigned culpability to those that were guilty of the attacks:

Figure 7: More Twitter and Google references to fake narratives around the Syrian gas attacks

While that narrative was quick to spread in local terms, in the areas in and around Syria, it did not take on a life of its own until the narrative reached a prominent influencer. In this case, it was an alt-right influencer on social media named Mike Cernovich, who has more than 531,000 followers on Twitter alone:

Figure 8: A tweet from social media influencer Mike Cernovich referencing the Syrian gas attack and the resulting fake propaganda stream

Because of his influence and large audience after he began interacting by posting items from this particular narrative, the campaign reached a fever pitch. In less than 24 hours, the #SyriaHoax hashtag was the number one trending topic on Twitter and was only eclipsed by President Trump tweeting about an actual missile strike that he ordered as a response to Assad's gas attacks:

Figure 9: A follower aiding in the trending of the #SyriaHoax narrative

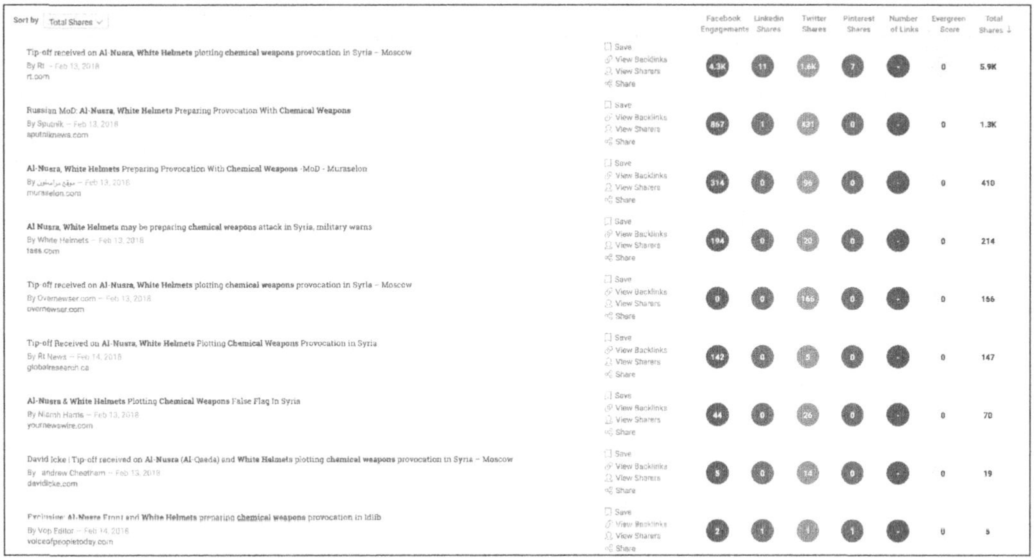

Figure 10: Statistics showing the spread and viral nature of the disinformation campaign

The spinning of a narrative might not seem that damaging or even really part of a cyber warfare campaign, but consider the inclusion of malicious links and shortened URLs into the tweet storm and one can begin to understand that there is a further weaponization potential. According to sources, on average a generic user of Twitter encounters roughly 17 tweets per day that contain potentially malicious links or embedded malware (Waugh, 2011). Added to that roughly 1 in every 500 web addresses posted on Twitter lead to sites hosting malware. According to research by TrendMicro, the percentage of malicious tweets in just a 2-week period, those that contain malware or links to compromised domains, can be as high as 8% on any given day (Pajares, 2014):

Day/Date	Number of Tweets with URLs	Number of Malicious Tweets	Percentage of Malicious Tweets
Wednesday, 09/25/2013	39,257,353	2,292,488	5.8%
Thursday, 09/26/2013	47,252,411	3,190,600	6.8%
Friday, 09/27/2013	49,465,975	3,947,515	8.0%
Saturday, 09/28/2013	37,806,326	2,018,935	5.3%

Figure 11: A table from the TrendMicro research showing statistics on malicious links in Tweets over a 4-day period (Pajares, 2014)

Interestingly, Twitter does use a filtering system developed by Google (the Safe Browsing API) that is meant to detect malicious URLs in near real time. That system checks posted URLs against a blacklist, and will block malicious links from being posted, or warns Firefox and Chrome users to think before they click. However, that filter works only on URLs that are shortened using the bit.ly service. But that is only one of more than a few hundred URL shortening tools that are available on the internet. Should a malicious user or threat actor campaign include those techniques or tactics, their embedded shortened URL will likely not be caught by Twitter's filter.

Conclusion

The goal of these new attack campaigns is not just to twist the narrative on any singular particular topic; it is to use the topic and the inherent shared nature of social media to not only spread false or misleading information but also include misdirection and malware links within the narrative itself to spread exploitation.

In other words, the goal of the new type of attack campaigns that are present today and in the future is to overtly try to spread fake news and confuse a target population as to what is the truth. Additionally, it is also to use the reactions, shares, trends, and influencer capabilities of these platforms to spread technical exploitation. This is altogether a much easier way for the malicious actors, especially nation state agents and operators who have coordinated activities and deep funding capabilities behind them, to increase the likelihood that their exploits are interacted with and ultimately activated.

This campaign method is much broader in scope and not nearly as "elegant" or "focused" as legacy spear phishing or technical exploitation, but it is more effective in its scale and the likelihood of success is much higher as the numbers are exponentially larger. This is the new method that can be equated to "phishing with dynamite."

The new paradigm in cyber security warfare operations is different than it has been in the past and requires a change in thinking in order to potentially classify and understand the new attack vectors. This new approach looks like this:

- Analyze trending news items and articles
- Track overtly fake disinformation campaigns
- Intercept and analyze potentially malicious URLs and domains
- Track influencer shares of false news and narratives and notify them and their followers of the veracity of the topic or item
- Respond and remediate potential infections, or at least notify those that interact with the infected links and URLs
- Carry out follow-on analysis and categorization of attack tactics and tools
- Create technical response actions for future instances of similar attacks
- Share updates and technical remediation items

For defenders, it is critical that they and their leadership are aware of these new campaign tactics, and that they understand the broader implications that these types of attacks might have. There is little value in working to chase attribution in this space when the space by its very existence is ethereal and dynamic and operates to counter specific attribution. Old methods of security are no longer totally applicable, and neither are those older methods of attribution or campaign modeling.

In the next chapter, we'll think about strategic planning in relation to the future of cyber warfare.

7

Strategic Planning for Future Cyber Warfare

"In preparing for battle I have always found that plans are useless, but planning is indispensable."

— *Dwight D. Eisenhower*

General Eisenhower, one of the finest tacticians and strategists in the history of American military leadership, and some might say in world history, makes an interesting point in the preceding quotation. He states that in preparing for battle plans are useless, but planning is indispensable. What does he mean by this? It seems counterintuitive to even contemplate that point, but he must have known what he was talking about, right? What he means is that it is impossible to plan perfectly for a battle that will be wrought with change, failures, maneuvering, and dynamism; yet, it is useful beyond measure to think about the realities of what is likely to take place and plan as thoroughly as possible in response. One should plan based on the realities of what will occur, align resources to counter potential outcomes, and act – but act intelligently, with a constant evaluation of how effective the actions one is taking are, in relation to the expected end goal.

With that in mind, in this chapter we'll consider the following:

- How can physical and kinetic warfare tactics and strategies be applied in cyber warfare?
- What techniques do and do not translate?
- What can we learn from observing past physical warfare actions as part of the cyber spectrum?

First, let's begin by looking at some corollaries between physical warfare and the digital combat space.

Everyone has a plan until they get punched in the mouth

At the start of this chapter, we considered a well-known quotation from General Eisenhower. Another famous quotation that could be applied in the context of strategy comes from Mike Tyson, the former world heavyweight champion: "Everyone has a plan until they get punched in the mouth." In other words, there is a benefit to having a plan, and there is merit to preparation, but ultimately it comes down to how you respond once you take that first vicious hit. In cyber warfare, this is just as true. Through the massive data breaches and nation state compromises in recent history, we have all been collectively punched in the mouth, and in many instances, knocked to the canvas. What matters now is how we leverage the knowledge we gained from getting smashed and respond intelligently to try and fix the problem. In boxing terms, we need to learn to dodge and counter.

As has been discussed, past approaches to cyber security were mainly in the form of technical fixes. These "fixes" have been in response to what is now increasingly becoming an almost unsolvable problem, and thus such approaches are proving to be woefully ineffective.

In order to have any real hope of being better prepared for the coming onslaught of cyber security attacks, it is imperative that those in power, both at the government and commercial levels, change the way we do business. We can no longer continue to attempt to string together technical solutions that are point fixes for a problem that requires a broader approach. A broader approach that is not anchored in just technical solutions and best-of-breed solutions provided by vendors that are, in most instances, more concerned with growing their businesses' bottom line than they are with the broader implications of fixing security for the masses.

The nature of cyberspace is not solely for commerce and global information exchange. It is a warfighting domain. A digital battlefield where every nation on the planet; every criminal organization; every user, device, and network; and a myriad of other technologies interact and exchange bits in an endless state of change. It is also the only place in the world and throughout history where rogue nations and impoverished countries – often so poor they can barely feed their own populace – can take aim at the superpowers of the world, and do so with efficacy.

If that is the reality, and if our systems are built on a house-of-cards perimeter-based model that is inherently flawed – as has been discussed in previous chapters – then there should be a realization that we must change our approach to fixing these issues. But that fix cannot be one of simply more technology. We cannot continue to "Frankenstein" our way forward and hope that eventually, with enough technology applied, we can ultimately fix the issues we collectively face. It is time to apply strategy, and specifically a focused strategy, to this issue so that we might be able to finally gain some ground and take back the high ground from the enemy.

What type of strategy?

If one understands and really accepts the reality of the cyberspace being a warfighting domain, an active digital battlefield, then the application of any strategy outside of one founded in a military-related strategy is clearly an exercise in futility.

But there is significant nuance in this space that requires a level of malleability for the strategy that an organization chooses to put in place. While cyberspace is a warfighting domain, it is also the new hub for business and enterprise for the foreseeable future. It is the conduit for nearly all business on the planet, and cyberspace is the most prolific avenue for information exchange the world has ever seen. Therefore the nuance that must be noted is that any strategy that is applied must be based on the tenets of effective counter actions in cyber security warfighting principles, but must be open enough to allow for business to thrive and for information to flow where it is needed. This is a difficult problem to solve.

The purpose of a strategic plan for security is to provide management and leadership with the information necessary to make informed decisions about specific investments in the security space. A strategic plan will link the security function with the business direction. Because cyberspace is a warfighting domain and a domain that is of extreme importance to businesses, the strategy must also present a business case to leadership. That business case must be one that describes key business benefits and outcomes related to security.

The best strategies for security will help achieve business objectives by identifying and addressing security requirements in business functions and initiatives and providing infrastructure, people, and processes that help secure those requirements. Although driven by requirements that may not be specific to business items, a good strategy must consider other factors that may impact on the achievement of those outcomes. The strategies must be revised periodically to allow for changes in business direction, technology changes, and new constraining factors or legalities.

As has been discussed and detailed in prior chapters, the old model of a perimeter-based security strategy has categorically failed and is no longer considered effective.

The strategy that can make a difference is one that focuses on the controls being applied where the threat is most active. Namely, one that extends the controls from an internally secured network or infrastructure outward toward the "Edge" of the control plane, applying controls based on strategic initiatives like host-based segmentation, multi-factor authentication, and a variety of others, for example. A strategy that recognizes that the network is not much more than an area of contested space that constitutes the most difficult area to gain command of requires a change in thinking.

In reality, the greatest and most exploitable entities on any infrastructure are the users and their devices, followed by the applications and cloud assets that the enterprise leverages to conduct and grow the business or to simply do their work, depending on whether the infrastructure is of a governmental or commercial nature.

An interesting corollary in how the demands of the battlefield require a change in the strategies that leaders employ to "win the war" can be taken from a brief analysis of the Iraqi conflict, which we'll discuss in the following section.

When the nature of combat demands a change in strategy

In 2003, the US military deployed its combined might – all of it – to invade and "liberate" the nation of Iraq. The goal was to remove the dictator Saddam Hussein from power and eliminate the Ba'ath party that had dominated the country for decades. While the veracity of the claims that motivated this offensive, and potential ulterior intents, will be debated for years, the fact remains that there was a war effort launched to enter a sovereign nation, remove its leadership, and transition the populace to a new and different way of living.

In April of that year, the US and its allied forces launched an all-out offensive to invade Iraq. As had been done for the last 100 years or more of US military engagements, the Army mobilized on the ground after a selective bombardment had taken place and the airspace over the country had been dominated. In less than a week, nearly the entire armored division of the US Army, along with coalition partners and the US Marines, had made their way from the Iraqi border to Baghdad. The invasion was complete, and the thinking at the time was that this was another victory that could be chalked up to the dominance of the American military machine and the US leadership's strategy having defeated the enemy.

We could not have been more wrong.

Infiltration does not equal dominance

While the Army and the coalition had done its job of dominating the enemy and infiltrating the country, what had happened was that the speed and effectiveness of the attack caused the Iraqi Army and its leadership to implode. The Republican Guard dissolved, and thousands of fighters literally dropped their uniforms and melted into the populace. The strategy of taking the grand objective, Baghdad, had tossed the Iraqi National Army and its affiliate operators and actors into turmoil and sent them scattering into their homes and neighborhoods.

Fast-forward roughly 90 to 120 days after the fall of Baghdad. Insurgents, either ex-Iraqi Army personnel or terrorist actors from a variety of organizations, began to exact a heavy toll on US and coalition forces; this toll primarily took the form of limited skirmishes within small sectors of urban areas, or via the use of **Improvised Explosive Devices (IEDs)**. In these attacks, the insurgents adopted tactics that had perplexed and confounded US military personnel during the Vietnam war, but they also escalated the perplexing nature of those attacks by ensuring that the combat took place in areas that were heavy with potential collateral damage.

The insurgents adopted the basic tactics that the Viet Cong had used with efficacy in the remote jungles of Vietnam, but adopted them in a jungle of concrete and structures instead. This change in tactics meant that the insurgents and terrorists had the upper hand. The insurgents were also bound by no rules of engagement and had no restrictions on the ways in which they could innovate and exact their attacks on enemy targets. The insurgency could strike any time against any target, and use any tactics that they found would degrade coalition and US forces. The balance of power in this case was in their favor.

Meanwhile, American and coalition forces were mired by using tools and tactics that had worked in the past – World War 2 to be exact – but were not successful in engaging this new type of threat. In truth, those tactics did not work well in Vietnam, but between Vietnam and the Iraqi conflict there was the Gulf War, where most of the most senior leaders in the US military had cut their teeth with those old large-unit tactics and strategies. Having entire battalions rapidly enter an area covered from the air and led by huge groups of tanks is an example of that archaic approach. Because of that exposure and the quick victory in the Gulf War – the 100-Hour War, as it was known – those same American leaders were now running the entire campaign of this new offensive and were confounded, as there was no quick victory. Where previously the enemy was smashed utterly through the *shock and awe* of US military might, this time the enemy had scattered, only for those shards to come back and strike independently, inflicting hundreds of small cuts upon the allied forces. This was a situation that the Gulf War veterans were entirely unfamiliar with.

The grand strategic approach of obliterating the enemy technically at a large scale, as had been done in the Gulf War, and systematically moving into an area and imposing the American military's will, did not work. The insurgency thrived on sniper attacks, cheap bombs, mortar attacks, and quick singular engagements. Added to this frustration for the American and coalition forces were the restrictions that were imposed upon them as part of their rules of engagement.

Those extremely restrictive orders mandated that the Americans and their coalition counterparts did not risk engaging with the enemy unless first fired upon, or if there was a high possibility of collateral damage, the likelihood of which was extremely high as the engagements often occurred in the middle of a city full of civilians.

The combination of those restrictions and the insurgents' ability to innovate meant that for a number of years the costs to the US and coalition forces would be high; thousands would make the ultimate sacrifice and even more Iraqi civilians would be affected, as what was thought to be a quick victory wore on and on for over a decade.

In cyber warfare, this relates to the reality that in most instances and infrastructures compromise has already taken place in some way. Most infrastructures have some open backdoor somewhere, and it is highly likely the enemy has already established a foothold in the network. Because of this beachhead inside of the defended perimeter, it is not possible to simply "dominate" the enemy and keep them out. No firewall at the perimeter is a high enough wall when the adversary is already inside. And using heavy-handed tactics to try and ferret the enemy out will likely only result in the degradation of network components and technology utilization.

Leaders need to have their "boots on the ground"

Another issue that plagued the strategy and ability to win decisively in the Iraq War was the fact that the ability to manage the response to the threats from the insurgency was relegated almost entirely to the most senior command leadership. This left officers on the ground unable to adapt to the evolving threats they were faced with. As had been the common practice in past wars, the ultimate decisions for actions at the grand scale were managed by the Generals and Admirals, who were often far removed from the battlefield.

This practice worked in World War 2, and in some instances was effective in general terms in Vietnam, but in a combat space that was as dynamic as the Iraqi theater, this method hindered the ability of those soldiers on the ground to respond. Other than in the case of very limited special operations groups who had more autonomy and specific directives to respond proactively to threats, such as Navy SEALs and Army Delta or Rangers, the legacy command infrastructure retained its stranglehold of control over the actions of those who were fighting the war.

In cyber warfare and cyber operations, there is a very real need for the leaders in the organization to be willing to "get dirty" with their troops. Often there are teams of technically oriented operators that are far removed from the higher echelons of command that are actually doing the work. If those troops do not really understand why their actions matter and how they are part of the survivability and prosperity of the organization, they will suffer from disenchantment. For effective command and control to be leveraged, the leaders in cyber warfare need to be ready to dive in and sit next to their operators and learn from "on-keyboard" actions. There is no better exposure that they can get than helping their cyber warriors execute the mission.

The environment determines what works, not the equipment

Even the tools and assets used by the US and coalition forces weren't prepared for the changes that were demanded of them in this new theater of war. In past engagements, the ability to move on the ground on the battlefield was best supported by lighter armored vehicles, Humvees, Jeeps, and military trucks led by heavily armored tanks and "up-armored" vehicles.

That approach works when the battlefield is open and the streets are wide. However, when the area where the fight takes place is in some of the oldest cities on the planet where buildings are close enough that the average human can reach out and span the entire alleyway, the benefit of those assets is limited at best.

Coupled with this, the light armor of the Humvees and Jeeps, which afforded them their mobility, made them perfect targets for the devastation that IEDs and roadside bombs could bring to bear.

Figure 1: Lightly armored Humvees were great assets for past engagements

Figure 2: The damage that a Humvee sustains from an IED thanks to its light armor

Helicopters and tanks had jet-powered engines that relied on sucking in and compressing air to function. In an area with fine particulate sand and dust, those same engines were afflicted with a constant need for cleaning and maintenance, which often grounded air support or hampered the ability of tank groups to support US forces engaged in combat. Everything in the area was essentially customized to limit the power that those assets would have had if they were in another area of operation.

Figure 3: Sand and fine particulate dust or dirt impacted engines and hindered operations

This same reality exists in cyber warfare spaces. Often the defenders are working with what they have been told is the "best of breed" or the most advanced solution, only to find out that they still end up with a breach. Billions of dollars have been spent on the sexiest, most advanced cyber security solutions that the industry has to offer, but the defenders still suffer failure and infrastructures are still compromised. While defenders pursue the most powerful and advanced solutions they can find, the enemy needs only a single user with a bad password or an unpatched application to derail an entire defensive position.

Intelligence and "Intel" may not be the same thing

The intelligence life cycle in the Iraqi war was also vastly different than what US or coalition forces were prepared for. In past engagements, including Vietnam in many instances, the enemy was large enough and aligned with a significant enough political motivation or group for intelligence collectors and analysts to decipher their actions and plan accordingly.

Even in the earlier Gulf War with the Iraqi Army, the intelligence apparatus was well set to monitor and react to the coordinated forces of hundreds of thousands of Iraqi Army soldiers and large tank battalions. Satellite coverage and the large backend decision-making matrix that drives the outcomes in the intelligence machine for US forces were able to keep pace with the slower-moving advances or retreats during that conflict. When that same intelligence capability was needed to intercept and cover small units, hundreds of politically different threat groups, more covert communications mediums, and a myriad of new avenues of attack all confused and impacted the US and coalitions intelligence efforts.

There was no time for long-term analysis of tactics and then plotting counteroffensives to combat the threat. Often by the time an action or potential attack could be discovered, it had already occurred or the insurgents were aware of the impending response and their plans had therefore changed. There was no means of using intelligence to influence vast groups of the population as the entire country had politically fragmented into hundreds of individually affiliated factions, each with its own motivations.

There were no large points of infrastructure to collect specifically military-related information or intelligence as in this theater of war every user on every phone and in every internet café was potentially a member of an attack team. Everything had to be gathered, analyzed, deciphered, and leveraged to have any potential benefit for intelligence operations.

While the ability to communicate via technical avenues had vastly increased over the half century since World War 2, the reality was that ground commanders would often have to ask for permission to operate or engage the enemy from commanders that were thousands of miles away. Meanwhile, insurgents could ask for guidance from their leaders who were either on-site or nearby, meaning that the insurgency was faster and more proactive at command and control than the vaunted US and coalition forces. While the counteroffensives were able to adapt to actions on the ground in near real time and maneuver or manipulate their force planning and positioning, the US and coalition forces were often restricted in their ability to respond in kind.

Again, it is possible to see how this relates to cyber security and cyber warfare. Organizations including the US DoD and civilian agencies try constantly to find valuable intelligence to enable them to respond better to threat actors and nation states. But the adversary knows this and works constantly to subvert those actions. Fake attacks, bogus domains, stolen exploitation tooling, and a variety of other tactics hinder cyber intelligence collection and its use. Adding in the explosion of data that is present on contemporary networks thanks to device and account proliferation and the ability to find useful data for intelligence-based cyber actions is even more difficult.

Too much may be too much

Another confounding issue for the leadership and soldiers on the ground in the Iraqi conflict was the massive sprawl of projects that were necessary for the conflict to have any semblance of victory. Thanks to decades of sanctions and restrictions combined with the corrupt nature of the ruling Ba'ath party and their mismanagement of the infrastructure of the country, essentially everything the populace needed for basics was either in disarray or non-existent.

Other than the roads, which were mostly usable, the infrastructure of the country was in a state of woeful neglect. Thousands of civilians had no water, electricity, or the logistical support necessary for dependable food access. The banking system was eviscerated during the sanctions and the invasion, and the political stability of the country was tossed into a state of flux as the ruling party was ousted following the invasion. The entirety of the country was teetering on the brink of total collapse.

Because of those issues, the US and coalition forces had to try and respond to everything all at once. Yes, there were obviously more pressing matters at each step of the process of improving the country's ability to rebound, but the reality was that it was a massive undertaking, one that was too large for a force even as large as the US Army and a coalition of many other countries.

The approach of trying to solve all of the nation's problems at once, with many moving parts that were all intricately interwoven, added to the quagmire and led to increasingly long delays and the bifurcation of projects. Because of this, delays in promises and projects lagged on and on for years, and in some cases decades.

Those delays helped add to the frustration of the populace and were likely at least influential in adding to the strife and following continued violence in the area.

In cyber warfare and defensive cyber operations, we see the relationship here as well. Most times when one looks at the defensive planning and operational focus of a larger organization, the approach is one of "solve everything now." And while that makes sense as there is certainly urgency needed, taking on too many projects simultaneously is an error. This only leaves pieces of the infrastructure reaching a completed state of security and often hinders defensive planning and execution. To achieve efficacy, one project must be completed before another one is undertaken, or at the very least projects and planning must be "piggybacked" so they get done in rapid succession. Only having 90 percent of a multi-factor technology deployed means 10 percent of the organization is still under threat. Projects must reach completion before they are considered finished.

Big walls can mean big problems

A final aspect of the conflict in the Iraqi theater that perplexed US and coalition forces and helped the insurgents continually inflict damage was related to the use of the civilian city infrastructure itself as the arena for combat. In many instances in past wars, the civilian population had either vacated the combat zone or had been somehow relegated to areas that were at least away from the most heated areas of engagement. This often occurred because in those past wars things were slow to move, and the actual fighting typically took place in areas where there had been enough significant conflict to indicate to the civilians in the area that for their own safety it was imperative that they vacate the area. In the Iraq War, this was not usually the case.

The US and coalition forces had invaded so quickly and disbanded the Iraqi army so fast that it was literally within days that the spidering of skirmishes had begun as the now unemployed Iraqi soldiers corroborated with outside insurgents to attack the US invaders. Those insurgents knew that the invading forces were unprepared to move house to house and street to street to take back ceded ground from the enemy. The insurgents lay in wait inside the pivotal areas in Iraqi cities and slowly took control of entire city states as they overtook civilian areas and either killed or intimidated the local leaders in the area.

In doing this, the insurgents were able to "dig in" to the area and make any attack by the US and coalition forces ineffective unless they were willing to engage in almost singular combat and retake the area brick by brick. The longer the US took to realize this and stop the insurgents from continuing to move laterally and spread through the network of city streets and homes, the deeper in they were dug.

The US initially thought they could cordon off areas of high threat and contain the spread of the insurgency, as had been effective in the German theater during World War 2, but all that did was increase the insurgents' ability to defend the area and allow them time to figure out new ways to outflank US forces.

Those walls also actually aided the insurgency by further isolating and frustrating the average innocent civilian, who in many instances went to bed and woke up the next morning with concrete barriers now isolating them from their neighbors.

Those walls and the increase in isolation and "security" control points in what were once just streets in a city were then seen as hindering and confounding to daily life and would alienate and drive more civilians to join in the conflict against the invading US forces. Added to that, those innocent civilians who were unfortunate enough to be caught inside those cordoned-off areas were trapped inside a kill zone.

Large infrastructure segmentation based on legacy firewall approaches is very emblematic of what is described in the preceding illustration. Threat actors' and hackers' greatest victory is not in gaining access to a system; it is when they can dive deeper into a network and find areas to set up future operations. Their aim is long-term access and cross-domain maneuverability. Using those big segments may seem like correct segmentation, but it is only a piece of the larger need. Host-based segmentation and the granular enforcement of access controls and the elimination of any possibility of lateral movement are what make the threat from those types of hacker actions minimized.

Figure 4: A picture of the author taken during the invasion phase, April 2003, of Operation Iraqi Freedom

Figure 5: An image of US President George HW Bush showing the "MISSION ACCOMPLISHED" banner. This was in May 2003; the war in Iraq raged on for over another decade

The mission was not accomplished...

It wasn't until US and coalition forces scaled down full combat operations in the Iraq theater roughly in 2016 that the losses to the American and coalition forces started to significantly decline. The position of power in the Iraqi warfare domain remained in the hands of the insurgency because they were better able to operate outside the bounds of any rules that would have hamstrung them, whereas the US and coalition forces were never able to adapt enough or to be dynamic enough to overrun or beat the insurgency outright.

This entire scenario can be used as a parallel for the problem that we continue to see in cyberspace. The adversary is in the position of power and has the authority and ability to operate at will. Cyber security "insurgents" engage with the defenders at will and employ tactics that are deviant from what cyber security defenders are prepared for. The insurgents in this space use what were thought to be points of strength for networks and infrastructure to dig deeper into systems and circumvent the controls those tools offered. Just as with the insurgents in the Iraq War, the adversary in this digital space knows that they have the initiative and capacity to dictate where and when engagements happen.

While cyber security defenders typically seek perfection, or very high levels of certainty, to try and react or to respond tactically to the adversary, the adversary is staying two steps ahead. There are no rules of engagement for the "insurgency" in this digital battlespace and the threat actors know that. They thrive on their ability to operate outside of any rules or restrictions. The insurgents in this space knowingly and willfully maneuver and manipulate command and control infrastructures for their nefarious purposes. Hackers and enemy nation states are not bound by compliance regulations nor are they hindered by budgets or keeping business applications operational.

Even when one thinks about the response and reaction of the US and coalition forces to try and cordon off insurgents into "controllable" areas, one is reminded of a network or digital infrastructure being segmented. In the case of the Iraqi campaign, the US Army literally built giant walls around entire neighborhoods to try and contain threats. This is eerily like the way a network engineer firewalls off segments of networks to contain digital threats. And in truth, this basically fails just as the army's strategy did. In the Iraq War, the insurgents learned very quickly that either they could simply have someone with validated paperwork operate clandestinely for them and move beyond the walls, or in other cases they simply climbed over the structures in the dark. Either way eliminated the benefit of the segmentation that was being offered. In the digital space, the moment an enemy recognizes that if they can move laterally they can further infect an enterprise – and in most cases all that is needed is an administrator password or network share to do so – the control or power that a segmented network offers is rendered moot.

Figure 6: An example of a "firewall" for street-level areas of operations in the Iraqi theater

When one considers the intelligence life cycle that is so pervasive as an offering from cyber security vendors and compares that process to the one that plagued US and coalition fighters in the Iraq War, the same issues apply. In the Iraq War, quick decisions were needed to act decisively on combat threats. Often the archaic intelligence life cycle combined with a multitude of forces needing and sharing that information, also known as threat intel, added to the time that would be needed to process that information. This would result in casualties at worst or often operational losses at least. In the digital space, this appears when one considers how threat intelligence can be beneficial, for sure; but when the speed of the digital space and the intricacies of that dynamic space become intertwined with business demands and operational requirements, things become muddied very quickly. Additionally, in the digital or cyberspace, **Security Information and Event Management (SIEM)** solutions (tools for analysis and visibility in infrastructure) have been touted as the "single pane of glass" but have typically not lived up to that billing.

In a battlespace with so many hidden and dark corners and no established baseline, how does any tool ever actually know when an anomaly occurs? Just as in the Iraq War, where there was oversight and analytics being combined with threat intelligence and data points, but there was no way to truly know what "normal" looked like, the possibility of predictively determining a necessary action is difficult at best in cyberspace.

Pointing to the issues that affected the decision makers in the Iraq War and led to severe difficulties in making progress and subduing the enemy in that area can be correlated with issues of a similar nature in cyberspace. Often in cyber security, the leaders that are in charge of or tasked with defending the enterprise are limited in their authority to implement change in the infrastructure.

It was not until the last 18 months that the first **Chief Information Security Officers (CISOs)** in cyberspace became broadly accepted as "critical" leaders in many organizations. In many cases today, CISOs report up the chain of command to a **Chief Information Officer (CIO)** or another executive as part of their hierarchical command structure.

This can be problematic when, in many cases, the folks that the CISOs report to have little if any knowledge of cyber warfare operations or technologies and can be far removed from the "action on the ground." Just as in the Iraq War, the lack of insight and familiarity with what is needed to respond to threats and the enemy in this space is dynamic and requires command authority to make an impact. Those organizations that subscribe to this older methodology and command structure enable confusion and a lack of decisiveness that is so critical to victory in any warfighting domain, especially a digital one.

As with the assets in the Iraq War – the helicopters, tanks, Humvees, and Jeeps – the assets we use in cyberspace have inherent flaws as well. In cyberspace, businesses now rely on applications to generate revenue and act as the interface with the customer base. Those same applications are also reliant on regular patching and secure code development processes to ensure that they remain safe. Often the very nature of the speed of business and the need for uptime for those applications makes them "unpatchable" or keeps them operating for years, in some instances decades, without necessary patches or updates being applied.

The devices that we all use to access those applications have embedded flaws, installed backdoors, logic programming errors, excessive network capabilities, and default credentials that hinder their security posture. They are manufactured in countries that are openly hostile to the US and allied nations or have at least a known clandestine program that targets our collective interests. Developers and code builders introduce threats to these applications and devices as well.

Many times, developers for applications and devices are working for reduced pay bands in countries that have noted criminal syndicates and organizations with ties to less than reputable entities. All that is needed to introduce backdoors and flaws into those applications or devices is for a backdoor payment to be made to an underpaid developer and a hardcoded, deeply embedded flaw into a system can be introduced. Even the nature of the user can be an issue for these assets.

Enterprises and governments have increasingly moved to a BYOD approach to enterprise IT. But as that approach proliferates and more users have more devices, with more bad security management, passwords, and often questionable online interactions, the possibility that threats will be introduced increases exponentially.

Standard network security practices can also be an interesting corollary when compared to the failures in the Iraqi theater. In the Iraq War, the US Army sought to isolate and control areas of potentially higher threats by physically segmenting cities and neighborhoods. While this helped to isolate and limit civilian interactions and deaths in past wars, in Iraq it only helped to alienate the populace and generate more insurgent agents.

In cyberspace, by simply applying old firewall rulesets and broadly limiting traffic at certain points, the network becomes a less optimal avenue for commerce. More and more firewall rules are continually applied and in some instances, millions of rules are piled into the network that ultimately hamper throughput and limit security analytics and response. By just trying to firewall off sections of the environment based on "best practices" and legacy thinking, the network can become far more vulnerable than it was previously.

Tying into this issue is the general application of security tooling to the user population. Often, security tools like **Data Loss Prevention (DLP)**, password management, encryption, and other security solutions negatively impact users. As soon as a user has a negative experience with one of the restrictive actions of those tools, they will attempt to circumvent it. This negates the benefit of the security control and degrades the overall security posture of the environment. In other words, broadly applying misaligned and highly restrictive security tooling to users, networks, devices, and the variety of other assets in cyberspace can help cause security problems.

The political points for or against the Iraqi conflict aside, the point of the discussion in this section is to show that while an older strategy might have been effective in past engagement, even massively so in the case of World War II, the demands of new battlefields and enemy tactics can negate the benefits that came from what was a winning strategy.

All the points that made that past grand strategy so effective were what doomed that same strategy when applied to a new battlefield with different adversaries in the Iraq War. Those outdated approaches combined with an insurgency that did not play by or even recognize any of the "standard" rules of engagement were so problematic for the US and the coalition that there really was no true victory. Everything from communications to logistics, intelligence operations, command and control, and even the very assets employed by commanders to try and win the war were not strategically viable based on the intricacies of the battlespace.

The high ground in the digital battlefield will remain firmly in the control of the enemy if defenders continue to subscribe to failed strategic approaches that are outdated and do not deal with the reality of the threat space.

What does an effective strategy in cyberspace look like?

New threats and a new era of realization that the majority of the infrastructure that is currently supporting federal and commercial infrastructures is built on a failed perimeter-based security model has prompted the industry to move toward a new cyber strategy. The new strategy that must be adopted is one that enables better responses to new threats, reduces vulnerabilities, deters adversaries, and secures systems with a focus on what is most practically achievable. In order to have any hope of better securing cyberspace, there is a fundamental thing to realize, which is that part of this new strategy will require technical advancements and managerial and administrative change to take place across the federal government and the private sector. We cannot collectively continue to do the same thing and expect a different outcome.

Changing strategic concepts

Those leaders who are in place to implement change should also recognize that a purely technocratic approach to attempt to remedy the larger strategic issues in cyberspace are insufficient to address the nature of the new problems we will face in the coming decade and beyond. Leadership cannot subscribe solely to a focus on "checking the box for compliance" and think they have achieved any real level of security. If that strategy of compliance chasing worked, we would never have had a single **Payment Card Industry** (**PCI**)-related breach, or an HIPAA (a healthcare compliance standard)-related breach, as those compliance mandates have been in place for a decade or more.

Securing information and systems against the full spectrum of threats and expecting a zero-sum output of no compromises or exploits ever is an exercise in futility. In order for that to work, an organization would be required to be perfect all the time on every bit and byte and never have a single flaw in any system. This is an impossibility. Instead, what should be the intelligent approach is to enable the use of multiple, intersecting protection solutions that address the components of what makes up functional infrastructure: namely people, technology, and operational or business assets of information systems.

It is a fact that no single system will ever be "unhackable," and it is also true that no system cannot be secured unless any and all interconnecting systems that touch or access that infrastructure are also secured. Therefore, logic suggests that to be effective, an organization must use multiple, overlapping protection solutions that work in tandem. In doing so, the failure or circumvention of any individual protection approach does not compromise the entirety of the infrastructure.

The correct strategic approach in this space is one that recognizes that in order to best counter a threat, organizations must focus their efforts and align their technologies to counter the threat at the correct intersections within the technology ecosystem.

This is done correctly by applying a strategic approach that focuses on gaining control of user-enabled devices and systems, secures data wherever possible, and leverages the power of the cloud as often as possible. Additionally, a key aspect of this strategy is to consider every network, device, user, account, access, or other related item compromised until proven otherwise. Everything is a threat, all the time. Nothing should be allowed to operate by default and any and all access must be explicitly proven valid before it can take place.

Lastly, for this strategy to be effective, the leadership in place must realize that the network is always a contested space. The network is where the battle is being fought and also the most dynamic area of threat; whether the "network" is cloud-based or on-premises does not matter. For this approach to be effective, there must be a focus on using a control that can be offered at key control points as part of that network in order to gain insight into the operational situation in the system; but this point of control is always going to be tenuous.

There are many current terms for what this strategic approach should be coined, but for the purposes of this book, we shall term the strategy **Edge and Entity Security (EES)**.

Strategically defending the "Edge"

What most leaders and management in the cyber security space tend to forget, or at least fail to recognize, is that we all follow a "leader" as we work to better secure our systems. That leader is the US DoD, or "the Fed" as it is often called in cyber security circles. The reason for this is that it is (and was) the US DoD that was "first to market" with the clear delineation on what threats were taking place in cyberspace, and especially cyber warfare. It was (and still is) the US DoD that possesses the largest singularly aligned effort to actively counter cyber threats. Therefore, it makes sense to leverage the tenets of the US DoD's strategy that are in sync with EES.

The seminal document that is guiding the DoD toward this strategy is NIST 800-207, otherwise titled "Zero Trust Architecture." NIST, or the National Institute of Standards and Technology, is a science laboratory and is a non-regulatory agency of the United States Department of Commerce. Within NIST is the **Information Technology Laboratory (ITL)**.

According to the NIST website, the ITL "develops tests, test methods, reference data, proof of concept implementations, and technical analyses to advance the development and productive use of information technology. ITL's responsibilities include the development of management, administrative, technical, and physical standards and guidelines for the cost-effective security and privacy of [data] other than national security-related information in federal information systems. The Special Publication 800-series reports on ITL's research, guidelines, and outreach efforts in information system security, and its collaborative activities with industry, government, and academic organizations."

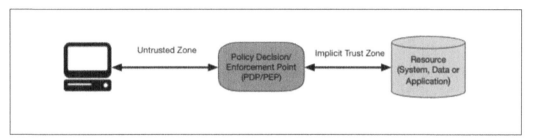

Figure 7: A sample access model from NIST 800-207

It is the ITL that is most directly responsible for the 800-207 document that is being used to help align different DoD agencies toward the strategic approach of enabling a zero trust architecture, or as noted here EES.

In an EES strategy, the focus is not on the defense of any perimeter or large area network, as that has proven indefensible. EES mandates that the focus for security should be on the "Entities" and how they access or touch the "Edge" of the infrastructure. There are very specific points to understand about this concept.

When detailing what an "Entity" is, the simple way to detail this is by taking a position that every user, device, application, or asset that might have access to vital data should be considered an Entity and must have granular security controls applied to it.

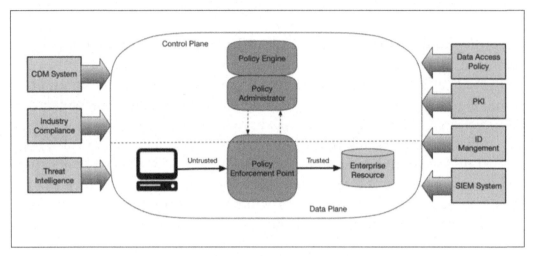

Figure 8: Sample core components from NIST 800-207

The "Edge" is different than the perimeter. Whereas the perimeter concept essentially states that far at the boundaries of the network there is a defensive "wall" that borders the infrastructure and keeps the enemy at bay, the "Edge" concept states that the edges of the infrastructure travel and move with the entities and therefore must also have controls bound to the fabric of the medium that the Entity will use to gain access to critical data.

As part of an EES strategy, it is paramount that those involved in the future migration of the infrastructure accept that, because a typical infrastructure has now grown increasingly complex and possesses no real defensive wall, that their security strategies singularly defend that network's perimeter. Any system in use today will likely operate several, if not hundreds, of networks and subnets, each with their own local infrastructure, user base, data repositories, and cloud services. The complexity that is so prevalent in today's infrastructure means that there is no single perimeter for the enterprise.

The very nature of the way that systems function today and the means by which those systems and users "do their jobs" entails that differing approaches to securing what matters most be part of the overall strategy.

Often, when considering the implementation of a strategy in cyber warfare, users and leaders ask the question, "What is the one thing we should focus on first?" This is a valid question, but a more well-aligned version of that same question would be, "How do we fail the most first?" In other words, when engaging in a new strategic plan like EES, those in charge of engaging in this effort should not try and come up with a singular "thing" to complete first. Instead, they should look at the chance to implement a new strategy with an eye toward fixing first those items that would be most damaging to the organization when, not if, an attack occurs. What is the most important point in the infrastructure that, were it to be the victim of a cyber attack, would cause the most detriment to the organization? That asset, item, database, or whatever it may be is what should be addressed first.

Eat the elephant

Another point to be aware of as one considers how to engage in an EES-focused strategic plan is that there is a process to engaging in a strategy. It is not a strategy to try and solve everything at the same time. It does not work in warfare, as noted in the section on the Iraq War, and it is not advisable in strategic endeavors for any federal or commercial cyber-related endeavors. The process for EES mandates that each Entity be fully secured and programmatically completed before another piece of the strategic plan is undertaken. This helps to eliminate parallel work threads and reduces the likelihood of too many items being processed at any one time. In many instances, this is a key point of failure for organizations in the cyber warfare space. In a variety of studies, the impact of the non-completion of specific tasks before another action is undertaken in cyber security projects can be as high as 30%.

If that is the reality, one can easily see how having multiple project items all running in parallel streams in an infrastructure that may include millions of Entities and a dynamic Edge can lead to non-completion of important items that ultimately lead to a breach or exploit.

Just as in real warfare, a key component for a winning EES strategy is to gain visibility into the battlespace. As noted in the section *When the nature of combat demands a change in strategy,* on the issues that plagued the Iraqi conflict, the intelligence life cycle is only as good as the collection and analysis capabilities of the assets that need to leverage that telemetry data for intelligence purposes. In conventional warfare, the best visibility comes from taking the high ground, being on a hill, or having satellite imagery of an area of conflict.

In cyber warfare, the "high ground" is taken when an organization can "see" everything. This means that all Entities and their interactions with Edge components and the infrastructure are all observable and provide useful data points that improve the defender's ability to respond. A key point is to make sure that the data and the analytics that are being provided enable an action or outcome.

Analytics and data, no matter how innovative, are effectively useless if they cannot be used to respond to an issue within the enterprise. What good would satellite coverage of an area be if the high-resolution imagery that the satellite provided was not able to be used to stop a convoy from driving over an IED? The answer is none. If the analytics and data that are provided by the intelligence collection apparatus are not used to actually fix the issues that are present, then they literally add to the problem by increasing the load on analysts and defenders.

EES as a strategy requires that analytics and data are used to improve intelligence and prompt action, not to simply "do analysis." In warfare, when analysis and data do not help the warfighter, it is known as "analysis paralysis" – this is not the desired state for EES.

Consider one version of a more optimally configured EES-focused security implementation. For this case, let's focus on the Entity that is most likely to cause an actual compromise of the infrastructure: the user. In order to secure a user – a notoriously difficult matter – there are a variety of steps and overlapping solutions that must be in place.

The point of a user trying to access an asset or portion of a network is always going to ultimately be to leverage some resource within that infrastructure. It might be an application, a piece of data, or some other asset, but certainly at some point the user is going to request access to "use something." Therefore, the user must be considered as a threat until they are validated as not being compromised and they have a valid and justified reason to be attempting to connect to the infrastructure.

A variety of controls could be put in place to enable this defensive position. Technologies like multi-factor authentication should be used to aid the validation of who the user is and to enact an out-of-band authentication request. In other words, a means of prompting the user who is requesting access to use an additional step to ensure that they are who they say they are before they are provided access to the requested asset. Multi-factor authentication tooling should be part of an overall **Identity and Access Management (IAM)** program that is built to enable smooth user access requests and eliminate overly complex access control issues.

The orchestration enables the strategy

Another part of this approach requires the use of orchestration and analytics to aid in controlling user access requests. Part of that orchestration and analytics should be that the user's device is checked for patch levels and is managed by the infrastructure for security purposes. The use of monitoring software can also be part of this EES approach – not in the legacy DLP method of blocking a user from accessing information or data by default, but in a manner that allows access based on the IAM controls and that logs and tracks the user as they access or leverage the assets they seek.

Analytics and the validation process should be applied to filesystem permissions as part of the EES process as well. Before the user is granted access to the asset, there should be logic in place that uses telemetry and analytics to make real-time decisions on the level and type of file access requested and to react should any of those parameters be outside the bounds of what is a normal valid request.

Some of the most basic tenets of this strategic approach to enabling EES for an organization can be succinctly stated as follows:

- All data sources and computing services are considered Entities that must be secured.

- All communication is secure regardless of its physical or virtual point of origin.

- Access is granted only to singular resources based on a per-connection basis and is reliant on a time-based connection.

- Technical policies must be applied to all Entities and be enforceable at the Edge of the system and should include behavioral attributes that are used to determine the validity of the transaction.

- All systems are always maintained in the most secure state possible, and monitoring and analysis is used to ensure that that the infrastructure and all associated Entities remain in the most secure state possible.

- Entity authentication is dynamic and strictly enforced before access is granted.

- The infrastructure lives in a constant cycle of access control, analysis, scanning and assessing threats, limiting lateral movement, and continuously validating requests for access.

- The network is contested space and is considered an area of constant threat.

- Controls must be extended from the controlled space within the infrastructure and outward through the fabric of connectivity to the Edge of the system, and applied to the Entities of the enterprise.

In warfare, change is a necessity, as are strategy and tactics. Defending more effectively requires leaders and those in a position of influence to adapt their approach to one that deals with the current and near-future state of infrastructure. As noted previously, the "Edge" and the "Entity" can be better secured, along with the whole of the infrastructure, if the problems in that space are dealt with strategically.

Conclusion

This chapter's aim was to open the reader's mind to the intricacies of what warfare in the physical space looks like and to help frame the points around how the realities of new warfare tactics demand a change in strategy. There are many other potential warfare references throughout history that could be analyzed to provide similar insights into the failures or benefits of different strategies. Regardless of the specific engagement, the truth of the matter is that warfare by its very nature is ever-changing and is wrought with potential failure points. The Iraqi conflict is just one of the most recent examples and is well suited to showing how older winning strategies can fail when they are met with new variances in a combat environment.

The most important objective of this entire chapter is to help the reader understand that there is a need to change the approach at a grand level to strategically change the way we engage and interact with the enemy in cyberspace. To do anything other than adapt and modify our collective strategies in this space will only continue to enable breaches and exploits to succeed. It is incumbent upon practitioners and leaders in the space to plan for the long term and to focus on areas where ground can be gained and threats can be mitigated based on the realities that they require to function.

8
Cyber Warfare Strategic Innovations and Force Multipliers

*"But magic is neither good nor **evil**. It is a tool, like a knife. Is a knife **evil**? Only if the wielder is **evil**."*

— *Rick Riordan*

Tools are just that: tools. There is no innately good or evil tool. The user is what determines what that tool is going to be used for and is ultimately responsible for the impact that the tool might have. A shovel can be used to dig an irrigation ditch and provide needed water for crops and homes. It can also be used to bash someone's skull in and bury them in a shallow grave. A visceral image and a violent one, but sometimes it is necessary to be a bit shocking to get a point across.

In cyber warfare this is just as true. While there certainly have been specifically developed weapons that have emerged from nation state actors and groups, the majority of what has been used as the tools to engage in cyber warfare actions were actually simply functional pieces of the infrastructure or tooling that could be used for innovations or securing systems. The tools that are in this space most often have a double edge. One can be used to help secure systems and improve the quality of an infrastructure, and the other edge is ever ready to be turned on the defenders and used to eviscerate those same systems and its users.

In this chapter, we will point out some of the more overly malicious tools that are either actively being used for malicious purposes or that are in the early stages of usability as potential tool sets. Additionally, we will delve into some similar tools that can be used to possibly defend an enterprise from a cyber warfare action. However, keep in mind that a tool is just that, a tool. It is only as good or as evil as the user behind it.

In this chapter, we will discuss some tools and techniques that can act as force multipliers for defenders if they are leveraged correctly:

- We will detail ways to plan for real-world defense operations
- We will talk about ways to address issues around passwords
- We break down how the Software-Defined Perimeter can be part of a stronger infrastructure

Defensive tooling and strategic enablers

When it comes to defending an organization from future related attack vectors, there is a requirement that the defender changes their way of thinking in order to better prepare for what might be heading their way. The old paradigm of simply trying to predictively stay ahead of the threat by using anti-virus tooling, or having segmented VLANs that are bound by firewalls, is no longer sufficient.

Attack tooling and threat vectors have proven these outdated approaches to be ineffective, and to continue to try and defend anything with approaches and tools that have proven insufficient is tantamount to madness. Changing the way in which one plans for coming attacks, and using newer, more innovative solutions that operate in the way infrastructure, users, and the ever-changing workforce are evolving, is not optional: it is the only way to have any chance at survival.

In order to understand how best to defend something, one must first understand what types of attacks are most likely to succeed. In doing this, what happens is that the organization can better understand what priorities must be prescribed to address the most immediately impactful areas of concern. Just as in combat within the physical space, a defense is best when it is based on reality and when the defender aligns their strategy and technologies to defend where an attack is most likely to occur.

Meet the Monkey

In cyberspace and in cyber warfare exploitation, attacks succeed because they locate and leverage the weak points in systems and networks. They do this by looking for technical and human vulnerabilities and then slowly and carefully zeroing in on the fail points that are found.

In order to defend from this type of attack cycle, it is necessary to continually test the system for those likely weak points. But this can be difficult, especially when dealing with large infrastructures that are bridged between cloud, non-cloud, on premises, off premises, and a wide variety of other potential configurations. One of the most well-aligned tools that fits this need is available as an open source offering.

It is called Infection Monkey.

Figure 1: The Infection Monkey logo

The Infection Monkey tool is designed to be an open source solution to help an organization test its infrastructure's and data center's ability to withstand a breach, and the follow-on lateral movement that usually results in more internal server or machine infections. The Infection Monkey system uses a variety of methods and tactics that allow it to automate the exploitation life cycle and autonomously self-propagate across an infrastructure. This system also includes a ready-built system that reports successful exploits and compromises to a centralized Monkey Island server.

This system has a wide offering of potential exploit tools and tactics that can be aimed at critical infrastructure components to help automate testing, which will allow the defenders to better focus their efforts on fixing what is most likely to be a fail point. A few of the more recent and often effective modules within the Infection Monkey tool are as follows:

- **Sambacry** – A remote code execution vulnerability, allowing a malicious client to upload a shared library to a writable share, and then cause the server to load and execute it.

- **ShellShock** – Allows remote attackers to execute arbitrary code via a crafted environment, as demonstrated by vectors involving the ForceCommand feature in OpenSSH sshd, the `mod_cgi` and `mod_cgid` modules in the Apache HTTP Server, scripts executed by unspecified DHCP clients, and other situations in which setting the environment occurs across a privilege boundary from Bash execution, also known as ShellShock.

- **ElasticGroovy** – Allows remote attackers to bypass the sandbox protection mechanism and execute arbitrary shell commands via a crafted script. The Infection Monkey will look for machines with an open port 9200 and attempt to execute commands. If successful, the Infection Monkey will use scripts to collect machine intelligence and configuration data and to also download an executable to the machine to further propagate Infection Monkey tooling into the infrastructure.

- **Struts2** – Allows an attacker to perform a **remote code execution (RCE)** attack with a malicious `Content-Type` value. If the `Content-Type` value isn't valid an exception is thrown, which is then used to display an error message to a user. The Infection Monkey will discover if the attacked machine is vulnerable and if so, will craft a specific payload to exploit the vulnerability. Following that the Infection Monkey uses this exploited machine to continue its propagation further into the network.

- **WebLogic** – Oracle's WebLogic server has a blind RCE that can be attacked and exploited with a crafted packet. To do this, the Infection Monkey installs a server that listens for incoming traffic that is indicative of the vulnerable server communicating on the network. The Infection Monkey then sends crafted exploit packets to different components with intrinsic commands to each component of the WebLogic server. The server will respond due to the vulnerability, and the Infection Monkey system then uses scripted commands to launch an exploit against the WebLogic server.

- **Credential Harvesting** – Because of the proliferation of administrator and overly empowered user accounts and their associated passwords being so prevalent on networked systems, the Infection Monkey tool also includes a module for credential harvesting. To do this, the Infection Monkey system targets Windows machines with a customized version of Mimikatz (a common exploit tool for harvesting password secrets from Windows machines). The Infection Monkey tool will also exploit Linux machines by scraping accessible SSH (Secure Shell) key pairs and attempting to use them to log in to other machines on the network.

Those are just a few of the capabilities this tool offers. While there are a variety of exploits built into the tool, usually most deeper infections result from the use of bad passwords and overly excessive shares and privileges that the Infection Monkey finds. It is not usually the power of any singular exploit that allows this system to dig so deep into the infrastructure.

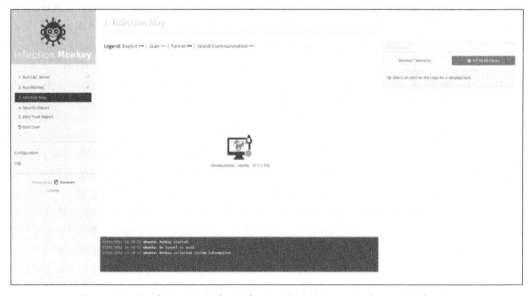

Figure 2: A singular instance of an Infection Monkey appears when testing begins

We'll get more into specific capabilities of the Infection Monkey in the following section.

More offerings from the Infection Monkey

The Infection Monkey also can help defenders decipher where there are avenues within their infrastructure for lateral movement, which is often when an exploit goes from problematic to a WannaCry-level event. The Infection Monkey tool does this by using a variety of detection capabilities that defenders can use to help automate their analysis of potential infection and exploitation avenues. The system does this by using an installed analytics tool that looks at machines that are in the same domain or work group and may have the same users and passwords present on them. This is done via a "pass-the-hash" attack that is a common penetration testing approach for gaining access to systems with shared credentials.

In a pass-the-hash attack, the attacker works to basically "become" a user and is authenticated without having access to the user's actual password. In a pass-the-hash attack, the goal of the attacker is to use the hash directly without cracking it. Doing that makes time-consuming password cracking less necessary. Because passwords are often stored in plaintext or use weak encryption and are also usually stored in a hash form, this attack is often successful. If an attacker obtains a valid password hash, they can use it to gain access to a system.

A hashing function is designed to take an input and convert it into an output that cannot be reversed. This method bypasses standard authentication on many systems and is a favorite for lateral movement. Using this technique, valid password hashes for the targeted user account are captured using a credential access technique. Once the attacker is successfully authenticated as a valid user, the attacker can further leverage the culled hashes to perform authenticated actions on local or remote systems.

Pass-the-hash attacks are most often noted in attacks on Windows systems. However, they are possible on other systems. Vulnerable web applications are also possible targets of pass-the-hash attacks. In Windows, this attack depends on using **Single Sign-On (SSO)** functionality in authentication protocols. With SSO, users enter their passwords once and are then able to access resources they have been given rights to without requiring re-authentication on the system. SSO requires the system to have the users' credentials stored temporarily within the cache. The Windows system then replaces that credential with a password hash (usually a ticket). Any follow-on authentication is then done by using that value instead of the actual credential. In Windows, those hashes are loaded into **Local Security Authority Subsystem (LSASS)**. That component is responsible for user authentication, among other things. Using hash dumping tools, an attacker will seek to dump the passwords' hashes for further use.

Additionally, the Infection Monkey system possesses the capability to test for proper micro-segmentation policies and controls via firewalls. The Infection Monkey system accepts a list of network segments that the administrator or tester thinks are segmented and "untouchable" for testing purposes. The monkey then attempts to gain access to those assets using common cross-domain exploitation tooling. If any of those exploits or login attempts work, the results are propagated to the Infection Monkey report server.

Finally, the Infection Monkey can act as if it were crafted malware and will even trigger malware alerts if the affected system has those tools in place. It can also work to act as more nation state related malware and attempt to tunnel out of the network. It does this by using its custom-built tooling to automatically attempt using common internal network protocols and ports to tunnel traffic out of the internals of the infrastructure.

The tunneling capability of the Infection Monkey system operates in a very similar manner to low and slow APT type exploitation events. The system tests for this by installing two Infection Monkey machines in the same network subnet or VLAN.

Those machines are then connected via a common TCP connection or over HTTP (or HTTPS, if configured), depending on what is allowed by the network. One machine waits for incoming messages sent via local multicast addresses to the second Infection Monkey instance. That second machine continues scanning and looking for open tunnels or avenues of communication between subnets and when one is found the process repeats. This can repeat until the Infection Monkey machines ultimately communicate with the central Infection Monkey server and will show potential fail points in the infrastructure that are open to these types of exploits and malicious communications.

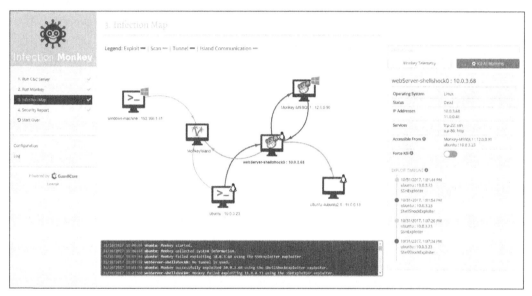

Figure 3: The same network port as the Infection Monkey system finds avenues for tunneling and shared credentials

But the power of the monkey doesn't stop there. If harnessed correctly, this tool can help with more advanced defensive planning as well.

Advanced uses of the Infection Monkey

Using the Infection Monkey system is a solid approach to discovering misconfigurations and potential avenues of lateral movement within an infrastructure.

Additionally, as defenders often note, one of the most difficult issues to solve in cyber security is manpower. With the use of the Infection Monkey as an automated penetration tester, this issue can be solved. For those that are engaged in realistic cyber defense strategic planning, a tool like Infection Monkey can be the difference between a successful defense or yet another exploit that leads to a breach.

Virtual modeling has also come a long way in recent years and can be used to iterate on infrastructure to build more secure systems. This is akin to the way one would architect a physical building. When one wishes to build an actual physical piece of infrastructure, the first thing that is undertaken is to design and plan for the ultimate edifice. Those involved will draw designs on paper, or in most cases today they will use software that allows this design to take place. Regardless of the medium, the process is to first design, then plan, then procure components, then begin building, and finally to construct the physical building. In the digital world or cyberspace this should be no different. Correctly leveraged virtual design tooling now allows this to work. And it can be much more innovative and interactive than simply a design on a piece of paper or a sketch on a whiteboard.

Using this approach allows a security engineer to leverage the dynamism of virtual environments to iteratively deploy and re-configure critical components of the infrastructure. Using clones and virtual copies of those components can help an engineer ferret out potentially useful security tooling as well as identify and remove or remediate weak points or misconfigurations. In the same manner that a physical architect or engineer can use design software to add and remove load-bearing walls or structure points on the fly, this can happen in the virtual context.

An additional benefit here is to use the virtual space and configuration capability to test the system's ability to withstand or respond to malware and viral infections. This is commonly known as "sandboxing." In this manner, the security engineers and designers can deploy potentially malicious code and applications into the virtual infrastructure and allow the malicious activity to propagate.

Any fail points or design flaws can be observed and remediated without any negative impact on any real operational systems.

The design process can, and should, be conducted using virtualization platforms that make this possible. One of the more specialized tools crafted specifically for this is from HyperQube.

The main purpose of these solutions, in this case that of HyperQube, is to allow security engineers and leaders to understand the variety of intricacies that make a system functional, and to determine what solutions and technologies can be used to bolster the infrastructure. In older instances, this was attempted in virtual laboratories primarily using the VMware suite of products. While this is possible, it is time-consuming and labor-intensive, both of which run counter to the business of designing and deploying secure infrastructure in the virtual space.

The reason for the past inefficiency of this approach when one uses the default copy for a virtual environment in vSphere is that the deployment duration can be lengthy, and the storage requirement is too large. The extended time needed to build an effective copy of the associated VMs occurs because by default VMware's vSphere product makes an extremely detailed clone of every single VM in the infrastructure. This means that the engineer or designer is building an enterprise environment for which the time and storage requirement equals over a terabyte of data.

That vast chunk of virtual infrastructure configuration data must be sent over the network to clone it, and it must be stored in its entirety. But the VMware vSphere system does not copy the networking, which increases the labor time on the final steps as the system must be "re-networked." That means each network connection in the copy will have both a new IP address and a new MAC address as the new infrastructure is deployed. This is problematic for the security engineer, as most security tools require those configurations specifics to work, therefore the copy is flawed in the VMware instance.

HyperQube's technology remedies this issue by functioning differently than the vSphere model. The way HyperQube facilitates virtual infrastructure design at scale is by using the VMware vSphere API and creating new virtual switches when an environment is copied. The HyperQube system creates new virtual switches every time a copy of an environment is made. Then the API program crawls through all of the outdated **network interface card (NIC)** configuration files, stores the IP address and the **Media Access Control (MAC)** address, correlates that to machine information to the new machine it's attached to, and then creates new virtual NICs and gives them the same (correct) IP address. Then, via API programming, the HyperQube system attaches the new machines to the new virtual switch that has been created.

Next, let's take a look at a key security enabler for future defense strategies: the **Software-Defined Perimeter (SDP)**.

The Software-Defined Perimeter

Another defensive enabler in this space that should be part of a next-generation security strategic enabler is to focus on extending the security fabric that is inherent to the core infrastructure outward to the endpoints. Today, in most instances this is commonly known as Software-Defined Perimeter, or SDP.

In past iterations, this approach may be noted as an unknown zone or a "Black Cloud." SDP is an approach to infrastructure security that evolved from research done at the **Defense Information Systems Agency (DISA)** as part of a project called the Black Core Network that took place in 2007. In an SDP strategic approach to securing infrastructure, connectivity is based on a need-to-know model. In this approach, every device and identity is verified before that entity or instance can access any application. For SDP implementations, the entire application infrastructure is effectively "black" (a common **Department of Defense (DoD)** term meaning the infrastructure cannot be detected).

Using an SDP approach, one can eliminate a myriad of issues by allowing application owners the ability to deploy "micro" perimeters that retain the traditional network's security controls and inaccessibility to unauthorized users. However, thanks to the dynamism of virtual networking and internet connectivity, SDP can theoretically be deployed anywhere. There are products on the market that enable this, and many are still being developed as well. This model offers an extension of organizational security tooling and control on the open internet, or in the cloud, a hosting center, a private corporate network, or potentially even on some or all those locations.

The SDP approach is reliant on technologies that can provide application owners with the ability to deploy internal security control functionality on demand to help protect their servers and even endpoints in many instances. This can be achieved when the organization adopts virtual components instead of solely physical appliances. In simpler terms, the "more virtual" the better. In SDP, the virtual security apparatus is controlled by the application or service and serves as the security policy enforcement mechanism.

An SDP infrastructure only allows access to a client's device after it verifies and authenticates the identity and validates that the device has the correct patches and security controls present. This approach to virtual systems architecture has already been in place for a variety of organizations within the DoD. In that SDP implementation, the servers for the DoD classified networks are virtually positioned behind an access gateway that acts as the SDP broker for all connectivity.

For this version of SDP to function, the client (a machine) must first authenticate to the SDP gateway before it is ever allowed access to any servers or that server's applications or services.

The basic tenet herein is that all client's devices, applications, and users are first authenticated, then authorized, validated, and tested before the SDP broker deploys an encrypted connection in real time to the requested asset within the infrastructure.

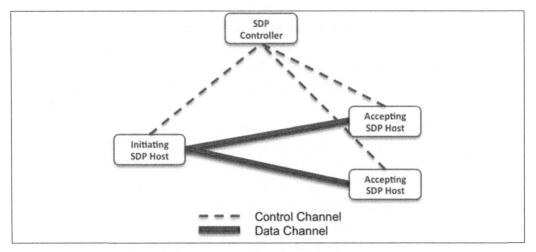

Figure 4: A sample SDP architecture (by Brent Bilger)

According to a paper authored for the IEEE, an SDP architecture should typically consist of five component security pillars (Abdallah Moubayed, 2019):

- **Single packet authorization (SAP)** – SPA is the key aspect of device authentication. In an SDP infrastructure, the system uses SPA to only accept traffic that comes from an authorized device. The first packet in the request is cryptographically sent from the client's device to the SDP controller. The controller is where the authorization is validated before access is granted to the infrastructure. The SPA is then sent by the device to the SDP gateway as part of a process of continual analysis to help it determine if the device's access should continue to be allowed. Additionally, using SPA can help reduce the threat of DoS attacks as the system processes only validated packet streams. SPA is helpful for analysis as well because if an SPA controller receives any packet that is not correct, it is considered as an attack.

Using SPA helps to locate and determine an attack based on a single packet instead of a stream of packets or an entire byte.

- **Mutual transport layer security** – In an SDP instantiation, the system will utilize the full capability of the **Transport Layer Security (TLS)** standard in order to enforce two-way cryptographic authentication. Using mTLS enables the authentication schemes that tie certificates to a known valid root certificate authority and will not be hindered by the management of potentially hundreds of certificates trusted by most browsers. mTLS mitigates fake certificate attacks when an attacker forges a certificate from a compromised certificate authority.

- **Device validation** – Device validation adds security by ensuring that the cryptographic key used is held by the proper device before access is allowed. In SDP, this happens because of the use of the mTLS approach. Using mTLS makes sure that the device authentication and validation key being used has not expired, nor has it been revoked. Because the controller cannot, however, determine if the key is fraudulent or stolen, device validation verifies that the device belongs to an authorized user and that the device is running trusted software. The use of this type of device validation and tracking helps to ensure that all packets can be analyzed and correlated for forensics, should the need arise. Requiring device validation means that all connections can be forensically recorded with data and telemetry about what device and which user made each specific connection to which specific service. A follow-on benefit of device validation is the ability of the device itself to prove that the device holds the private key required for access, and that the software running on the device meets the policy standards of the organization. In doing this, device validation eliminates credential theft and the potential impersonation attacks that might follow. Lastly, because users are granted access to only authorized applications, and because all connections are session-based, the threat of lateral movement from compromised devices is greatly reduced.

- **Dynamic firewalls (DFs)** – In order for SDP to work there must be **DFs** in place. In a DF, the default firewall rule is based on denying all connections, rather than having tens of thousands of singular rules that each have their own intricacies. This is a much simpler approach, but is much more difficult to achieve in such a dynamic and ethereal network space. The SDP policy at the gateway operates by dynamically adding and removing rules in real time. This occurs before the request to access is authorized and only allows authenticated and authorized users to access the protected applications and services.

- **Application binding** – This part of the SDP process forces all authorized applications to use the encrypted TLS tunnels. This is done once the device and the user are authenticated and authorized and have passed through the other outward-facing SDP controls. In using this approach, the SDP system ensures that only authorized applications are allowed, and that they can only communicate through encrypted tunnels. Any communication outside of those tunnels or that is unencrypted is blocked by default.

Given that these are the suggested components for an SDP system, there is also the common question of how this method of modernizing infrastructure should be adopted. The SDP approach can be applied to the vast majority of systems infrastructure. For example, in a normal core infrastructure an SDP approach can be leveraged to aid in dynamically creating, managing, and controlling security zones at a more granular level than with typical subnetting. This occurs because of the use of automated virtualized firewalls that are capable of dynamically creating a series of dedicated software-enabled firewalls on demand.

In a mobile-based or -focused infrastructure, SDP can help eliminate the problems that are present with mobile devices and the threats that IoT-enabled assets present. In SDP, this happens via the SPA system. In this model, a packet broker can replace or remove the username/password login on devices and IoT-enabled assets.

Also, thanks to the SDP approach, devices are stopped from openly transmitting information and default configured communications mechanisms are blocked as the devices are "black" and therefore undetectable by any non-validated users or hackers in the infrastructure.

Additionally, in an SDP system all SPA packets are encrypted and authenticated with an **Hash-based Message Authentication Code (HMAC)**. Doing this means that for a hacker or threat actor to attack these assets, they must first steal the SDP credentials and then attempt to spoof an individual SPA packet, an extremely difficult operation that would likely be discovered via alerting or security operations analysis. Because of the implied use of logging and analytics of all validated SPA packets by the SDP gateway, there is almost no threat posed by a faked and replayed SPA packet.

This approach can be beneficial for internal network infrastructures as well. Using the SDP approach allows cloud resources to remain "dark" to unauthorized users and unvalidated devices. Contrary to having the older paradigm of a **demilitarized zone (DMZ)** acting as a "moat" for a system, the SDP approach facilitates the management and security of organizations' cloud resources by "darkening" assets and applications that are not explicitly broadcast to those who have no "need to know." By using SDP tooling, the system is constantly authenticating and verifying a host for every session and making sure that each connection, packet, host, user, and device is validated and authorized before any connection takes place. In doing so, SDP minimizes the ability of a threat actor or hacker to move laterally following an exploitation event.

Even with port scanning and network enumeration the benefits of SDP are readily apparent. In the following screenshot, the first instance shows a port scan against a potential target host. The attacker machine performs a port scan on the target system.

The port scan then reveals that the target machine does not have any open ports between 1 – 1000. In the second instance, the same machine is scanned, however this time it is in a "dark" state as it is cloaked within the SDP infrastructure and no ports are discoverable (Abdallah Moubayed, 2019).

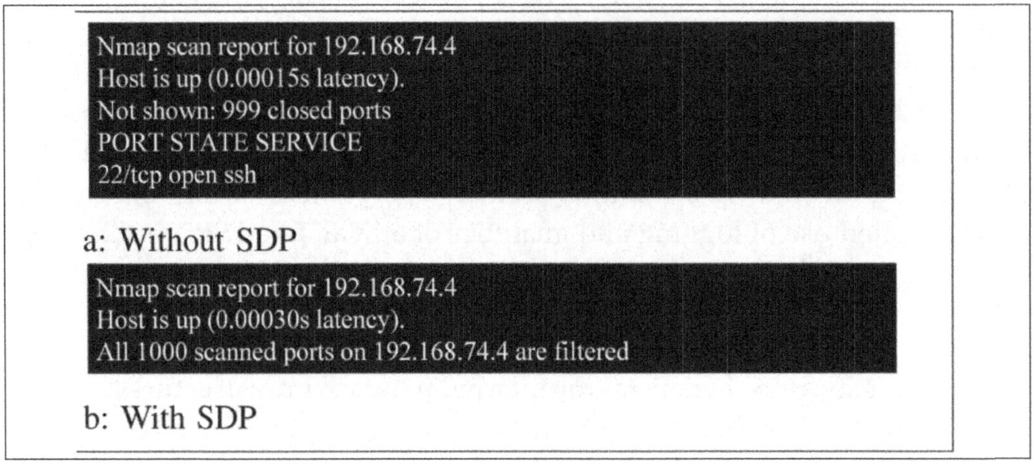

```
Nmap scan report for 192.168.74.4
Host is up (0.00015s latency).
Not shown: 999 closed ports
PORT STATE SERVICE
22/tcp open ssh
```

a: Without SDP

```
Nmap scan report for 192.168.74.4
Host is up (0.00030s latency).
All 1000 scanned ports on 192.168.74.4 are filtered
```

b: With SDP

Figure 5: Note the differences between detected ports on the "with" and "without" image

The use of an SDP-based approach to infrastructure is well aligned to help eliminate the dark corners within a system that plague defenders. Correctly implementing this particular approach does require a change in the overall system configuration and will require security engineers to change not only their configuration but also their concept of secure infrastructure. However, if this is done correctly the possibility of a truly secure and dynamic infrastructure is possible. This is precisely the model that Google has had in place for over 3 years with more than 85,000 employees in hundreds of countries and has had zero notable breaches or exploitation events. In short, this defensive strategic initiative works.

In order to really leverage the power of virtual infrastructure, it is necessary for the defenders in this space to use SDP to extend their control and security fabric outward toward the edge and the entities that reside there.

Application whitelisting

Along the same lines of SDP is the use of application whitelisting and ringfencing as a type of next-generation defensive tooling. While in an SDP implementation, the "power" of the system is reliant on the use of virtualization and a potentially heavy lift as systems are rebuilt to enable this approach, in the use of application whitelisting and ringfencing the change required for infrastructure is lessened and the most important assets in the system are secured with targeted policies.

Application whitelisting is a method of selectively specifying an index of explicitly approved software applications or executable files. Only those files are then permitted to be present on a computer or server. As opposed to blacklisting, whitelisting is more restrictive and allows only programming that has been explicitly permitted to run. Part of the first steps of whitelisting is the time spent compiling the initial whitelist.

To be effective, this list must be intricate and detailed and include a variety of data points such as detailed information about each users' tasks, machine configurations, and all the applications they need to perform their work. Most often, the ability to maintain the list is noted as being demanding because of the complexity and interconnections of business processes and applications, and the adoption of the BYOD approach. Often, users don't like the IT groups having explicit command and default blocking policies on their individual machines, which can lead to resistance to this approach.

However, if implemented, a whitelist approach offers more specific protection against malware. This is because only specific applications are allowed execute or run and all others are denied by default. Application whitelisting solutions can also help with monitoring an OS in real time. Application whitelisting should also restrict the use of PowerShell scripts and other types of scripts, which can eliminate the possibility of a ransomware attack.

Application whitelisting is more adept at eliminating malware and ransomware because it is not bound by a signature to identify and respond to a threat. If the software is not approved it does not execute, no signature is needed, as opposed to traditional antivirus software, which is signature-based. Usually, antivirus software works by explicitly forbidding the execution of software that is known to be malicious, but it is reliant on a signature or previous identification of the threat.

The problem with that is, however, that new malware is created hourly. It is therefore unlikely, if not impossible, for antivirus to maintain a completely comprehensive database of all the potentially malicious code that is available. Conversely, application whitelisting is more restrictive. No executable code can run unless an administrator has explicitly granted approval and the application is part of the whitelist. This, if implemented correctly, effectively eliminates the possibility of any ransomware or malware executing on the system or machine.

According to **National Institute of Standards and Technology (NIST)**, there are a few main types of application whitelisting that are most directly applicable:

- **File path for application whitelisting**. This is the broadest and most generic type. This method allows all applications in a path (directory/folder) to function. If used as a singular method, this is a flawed approach and does not leverage the full benefit of application whitelisting. This flaw is because this method allows any malicious file or files in the approved directory to execute. To make this more secure, the path to the file or folders must also be protected by access controls.

- **Filename method**. Using the name of an application file for whitelisting is implied here, but that is too generic an approach and leaves too many potential compromise avenues open. For instance, if a file is malicious or is replaced and its name was unchanged, then the file would still be executed. Additionally, a host could allow a malicious action to occur by placing a similarly named malicious file.

Due to these limits and potential flaws, this method should not be used on its own. The best method is to combine path and filename attributes with access controls methods or to tie the filename attribute to a digital signature attribute.

- **File size for application whitelisting**. This approach should be used only in conjunction with another approach with another attribute, such as the filename or file path method. In the simplest terms, this method uses any change in the file sizes to detect potentially malicious activity. As with other methods and approaches, this should be combined with an additional capability.

- **Digital signature for whitelisting**. Many application files are digitally signed. These digital signatures offer a specific, unique numeric value for each application file that must be verified by the recipient. Doing this helps ensure that the file is valid and has not been altered. One of the benefits of using this means of application whitelisting is that the whitelist must only update when a new digital signature is provided (by the software vendor) or when a vendor updates their application's signature keys. Using this approach also necessitates coupling with another application whitelisting method.

- **Cryptographic hashing for application whitelisting**. In this approach, each individual application is provided a unique cryptographic hash. If the hash is unchanged and correlates with the stored hash value, the file is considered good and safe to use. If the type of cryptography is strong and the whitelist maintains a running update, this approach is very sound in its use. However, if the hash database is corrupted or the whitelist is not continuously updated, as new software patches are issued, there is a high risk of an application failing to function, or potentially being compromised. Again, as with the other methods, using a combination of these approaches offers the soundest approach and eliminates the broadest swath of potential fail points.

- **Application whitelisting tools also typically have reporting capabilities**. This can help administrators and security professionals become aware of which users are engaging in risky behavior or acting maliciously. Also, this feature can help justify the expense of the application whitelisting solution as the leadership can see what activity is present on the network that was intercepted or nullified thanks to the approach leveraged. Application whitelisting can help an organization to act to preemptively block malware and risky activities before they become a problem, and can validate the security posture of the infrastructure. Lastly, thanks to the reporting and analysis that can be provided, the issues around compliance can be made easier as a full inventory of the running software on all systems and endpoints is readily available.

The old, outdated approach of blacklisting is not well suited for today's defenders' needs. Using application whitelisting helps to restrict what can and cannot function on an entity and can eliminate large areas of potential compromise. By eliminating easy fail points, the infrastructure can be made more secure by default.

Offensive tooling and strategic enablers

Just as there are defensive tools and strategic enabling technologies, there are also offensive solutions and tools that are available. As with any good offensive strategy in warfare, the need for intelligence collection and selective targeting is ever present. In cyberspace, and in cyber warfare specifically, the need to gather and collate effective data that can be used to plot the exploitation actions is even more present than in traditional warfare. With so many possible targets and such a vast possible target area, it is critical for an attacker to vector in carefully on potential avenues of compromise.

Why kill the password?

As detailed in past chapters, one of the most readily available avenues of exploitation is via the password. There have been literally billions of compromised usernames and passwords that have been stolen in past exploits. Thanks to that, the reality is that any good threat actor should first seek out those available passwords as part of their action planning and intelligence collection.

The reason this simple method of targeting and exploit planning is so useful is that the password and username paradigm is so prevalent and so widespread that the likelihood of finding a pair that work on some system and then using that foothold to dig further into the network is almost a certainty. In a variety of studies, users noted that they average 6.5 passwords, each of which is shared across 3.9 different sites. Other studies from organizations like the Ponemon Institute show that roughly 69% of users admit to using the same password for more than one device or site (Ponemon Institute LLC, 2019). In simpler terms, that's a lot of passwords to manage!

In other studies, companies like LastPass note that the average business employee must keep track of around 200 passwords. According to that same report, more than 80 percent of confirmed data breaches are password related. It has been found that in most cases, users underestimate the number of accounts they have. According to the report in a 250-employee company there might be as many as 40,000 passwords being used to access business-related applications. Studies show that nearly 3 in 4 users use the same or similar passwords (Gott, 2017).

Thanks to the interconnected nature of infrastructure and the often weak approach taken to security authentication and privilege management, all any attacker needs is a single compromised password.

In the `rockyou.txt` username and password dump there are over 14 billion usernames that relate to over 32 billion potential accounts.

rockyou. txt contains 14,341,564 unique **passwords**, used in 32,603,388 accounts.
Jan 13, 2019

Common Password List (rockyou.txt) | Kaggle
https://www.kaggle.com › wjburns › common-password-list-rockyoutxt

Figure 6: A Google search showing how many passwords and usernames
are available in a single password list (Kaggle.com)

There are a variety of means that can be used to gather and leverage username and password collections to help a threat actor begin the targeting cycle. Everything from simply buying lists of passwords on underground websites to simply looking at a site like *pastebin.com* can be a simple means of collecting potentially usable assets.

In the next section, we'll consider one of the popular and effective means of obtaining credentials.

WhatBreach

Using an open source tool is a viable means for collecting this type of information. One of the most well suited for this specific offensive intelligence collection means is WhatBreach, which is available via GitHub.

According to the GitHub posting, WhatBreach is an **open source intelligence (OSINT)** tool that can be used to find breached emails, databases, pastes, and relevant information.

A few more detailed specifics on WhatBreach are as follows.

WhatBreach is capable of downloading a database if it is publicly available, downloading the pastes the email was seen in, or searching the domain of the email for further investigation. WhatBreach uses the following websites and/or APIs:

- WhatBreach takes advantage of `haveibeenpwned.com`'s API. HIBP's API is no longer free and costs 3.50 USD per month.

- WhatBreach takes advantage of `dehashed.com` in order to discover if the database has been seen in a breach before. WhatBreach provides a link to a dehashed search for effective downloading.

- WhatBreach takes advantage of `hunter.io`'s API (which requires a free API token). This allows simple and effective domain searching and will provide further information on the domain being searched, and stores the discovered results in a file for later processing.

- WhatBreach takes advantage of pastes from `pastebin.com` that have been found from HIBP. It will also provide a link to the paste that the breach was seen in and is capable of downloading the raw paste if requested.

- WhatBreach takes advantage of `databases.today` to download the databases from the website. This allows a simple and effective way of downloading databases without having to search manually.

- WhatBreach takes advantage of `weleakinfo.com`'s API (which requires a free API token). This provides an extra search for the email in order to discover even more public breaches.

- WhatBreach takes advantage of `emailrep.io`'s simple open API to search for possible profiles associated with an email. It also dumps all information discovered into a file for further processing.

The features of WhatBreach include the following:

- The ability to detect if the email is a ten-minute email or not and prompt to process it or not
- The capability to check the email for deliverable status using hunter. io
- The ability to throttle the requests in order to help prevent HIBP from blocking you
- The capability to download the databases (since they are large) into a directory of your choice
- The ability to search either a single email or a text file containing one email per line

Here's an example of an email search using WhatBreach:

```
python whatbreach.py -e user1337@gmail.com
```

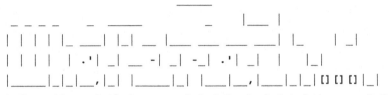

```
Find emails and their associated leaked databases.. v0.1.5
```

```
[ i ] starting search on single email address: user1337@gmail.com
[ i ] searching breached accounts on HIBP related to: user1337@gmail.com
[ i ] searching for paste dumps on HIBP related to: user1337@gmail.com
[ i ] found a total of 9 database breach(es) pertaining to: user1337@
gmail.com
----------------------------------------------------------------------
---
Breach/Paste:         | Database/Paste Link:
Dailymotion      | https://www.dehashed.com/search?query=Dailymotion
500px           | https://www.dehashed.com/search?query=500px
LinkedIn         | https://www.dehashed.com/search?query=LinkedIn
```

```
MyFitnessPal      | https://www.dehashed.com/search?query=MyFitnessPal
Bolt              | https://www.dehashed.com/search?query=Bolt
Dropbox           | https://www.dehashed.com/search?query=Dropbox
Lastfm            | https://www.dehashed.com/search?query=Lastfm
Apollo            | https://www.dehashed.com/search?query=Apollo
OnlinerSpambot    | N/A
```

And this is how to download a public database with WhatBreach:

```
python whatbreach.py -e user1337@gmail.com -d
```

```
                                   _____
                                         |___ |
   _  _  _  _      _  _____         _    |____|
  | | | | | |_  ___| |_| __ |___  ___  ___  ___| | _     | _|
  | | | |   | .'|  _| __ -| _| -_| .'| _|   |   |_|
  |_____|_|_|__,|_| |____|_| |___|_,|___|_|_|[] [] []|_|
        Find emails and their associated leaked databases.. v0.1.5
```

```
[ i ] starting search on single email address: user1337@gmail.com
[ i ] searching breached accounts on HIBP related to: user1337@gmail.com
[ i ] searching for paste dumps on HIBP related to: user1337@gmail.com
[ i ] found a total of 9 database breach(es) pertaining to: user1337@
gmail.com
-----------------------------------------------------------------------
---
Breach/Paste:        | Database/Paste Link:
Dailymotion    | https://www.dehashed.com/search?query=Dailymotion
500px         | https://www.dehashed.com/search?query=500px
LinkedIn      | https://www.dehashed.com/search?query=LinkedIn
MyFitnessPal       | https://www.dehashed.com/search?query=MyFitnessPal
Bolt          | https://www.dehashed.com/search?query=Bolt
Dropbox       | https://www.dehashed.com/search?query=Dropbox
Lastfm        | https://www.dehashed.com/search?query=Lastfm
Apollo        | https://www.dehashed.com/search?query=Apollo
OnlinerSpambot    | N/A
-----------------------------------------------------------------------
```

```
---

[ i ] searching for downloadable databases using query: dailymotion

[ w ] no databases appeared to be present and downloadable related to
query: Dailymotion

[ i ] searching for downloadable databases using query: 500px

[ w ] no databases appeared to be present and downloadable related to
query: 500px

[ i ] searching for downloadable databases using query: linkedin

[ ? ] discovered publicly available database for query LinkedIn, do you
want to download [y/N]: n

[ i ] skipping download as requested

[ w ] no databases appeared to be present and downloadable related to
query: LinkedIn

[ i ] searching for downloadable databases using query: myfitnesspal

[ w ] no databases appeared to be present and downloadable related to
query: MyFitnessPal

[ i ] searching for downloadable databases using query: bolt

[ w ] no databases appeared to be present and downloadable related to
query: Bolt

[ i ] searching for downloadable databases using query: dropbox

[ ? ] discovered publicly available database for query Dropbox, do you
want to download [y/N]: n

[ i ] skipping download as requested

[ w ] no databases appeared to be present and downloadable related to
query: Dropbox

[ i ] searching for downloadable databases using query: lastfm

[ ? ] discovered publicly available database for query Lastfm, do you
want to download [y/N]: n

[ i ] skipping download as requested

[ w ] no databases appeared to be present and downloadable related to
query: Lastfm

[ i ] searching for downloadable databases using query: apollo

[ w ] no databases appeared to be present and downloadable related to
query: Apollo

[ i ] searching for downloadable databases using query: onlinerspambot

[ w ] no databases appeared to be present and downloadable related to
query: OnlinerSpambot
```

Another tool that is available via open source means, GitHub, that can offer similar capabilities or can be coupled with WhatBreach is **H8mail**. H8mail is a similar tool to WhatBreach in that it can help search for compromised usernames, email accounts, and associated passwords. This tool has also recently been updated to a newer version known as *Scylla*. It is essentially the same tool with the same functionality but also includes a few more specialized modules around open source domain enumeration.

While username and password collection are relatively simple intelligence collection points, the potential access they might provide is extremely valuable. With just one administrator account or point of access, an entire network is potentially threatened.

Using tools like this that can find already compromised passwords is of vital importance for the defender. Knowing what is already likely in use by the adversary and being able to proactively defend from those threats helps to reduce the attack space.

SNAP_R

Another offensive tool or enabler that is new (-ish) to the scene is a combination of the power of Twitter with vectored machine learning to send phishing links to potential targets. This was not even a concept until a few years ago, but thanks to researchers at the security firm ZeroFox, it is reality now. For research purposes, a team from that company tried to see if they could use Twitter to conduct an automated phishing campaign. They found that not only was it possible, but the clickthrough rates for the automated Twitter bot were actually better than when the same attack tactics were conducted manually. This entire tool set was made available to the public in 2018 via GitHub.

The tool they developed is called **SNAP_R** (**Social Network Automated Phishing with Reconnaissance**, pronounced "snapper"). The solution uses a machine learning capability to target a large sample of users while simultaneously whittling down that list to only the most valuable targets.

That smaller target list is then used to aid the development of select Twitter profiles.

Those profiles are finally selected based on previous Twitter activity. The final step of this automated attack is when the Twitter bot uses the profiles to help craft unique tweets that are meant to spark an emotional response from the target. At a specifically chosen time, the bot will send the tweet to the target. The time for targeting is based on the profiled user's most active time for interactions on the basis of previous Twitter interactions.

According to the GitHub repository, the requirements needed to run this tool are relatively simple. All that is needed is the following software packages and account accesses:

- Python 2.7
- Active Twitter developer API credentials, a Twitter account username and password, and a goo.gl API key (all to be placed in the corresponding variables in `credentials.py`)
- word-rnn, downloaded and installed from `github.com/larspars/word-rnn`

Let's take a look at how one might run the attack.

Running the SNAP_R attack (sample commands)

Follow these steps to run the attack:

1. Clone the repository for SNAP_R.
2. In the root of the repository, create and fill in `credentials.py` with user credentials from the various services.
3. Download `tweets_model.t7` and move into `word-rnn/cv/`.
4. Obtain a list of users and a URL that you want them to click on.
5. Run `pip install -r requirements.txt` inside a virtual environment.

6. Run `python main.py`. The various options and parameters are available if you run `python main.py -h`.

With that simple install, anyone can be off and sending attacks via an automated Twitter bot that has a high likelihood of success. The larger the target list, the greater the chance for a potential click. As long as the backend of the post-click activity points to a malicious site or has an automated download capability, the targeted user will be a victim of an exploit and the attack will be a success.

Comment faking for influence

In a similar approach, another attack tactic combining the use of AI and online media was exhibited during a study conducted by a researcher to see if his bot-generated comments would sufficiently trick human analysts on a site for federal agencies. This site for this study was the Idaho Medical Reform Site.

In the United States, each agency has a comment period that allows the public to provide, via online comment forums, input into federal policy decisions. For this study, the researcher tested, and proved, that federal comment processes were vulnerable to an automated, unique DeepFake test submission. Furthermore, this test was sufficiently successful at impersonating human interactions. The researcher's bot successfully generated and submitted a high volume of human-like comments directly to the federal public comment website for the Idaho Medicaid Reform Waiver. This bot was literally able to influence policy and decision makers and was operating in an entirely automated way.

The researcher's bot generated and submitted over 1,000 DeepFake comments to the public comment website at `Medicaid.gov` over a four-day period. These comments comprised over 50 percent of the total public comments submitted. The bot's comments were often extremely relevant to the Idaho Medicaid waiver application and the follow-on commentary by the public. This included discussions of the proposed waiver's consequences on coverage numbers, the potential impact on government costs, and unnecessary administrative burdens to taxpayers.

A sample of the comments submitted show the amazing accuracy that the bot was able to generate and populate the site with. The system was also used to change the sentiment, candor, and tact of the comments to further fool the human analysts. The largest share of the bot's comments shared a negative view of the federal waiver. Because of the volume of submissions and the system's prowess, the actual outcome of the referendum could have been negatively influenced. The comments generated and submitted by the automated bot were virtually indistinguishable from those that were written by human participants during the public comment period. Human analysts and moderators would have no viable means of identifying bot-generated comments.

Examples of supporting, neutral, and opposing DeepFake waiver comments that were submitted can be found here:

Comment	Response ID	Date/Time	Sentiment
I support Governor Little's efforts to overhaul Idaho's Medicaid program.	459669	10/27/2019 4:00:00 PM	Supporting Waiver
Medicaid is an important safety net program. It helps people who are losing their coverage to get back on their feet. We need to make health and wellness a priority for the Medicaid program in Idaho.	459825	10/27/2019 6:08:00 PM	Neutral
I am writing to you today regarding Idaho's Medicaid waiver proposal, I oppose the aspects of this program that create new burdens on people who are already struggling. The proposed changes to Medicaid could deny health insurance to sick individuals when they are most in need. I do not support this approach that creates barriers to access. I am hopeful that you change the proposed waiver.	460129	10/27/2019 10:36:00 PM	Opposing Waiver

All the DeepFake comments could have been negatively biased in sentiment, which could have swayed a vital democratic process. The cost of doing this activity was nominal, less than $100. Using publicly available information and a having a basic ability to code would allow one to automate bot submissions. This attack could be launched with less than a dozen lines of code. Additionally, this technique is easy to modify to any other platform that hosts federal or private comment websites.

If only the opinions of technologically powered malicious actors are the ones that are heard, then government agencies or private organizations could lose the opportunity for fair and unbiased input, which would mean that the public loses confidence in that specific process and the results are invalidated.

Conclusion

Most often in the news and across the media cycle the adversary is described as the one in the position of power in cyber warfare. While that is not necessarily untrue, the defenders in this space can take back that initiative. But to do that, the defenders must adapt their old archaic approaches to the problem and leverage tools and techniques that beat the enemy at their own game. It is never easy to regain lost ground in a combat space, but by being smart and using force multipliers there is a real possibility to retake the high ground.

In the next chapter, we'll take a look at some new innovations that will help defenders, think about defense strategy and planning, and think about damage mitigation in the event of a successful attack.

References

1. Abdallah Moubayed, A. R. (2019). *Software-Defined Perimeter (SDP): State of the Art Secure Solution for Modern Networks*. Retrieved from ieee.org: https://www.eng.uwo.ca/oc2/publications/ thepublicationpdfs/2019-SDP-IEEE-Network.pdf

2. Gott, A. (2017, November 1). *LastPass Reveals 8 Truths about Passwords in the New Password Exposé*. Retrieved from lastpass.com: https://blog.lastpass.com/2017/11/lastpass-reveals-8-truths- about-passwords-in-the-new-password-expose.html/

3. Ponemon Institute LLC. (2019, January). *The 2019 State of Password and Authentication Security and Behaviors*. Retrieved from yubico.com: https://www.yubico.com/wp-content/uploads/2019/01/Ponemon- Authentication-Report.pdf

9
Bracing for Impact

"The battlefield is a scene of constant chaos. The winner will
be the one who controls that chaos, both his own and the enemies."

– Napoleon Bonaparte

Cyber warfare is the single most dynamic battlefield that man has ever
seen. Threats move at the speed of light and the impact that is afforded
a well-crafted attack can be global in its span. While the initiative may be
with the attacker in this space, this does not mean that the defenders of the
world are wholly useless. In fact, it is because the battlefield is so dynamic
and so ethereal that defenders can be as effective as their attackers. For that
to occur, however, the defenders must realize that the nature of the space
is one that will increasingly change in its malleability. And that in order
to gain the high ground on the digital battlefield, it is a necessity that the
defenders selectively engage adversaries when they are at their most
effective, not simply respond when they are not in a position of power.
But how does a good defense work when it is the offense that appears to
have the most reliable avenue to victory at their disposal? How should
defenders respond when the control plane for that response is outside the
boundaries of their defined battlespace? Is there a most effective method
and practice to limit the enemy's ability to gain a foothold and their
capacity to wreak havoc?

The answer is yes, there are ways to take back the initiative from the adversary and to enable better remediation and response actions in cyberspace.

This is not a simple matter. It is not an easy thing to change the overall approach in limiting the user's ability to introduce threats into the battlespace, while simultaneously eliminating the threats that are posed by new technologies and changes in the adversaries' tactics. But it is possible.

In this chapter, we will explore the following:

- The use of micro-segmentation as part of a defensive strategy
- Extending the control and defensive plane from the internal network infrastructure outward to the users and their devices
- How intelligence can be beneficial in the defense of cyberspace

Let's begin by talking about some new innovations in the security space, and, in particular, the power of micro-segmentation.

Disclaimer

The specific solutions and vendor references provided in this section are offered as example references only; they are provided for informational purposes. All information and references to vendor tooling or technologies are presented without any representation, guaranty, or bias whatsoever. The inclusion of any tool or technology does not imply endorsement or support of any of the linked information, services, products, or providers by the author.

Micro-segmentation is a key to survival

If we accept the points about the issues with the concept of perimeter-based security being a categorical failure, it is, therefore, necessary to think about how one can leverage technology to move past that fail point.

When that realization is accepted, the next question becomes, how should we still work to gain the upper hand by isolating the enemy within the infrastructure but not subscribing to the "high walls will protect us" ideology? This is where micro-segmentation comes into the picture.

What is micro-segmentation?

But first, let's detail what we mean when we suggest using real micro-segmentation. In the traditional perimeter-based model, segmentation is reliant mainly on the use of a firewall. While firewalls are still needed to help apply boundaries to the infrastructure and to set clear limits on where the delineation between controlled space and uncontrolled space lies, the use of a firewall as the primary means of segmentation for modern infrastructure is too "big" to be considered micro-segmentation. Consider that in the use of a firewall, the main concept is focused on carving the infrastructure up into generic segments of networks wherein the traffic generated by the assets that touch the infrastructure is funneled toward more limited control points.

The use of firewalls in this context is mainly around taking large swaths of network infrastructure and making those smaller segments more manageable and enabling introspection into the traffic that might be transiting those inspection points. Typically, this consists of breaking the infrastructure up into internal, external, and DMZ "zones" via the firewall approach. The private, or internal, zone is for interfaces that move traffic around the inside of the organizational infrastructure. By comparison, the public, sometimes called external, zone is for interfaces facing the public network or the internet. The DMZ zone is for interfaces that act as a buffer between the interior and exterior zones that often contain public web or mail servers. This is not micro-segmentation, however; it is simply segmentation. This approach can be beneficial to those that are attempting to go from an overtly open infrastructure to one that is more isolated, but it is by no means granular enough in nature to combat the highly dynamic and transitory tactics that modern threats employ.

To leverage micro-segmentation, it is necessary that the security controls in place expand beyond just firewalls to enable the segmentation of a much larger but more effective control plane.

Legacy network segmentation tooling, or internal, external, and DMZ firewalls, are a mismatch for today's infrastructure and cloud-based networks. That old paradigm insists that the systems they are defending were only designed to filter traffic between physical devices in a data center; no thought was given to the power that could be afforded to virtual servers and hosts within those newer workloads. Micro-segmentation done correctly will effectively create small, discrete zones or segments within each tier of an application, each user on the network, each device as it accesses a resource, and each packet as it transits the infrastructure. Using this approach at the grander level means that the outcome will be exponential gains in the segmentation within the data center and across key points of control within the system. True micro-segmentation requires that there are dedicated security controls between the hosts, networks, users, devices, applications, data, and between all controllable entities that seek to access the infrastructure:

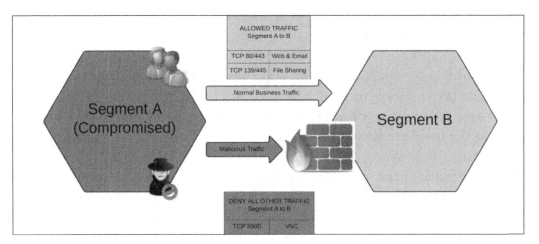

Figure 1: A basic firewall zone approach

For the network, micro-segmentation is the result of trying to protect hosts that reside in the same security zone or zones. The security zone could be a single subnet, VLAN, or broadcast domain.

By using micro-segmentation in the network, the granularity comes from enabling controls, host-based segmentation, dynamic rulesets, and others that limit the host's ability to communicate with each other directly without first traversing a security control. Using virtualization to enable this approach is a must for micro-segmentation to be feasible. By using a virtualized approach, each virtual guest machine will have its own firewall running at the hypervisor kernel. And will not be operating solely on a further distant firewall or on the virtual guest itself. If this is applied correctly, no communication can happen between virtual guests without first being inspected and, if necessary, blocked by the host's firewall:

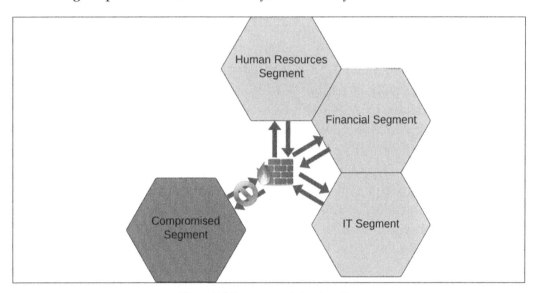

Figure 2: Micro-segmentation in action

We now have a better idea of what micro-segmentation is. Let's think about some of its underlying technologies.

Micro-segmentation tools and technologies

Micro-segmentation is possible because of two relatively new technologies that enable network layer controls to be abstracted at the hardware level (Bigelow, 2016). The first, and arguably most important, technology is commonly called **Software-Defined Networking (SDN)**.

By virtualizing the network, the control plane, where rules and controls are configured, becomes a separate control surface that is removed from the data plane, where the data and assets of value function, on a network switch or router. That control plane therefore no longer operates solely on the network hardware. Instead, it now operates on a dedicated virtual server that is known as the controller.

This central controller is the brain that instructs routers and switches and tells them how to move packets throughout the network. This is done using the southbound API. SDN can also throw this approach on its head thanks to the malleability of the now-virtualized infrastructure and use the northbound API.

This approach is beneficial to programmers as well as security and networking professionals, as they will have the additional ability to build applications that can have the ability to optimize the network based on the application's function. SDN is beneficial as it is the technology that can understand the requirements of the application and control network layer components. This facilitates the further improvement of components within the infrastructure, in order to optimize configurations that best serve users. Using this approach means that the network becomes self-optimizing and can, therefore, meet the performance requirements of the application "on the fly."

The second component of this approach that is "newish" to the industry but makes micro-segmentation possible is the **Software-Defined Data Center (SDDC)**. Contrary to the older, more simplistic hardware-focused data center, SDDC uses virtualization to abstract away the entirety of the infrastructure's layers in a hardware data center. In this approach, the SDDC carves the hardware into four basic components: computation, storage, network, and hardware (Rouse, 2017). In doing this, the application of virtualization allows a wide variety of differing applications, operating systems, and different network configurations to be present on a single piece of hardware, which greatly improves the operational capability and return on investment of those components.

Additionally, if more computing power is needed, additional on-demand hardware can be added to provide greater power to virtual resources across the hardware layer. Because of the broad industry acceptance of virtualization platforms, this approach helps us to easily move guest systems from server to server in a data center and between data centers. Essentially, by using SDDC, what was once a physical hardware-focused problem is completely virtualized and entire segments of infrastructure become portable and dynamic.

A pragmatic application for SDN

But because of the growth of SDN and SDDC, this means that micro-segmentation must be much grander in scale and spread, as what was once simply a few virtual instances needed to be segmented is now an entire virtual ecosystem must now be dynamically defended. For this approach to be effective, it is necessary to understand what exactly must be segmented and how. While, often, the concept of segmentation stops at the network layer, there is a very real need to extend that ability further toward the edge and the entity to enhance security control and manageability. Doing this pragmatically, however, is difficult in concept and can be even harder in practicality if one does not think about what to segment and how.

For better command, control, and visibility of the defensive surface, it is necessary to have visibility of all assets that communicate using east-west traffic, or internal network traffic, communicate within the same security zone. Doing this correctly can become "clunky" and could be costly (Miller, 2015). This is because doing this requires the movement of traffic outside of the security zone to a separate inspection point, and then returning that traffic, post-inspection, back to the security zone. Basically, this is a bit of a security "end-around." No matter the benefit to be garnered, the security team will need to determine specifically what must be protected, and what assets can be placed in less defensible zones.

Doing this helps to ensure that the "crown jewels," the items of true value to ensure the survivability of the organization, are offered the greatest protection and analytics for defensive purposes.

This helps to focus the visibility and defensive tooling along with vectored micro-segmentation onto assets that, if compromised, would be truly detrimental for the organization. In warfare terms, this is owning the high ground and applying combat effectiveness where it matters most.

An example of this might be if an organization was trying to protect a web application that runs in a virtual machine; they would use micro-segmentation to help make sure that asset is only available to select business partners in a controlled and monitored isolated segment. Using this approach, the partners would be restricted to using a selective IP address and a network tunneling protocol that terminates on the asset's nearest firewall (Bigelow, 2016). There would need to be follow-on security controls applied in this instance. Out-of-band authentication controls like out-of-band authentication for the administrators and users of that component or assets and the application of additional controls like automated patching and monitoring of traffic on the asset are vital.

Determining which high-value assets to protect first and deciphering which applications and operating systems are part of that "crown jewel" category, however, can be challenging. If done haphazardly and without planning or a real understanding of the infrastructure and the value of the internal assets, micro-segmentation can add significant complexity to an already dynamic environment. Most often, the approach to mitigating these issues stems from a concept around creating groups in those infrastructures that identify a certain workload and/or system category. Following that, security rules are added to those groups of assets in the form of a policy. As a virtual machine or asset comes online, its configuration is analyzed and compared to the policy. The hypervisor will then apply the policy rulesets dynamically to that asset. Should that virtual asset be moved or migrate to another physical host, if the policy is still in place, the policy rules will still be active (Miller, 2015).

By default, in this approach, the policy rules must be always enabled, even for new virtual machines. Not doing this with a default assignment will negate the benefit of the security policy for that resource and eliminate the benefit of creating secure components at runtime.

Operationally, this helps a security team as well. By using this approach and leveraging the power that the hypervisor and the virtual infrastructure possess means that the security team will not have to modify individual rules every time a new host, application, or service comes online. Using broadly applicable but technically enforceable policies helps enhance the security team's effectiveness and can help better enhance remediation.

Possible pitfalls in micro-segmentation

A potential counter to the benefits of micro-segmentation is that segmentation policies can be too granular. There is a fine line to walk between functional segmentation and a nightmare of administration for a segmented asset that is so restricted it is a virtual brick. For the benefits of micro-segmentation to be realized, there must also be consistency across the policies that are applied. The complexity of those policies will vary by organization, asset, network, infrastructure, business needs, and defensive requirements.

Added to that, the larger the organization and the more diverse the infrastructure, the more there is a chance that specific policies may not apply carte blanche across systems. Because of this reality, the chance exists that complex rules and policies will be created. As those diverse rulesets and specific configurations will require the security team to maintain granular controls for individual machines. If the policies are too granular, then more time will be required to analyze issues and then to make changes or remediate potential threat indicators. In other words, there are real benefits to this approach but there is no real way to "set it and forget it."

There are other issues that should be considered for those who are considering approaching segmentation at the micro level. One issue is that many current micro-segmentation vendor-based solutions are reliant entirely on network configurations and controls. In modern SDDCs, workloads, machines, assets, and applications can spin up, or power on, in seconds. Using only layer 2 provisioning slows that deployment down and takes a longer period.

That degradation and hindrance will slow down asset deployment and impact the use and scale of applications, all counter to infrastructure effectiveness.

Another issue is the lack of uniform policy configuration between cloud infrastructure providers. Because the cloud providers have command and control of the deeper virtual infrastructure, the cloud, there are often limits to the protections that can be deployed at other layers of the technology stack. Those cloud service providers attempt to build singular virtual private clouds that should match the layer-2 domain of the cloud customer. However, because of subtle differences that are specific to each cloud provider, each organization is forced to manage more and more security policies that will be different items of configuration than those from the cloud provider.

That lack of uniformity between the SDDC and public cloud provider helps to increase the likelihood of misconfiguration and adds to the complexity, which is counter to good command and control. Having some context of what actions and interactions are taking place within a security zone is required for good visibility and control. Only using network-based layer-2 micro-segmentation has no contextual insights into those changes. In most instances, this occurs because the segmented layer-2 domains are coupled to a firewall that has all the control over those interactions, but most firewalls do not enable contextual understanding. They only broker traffic going into and out of the domain. This lack of context can hinder security responses and remediations.

Without the contextual understanding that is available between the workloads, and other components in the virtual infrastructure, applying granular security policies that use micro-segmentation could potentially block useful, critical data flows. There is a need to use integrated tools to correlate, visualize, and adjust security-related changes as necessary. Not having this capability makes it difficult to realize the power that a micro-segmentation strategy can provide.

To more adequately leverage this approach, it is critical that security teams seek out capabilities that make it possible to micro-segment applications without relying solely on layer-2 networking controls. There are no open source solutions that actively enable this approach, but there are industry vendors that offer tooling that can be used in micro-segmentation strategies. One vendor, Illumio, offers a product called **Adaptive Security Platform (ASP)**. Their offering provides security enforcement across the workload via the **Virtual Enforcement Node (VEN)**.

As Illumio describes it, "the VEN is not in the data path, resides within the workload operating system, and enforces policy using the instruments that are in the operating system (that is, specifically, iptables for Linux operating systems and **Windows Filtering Platform (WFP)** for Windows servers)." Their security policies are computed via their centralized **Policy Compute Engine (PCE)**. This point of control receives contextual information about workloads through telemetry from all of the VENs that are distributed across the infrastructure. Illumio's PCE then uses the "relationship" between workloads to derive what policies should be installed into iptables for Linux or WFP for Windows.

There is no reliance on the network for security by approaching the control capability in this manner. All existing VLANs, physical separations, or segmentations will remain in place. The layer-2 network requires no change to its configuration and previously installed or built security protocols and tooling can remain in place. Using this tooling and technology allows for the use of virtual security tooling and does not negate the previously installed and deployed security tooling.

Reclaiming the "high ground"

A concept in warfare that is applicable here is to meet the enemy where they operate. In the case of cyber warfare this means that it is pivotal to take back the initiative from the adversary by focusing on reducing their ability to compromise or exploit users first. Users are the most common avenue for exploitation and are where there is the highest likelihood of a targeted attack gaining an initial foothold in a network.

Users are the most prolific instigators of compromising activities and are where the adversary focuses their efforts. While many might argue that the network or deeper into the infrastructure is the most powerful and correct area to try and gain control, this is not correct.

When one considers what is necessary to administer a firewall, which is a key piece of control for a network, the question should be "how does one manage that asset? And what is needed to leverage that firewall for security purposes?" In every instance, the answer will be an administrator account and a password. There has never in the history of cyber warfare or security been a single instance of an exploit simply operating entirely autonomously. At some point, either a human activated the exploit, or the exploit was instantiated leveraging human-related components before it moved to the proliferation stage.

If the goal is truly to improve security, then the need to apply controls toward areas that are most likely to be targeted makes more sense than focusing on areas of infrastructure that will always be needed to move electrons, and therefore is always an area of contested space. Just as with the roadside bombs and IEDs that were so deadly in the Iraqi conflict that the roads were always considered a threatened space.

Even if the road was secured and inspected, the moment that roadway could have traffic traverse it and drivers were able to access that transitory environment, the possibility that an explosive might lie just below the surface was ever present. The network itself is always an area of contention and will always be where the battle is fought in the cyber domain, it can never be "secure." If the network is the transportation avenue for both "good" and "bad" traffic it is and should always be considered contested space and should not be the first or the primary concern for security to be applied.

However, like anything else in warfare, this realization leads to a choice. Does one defend the users via their online profiles and accounts, which could be in the thousands, or work to defend the users via their devices?

It is much more likely that the defensive requirements will be less if one focuses on cohesively defending the users via their devices while simultaneously using approaches and tooling that will eliminate issues like VPNs and the password entirely.

Again, with this requirement there are no open source solutions that truly meet the muster, so we will explore industry vendor-provided solutions that could be strategic force multipliers for those that seek to approach the threat from this vector. One of the more broadly installed and openly used solutions that the US DoD Armed Forces uses for the defense of their users and their associated devices comes from *MobileIron*.

MobileIron recently released the industry's first mobile-centric security platform that makes the mobile device the ID that is used by the user to access the infrastructure. Because the mobile device is the ID, it is possible to fully eliminate passwords and enable a secure user authentication from user devices without requiring the user to remember or even type in passwords. This is how zero sign-on and conditional access works on any device, regardless of whether it is managed or unmanaged:

1. The user attempts to log in to a service from any device managed by MobileIron **Unified Endpoint Management (UEM)**. Once registered, the device is assigned an identity certificate and managed application configurations are pushed to the device.

2. The service redirects the device to MobileIron Access for authentication. Doing this requires the configuration of access as an **identity provider (IdP)** for managed cloud services. Access can also be configured as a delegated IdP to work alongside an existing IdP. This access enables split-tunneling on the device so that only the authentication traffic from the managed application is verified and all other traffic goes directly to the service after the next verification step.

3. This tooling verifies the user, device, app, threats, and other telemetry before sending a standards-based token (SAML or WS-Fed) to the service. User trust is established and is based on the assigned identity certificate.

The device and application trust is validated and is established based on the telemetry that comes from the MobileIron UEM and its managed application controls and configurations. Should an unmanaged application, a potential indicator of a compromised device, an unauthenticated device, or another detected potential threat attempt to connect, this system will detect that anomaly and provide the user with a remediation page that instructs them in how to remediate the issue and further improve their device's security posture. Additionally, this system combines integration with other threat defense tooling to help ensure devices with known malicious code, apps, profiles, or those that connect or attempt to connect over known malicious Wi-Fi access points cannot access the infrastructure.

4. Following that process means that the user now has access to the infrastructure on a controlled and secured device. This also ensures that the applications that are present on the device are patched and safe to use, and that the network being used for connectivity is safe and is not an avenue for introducing exploits or a compromised communications medium. This all happens without the use of a password.

For BYOD devices and desktops that are managed by a third party, such as an MSSP or remote **security operations center** (**SOC**), MobileIron can apply a standards-based zero sign-on using FIDO2 (FIDO2 is the overarching term for FIDO Alliance's newest set of specifications. FIDO2 enables users to leverage common devices to easily authenticate to online services in both mobile and desktop environments).

For this approach, the third-party management tooling is then used to help distribute the MobileIron FIDO2 client application to the device. The user will also have to register that now-managed mobile device with the FIDO2 application. This is completed by scanning a registration QR code from the FIDO2 app. Following that registration process, the managed device can be used to perform FIDO2 authentication without the need for a password.

In a similar fashion, the MobileIron solution can be beneficial to those that are not using a managed-device approach, which is increasingly common for small businesses and other less compliance-bound organizations. The method to enable this is, essentially, as follows:

1. The user attempts to log in to a cloud service from an unmanaged device.

2. The service redirects to MobileIron Access. MobileIron Access detects the device is unmanaged and displays a QR code to the end user (the QR code contains a unique session ID).

3. The user now uses their managed MobileIron mobile phone to authenticate to the QR code. The user first authenticates to the MobileIron UEM application on their managed mobile using biometrics (like FaceID) and then scans the QR code. Information from the scanned QR code is sent to Access including the unique session ID.

4. Access validates the user and other telemetry before enabling the session ID on the specific device. No password was ever required, and the user then logs in to the cloud service.

5. Based on the security posture of the device and user, Access can also redirect the user to a **remote browser isolation** (**RBI**) session. This is a service that is running in the cloud and instantiates an ephemeral remote browser session and only displays back pixels to the local browser on the desktop. The user does not need to download any application or browser plugin as the data is streamed using HTML5. The remote browser session provides a "secure containerized" display that can enforce data leakage prevention controls like disabling cut/copy/paste in the local browser or downloading/ uploading data to the remote browser session. Once the user closes the local browser, the remote browser session is terminated and there is nothing stored on the local browser or desktop.

We have been considering a number of ways in which defenders can prepare and equip themselves for an inevitable attack, but even the best defense is not impregnable. We should also consider what to do in the event of being compromised. In this case, the goal is to limit the damage as much as possible.

Kill the password, limit the pain

Diving deeper into the area around the FIDO alliance, and the efforts there to help defend devices and eliminate the threats that passwords introduce, it is imperative that one understands some of the concepts that are so key to this effort to eliminate the password for users and their devices. Often, **two-factor authentication (2FA)** as it is known is cited as the most powerful form of out-of-band authentication that can help eliminate password issues. While 2FA is a very useful solution and should be employed at large for all systems, it is not beyond compromise.

2FA helps add an additional point of authentication and splits the authentication protocol (password and authentication) between different systems and devices, but it's far from perfect; in the end, it really only means attackers have to crack two codes instead of one. And should an attacker phish a target with a focus on intersecting the 2FA process, it is possible that they might eliminate the benefit of this approach.

There are already noted instances of security researchers finding evidence that Chinese government-linked hacking groups have bypassed 2FA (Cimpanu, 2019). Those attacks were thought to be linked to APT20, a nation state cyber warfare group thought to be affiliated with the Beijing government. Based on those noted instances of compromise, the APT20 hackers exploited web servers as the initial point of entry into a target's systems.

While on the inside, the group dumped passwords and looked for administrator accounts in order to maximize their access. A primary focus of the threat actors was obtaining VPN credentials.

Having those passwords and accounts would allow the hackers to escalate their access and pivot deeper into the victim's infrastructure. They could also use the VPN username and accounts as more stable backdoors. As further proof of the need to secure user devices, the APT20 attackers gained large swaths of access, by manipulating legitimate tools that were already installed on hacked user devices. The threat actors did this rather than attempting to download their own custom-built malware, which would have been detected by local security software.

During a post-event analysis, investigators were able to determine that the threat actors had also managed to use those VPN accounts even though they were protected by 2FA. While the entirety of the details is still unclear, the concept of the means the group used to bypass 2FA is noted. It is most likely that the APT20 threat actors used a stolen RSA SecurID software token from a previously hacked system. Then, the threat actors used that stolen token on their own machines to generate valid one-time codes and bypass 2FA at will. In most instances, this would not work. In order to use one of the software tokens, the user would need to connect a physical (hardware) device, such as a key fob, to their computer.

That device and the software token would then generate a valid 2FA code. If the device was not present, the RSA SecurID software should generate an error and prevent authentication. The software token is generated for a specific system, but of course this system-specific value could easily be retrieved by the actor when having access to the system of the victim. The threat actor does not actually need to go through the trouble of obtaining the victim's system-specific value because this specific value is only checked when importing the SecurID Token Seed and has no relation to the seed used to generate actual two-factor tokens. That means the actor can simply patch the check that verifies if the imported soft token was generated for this system and does not need to bother with stealing the system-specific value at all. All the threat actors had to do was to make use of the 2FA codes was to steal an RSA SecurID Software Token and to patch one instruction, which results in the generation of valid tokens (Schamper, 2019).

Even the US **Federal Bureau of Investigation** (FBI) has sent advisories and notices that reference the issues that are present with relying solely on 2FA to aid in securing user accounts via 2FA on a device. The simplest method to bypass most 2FA approaches is SIM swap fraud. The method requires the attacker to convince a mobile network provider to provide details to a viable target's phone, or to simply bribe an employee of a provider, to port a target's mobile number to a different device. This will allow the threat actor to receive the 2FA security codes sent via SMS text:

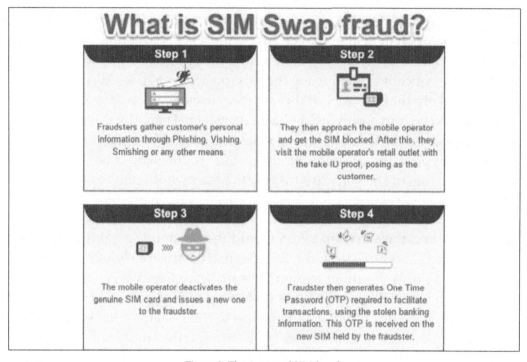

Figure 3: The 4 steps of SIM fraud

Another technique is the man-in-the-middle phishing attack that tricks people into entering their username and password and the associated 2FA code onto a fake site, which then passes it to the real one.

Following, you can see a fake web page for the ProtonMail hack. It is a simple but effective fake that has all the components of the real page:

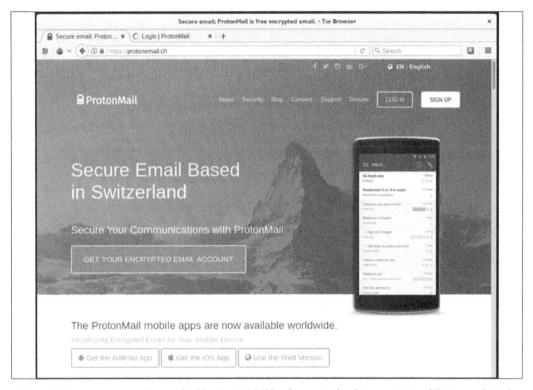

Figure 4: Even a secure email provider like ProtonMail has been noted as being a victim of this type of attack. Note the ".ch" ending to the domain name. That is not the correct domain for ProtonMail, but the site looks entirely accurate and is completely functional.

We can see more of the site in the following screenshot:

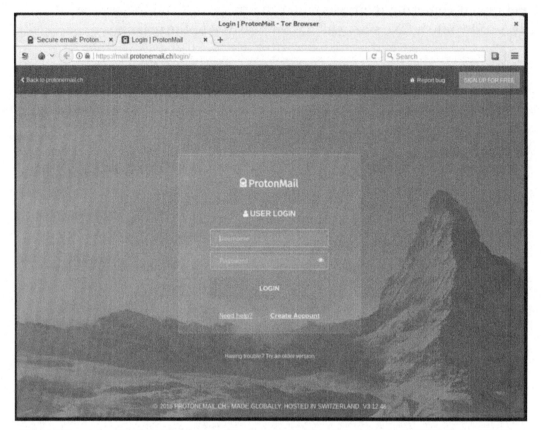

Figure 5: A user is redirected to the bogus login page, which will include a prompt for a 2FA login activation. All of the associated credentials will be compromised and stolen.

Even Google and Gmail have been victim to this approach:

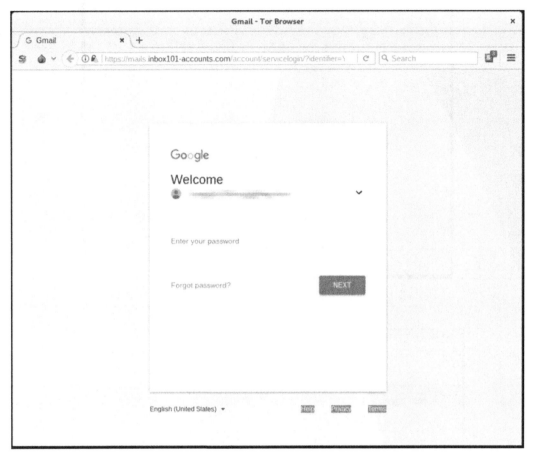

Figure 6: This is a well-crafted fake page where the threat actors hid the fake
domain information in the extended URL

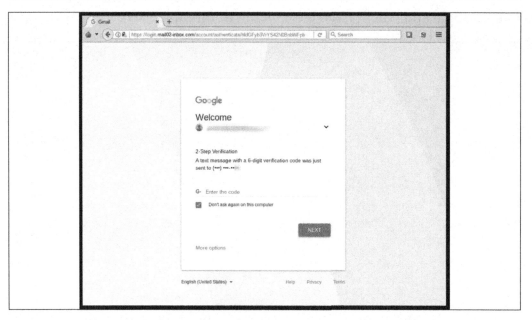

Figure 7: The follow-on link will prompt the user to enter their Gmail 2FA

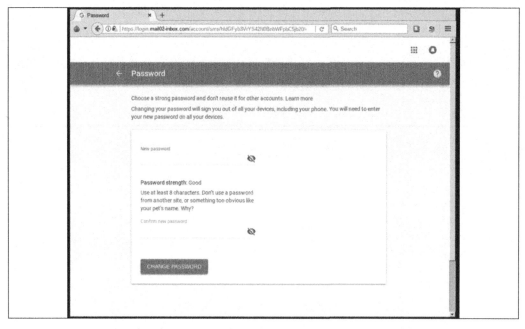

Figure 8: But then the users are redirected to create a new username and password,
which is actually being stolen and will be used to compromise the account

A third and much more advanced method is session hijacking. In this attack, the site is genuine, but the credentials and codes are stolen from traffic travelling to and from the user via the browser. Regardless of the specific technical approach, the point is that there are ways to circumvent the 2FA process and potentially introduce an exploitation cycle. Threat actors, especially capable nation state actors, are extremely adept at this and have been shown to be actively engaging in these tactics.

The goal in defending the user's device is to push the defensive "edge" as far outward as possible from the internal, and hopefully, better defended organizational infrastructure. While the user and their associated accounts and passwords will likely remain a key point of failure for the defenders, engaging security controls that reside on the user's device is a wise method of extending the defensive "edge" to the "entity" and limiting the impact that a compromised user can have should they introduce an exploit into a system.

Intelligence collection

Another key aspect of physical warfare that traverses well into the domain of cyber warfare defense is intelligence collection. In warfare in the physical space, this can come from a variety of potential sources. Everything from news reports, human conversations, financial records, and almost any other source of data can potentially yield vital insights into adversary actions or plans. Literally anything could potentially possess useful information, but gathering and actually utilizing that data is not feasible. The goal in warfare intelligence operations is to vector in on what activities and data points there are that might be of the most value and then integrate that information into the operational cycle. Doing this effectively can greatly increase the value of the data and improve the outcome of operations that are built and based on those detailed intelligence points.

In physical warfare, the intelligence cycle hinges upon leveraging correlated data points against targets that are operating in a manner that is most indicative of their participation in that intelligence cycle.

In simpler terms, one should look for behaviors that indicate an actor is operating in a manner that seems anomalous. Take as an example the intelligence collection operations in the Iraqi theatre. There was a large number of IED attacks taking place and, obviously, there were some human actors or operators within the populace who were responsible for deploying those nefarious devices.

Therefore, intelligence collection operations and agents were focused on seeking indicators that would be useful to determine which specific humans in the populace might be those agents of chaos. This meant focusing collection operations on behavioral indicators and technical data points that would be stitched together to form a profile of the most likely actors and then using further vectored intelligence to reduce the scope of the operation until the human actors who were responsible were discovered.

Without divulging classified means or techniques, this could have included human intelligence collection (interviews), open source collection, cell phone or internet activities, or even imagery that could prove useful. Those collection points would yield vital data that could be processed and analyzed to provide insights into the actions and behaviors of specific individuals that needed to be interdicted before they could harm anyone else. While this intelligence collection might have been intrusive at times, or even seen as being overly impactful by the general populace, it was a necessity to help prevent future attacks and was effective because the organizational defenses were tailored to the reality of the coming attacks, not best guesses.

The point here is that, in order to collect the necessary intelligence on actions and behaviors of threat actors and malevolent insurgents, there would be a perception of the intelligence apparatus impeding on the average innocent individual's privacy or daily activity. But in order to better secure the state and save lives, monitoring and data collection were non-negotiable and had to take place.

In cyber warfare and cyberspace operations, the need for intelligence collection and data used for intelligence operations can be just as valuable. Having key data indicators and intelligence telemetry from assets and entities can be very useful for planning defensive actions, aligning technology, and countering adversary actions. But just as in physical warfare intelligence operations there is a need to vector in the intelligence collection apparatus and the data and telemetry that are available into useful subsets so that there is a better chance of using that data for the betterment of the defenders. Not everything that can be collected should, and not everything that is collected is of actual value.

If one can step back from the often-immediate issues that arise when discussing monitoring behaviors for valuable intelligence, it is possible to understand the value that user behaviors can offer to the intelligence cycle for an organization. There aren't many solutions related to this capability that are open source or freely available. In the industry, they are commonly known as **UAM** or **user activity monitoring** solutions.

This capability typically consists of software tools that monitor and track end user behavior on devices, networks, and other IT resources. These solutions are broadly adopted across the US DoD, as there is a primary focus on using intelligence and telemetry to ferret out insider threats and to seek indicators of nation state compromises that are in play. In most instances, the range of monitoring and methods in the provided solution depends on the intelligence outcomes desired.

By implementing user activity monitoring as a focus of the intelligence collection system, the defenders can more readily identify suspicious behavior and anomalies that are potential indicators of threat activity.

Sometimes called user activity tracking, user activity monitoring is essentially a form of surveillance. But, in truth, it should be a vital intelligence collection capability that serves as a proactive analysis of end user activity. Using this approach will help the defenders to determine indicators of potential misuse of access privileges, exploit activity, compromised devices, or data either through ignorance or malicious intent.

The purpose of gathering user activity data points to aid the intelligence cycle is to enhance monitoring across the defensive area. In order to be useful, the capability leveraged here must be able to monitor all types of user activity, including all system, data, application, and network actions that users take. This may also include data points such as web browsing activity, whether users are accessing unauthorized data or files and more.

There are various methods implemented to monitor and manage user activity such as:

- Video recordings of sessions
- Log collection and analysis
- Network packet inspection
- Keystroke logging
- Kernel monitoring
- File/screenshot capturing

The specific data that constitutes inappropriate or malicious user activity will be open to interpretation by the organization using the solution. It is worth noting that this activity could potentially include anything that transits a digital system. Literally anything from visiting personal sites or various other online interactions that take place during work hours could potentially be part of one of these datasets. It should be noted that the point of this intelligence collection is not to impact the average user's day or ability to work, it is to bolster the efficacy of the defenders to better protect the infrastructure.

User activity monitoring as an intelligence asset is a valuable strategy to bring to bear in cyber warfare. Often, defenders suffer from a lack of visibility into how their user populations are accessing and utilizing sensitive data. This blind spot in the intelligence cycle leaves them susceptible to attackers who have gained access to systems and in many cases are operating as trusted users with all the associated credentials and privileges available to them. Correctly done, the approach taken in this intelligence cycle should be focused on:

1. Limiting privileged access to only users who need it for effective work production. System administrators and dedicated IT engineers as an example. Telemetry data should ensure that it is not possible for regular users to gain unlimited access or control.

2. Intelligence data should help to know what restrictions are in place or should be implemented to limit administrative tools and system protocols from being used by non-power users.

3. Intelligence data based on users' shared accounts and passwords can be beneficial to enable better defensive tooling.

4. Telemetry on user activity can help to deny protocols such as file transfers between group members, port-forwarding, and disk sharing.

5. Data therein can be used to help establish and enforce data protection policies, such as file-sharing activity, handling instructions for sensitive data, authorized services, and applications.

If a risky action is performed, such as downloading sensitive data, the security team should have the ability to respond based on the severity of the activity. Of course, this would require the defenders to have advanced telemetry and data on the users in the defensive space, and that they have detailed granular information on each user and edge device. Analytics and the behaviors that can be determined from the actions of the users and their devices as they operate inside and outside of the defensive area must be specific and detailed and must be focused on prompting remediation. Analysis without an outcome is just analysis. In military circles, this is called "paralysis by analysis."

Just as in physical warfare domains, there is a real need for intelligence collection and the resulting correlation of that culled data to help enable better defensive positioning. Users and their devices are where infiltrations begin, and they represent the furthest-possible defensive edge that defenders can leverage.

It, therefore, makes sense to gain the intelligence and analytic data that is available at that point to better enable defensive responses. And regardless of the user's personal issues with monitoring, the reality is that in order for an organization to survive they must have data to enable their defensive positioning. That data can only come from where the enemy will target and operate and that is the users and their devices. Everything else that is further inside the better-defended area can provide analytics and valuable data, but focusing analytics solely on that collection apparatus means that the actions are already "inside the wire." This is not the place you want to be doing analysis in warfare.

Conclusion

In this chapter, we discussed some of the larger principles that can be applied from physical warfighting practices to applications within cyber warfare. While, arguably, the two domains are different in form, there are approaches and useful capabilities that can be employed across the chasm between the two. There is a requirement in warfare to focus fire on the enemy where they are, not where they will be.

In cyberspace, the requirement is to do both of those things simultaneously. This means defenders must intelligently protect their internal assets as well as actively defend the users as they operate on their own personal devices "outside the wire." There are ways to enable this activity, but it often requires vendor-specific solutions and capabilities as open source solutions are not built to the scale and functionality that is needed. Using those solutions can be a valuable approach to addressing these issues.

In the next chapter, we will analyze the future impact of likely nation state attacks. We will also provide practical, reality-based examples of what the impacts from those attacks might be if the defenders are not prepared.

References

1. Bigelow, S. J. (2016, March). *Microsegmentation lets sofware define network security.* Retrieved from techtarget.com: `http://searchdatacenter.techtarget.com/feature/Microsegmentation-lets-software-define-network-security`

2. Cimpanu, C. (2019, December 23). *Chinese hacker group caught bypassing 2FA.* Retrieved from ZDNET.com: `https://www.zdnet.com/article/chinese-hacker-group-caught-bypassing-2fa/`

3. Miller, L. &. (2015). *Micro-segmentation for Dummies.* Hoboken: John Wiley & Sons Inc.

4. Rouse, M. (2017, April 30). *Definition SDDC (sofware-defined data center).* Retrieved from techtarget.com: `http://searchconvergedinfrastructure.techtarget.com/definition/software-defined-data-center-SDDC`

5. Schamper, M. v. (2019, December 19). *Operation Wocao.* Retrieved from foxit.com: `https://resources.fox-it.com/rs/170-CAK-271/images/201912_Report_Operation_Wocao.pdf`

10

Survivability in Cyber Warfare and Potential Impacts for Failure

"A good plan violently executed now is better than a perfect plan executed next week."

– General George S Patton

War is just that: war. Be it a "legacy" engagement on the front lines of some foreign chunk of soil, or be it on some digital piece of infrastructure, it is no less daunting and no less ugly. The battleground we find ourselves on today is one that is transitory in nature, ethereal in its definition, and dynamic at its core. Every man, woman, child, device, application, and anything else on the planet that is online and sending or receiving an electron is literally transiting a live fire battlefield. 24 hours a day, 365 days a year, this combat zone never stops, and never takes a moment's rest. The only way to survive in a space that is this fraught with danger is to have a solid strategic approach and to abide by a list of practices that translate equally well between physical combat environments and digital ones.

In this chapter, we will explore the laws of survivability for operations inside this combat arena. Notice we don't say perfection, or dominance, or something like that. Instead, we speak about a pragmatic approach that is focused on using the best technology and approaches to the problem while still being honest about the fact that there is no perfection here. This is about survivability and working to keep moving forward in a never-ending onslaught of attacks.

Focusing on a perfect solution and struggling to have a bullet proof network is part of what has led us collectively to the state we find ourselves in. In battle and in war, the best outcome is to survive long enough and with enough continued gas in the tank to keep moving forward. There is no perfection, and there are no perfect tools, but there are ways to be the "last one standing" when the digital smoke clears.

In this chapter, we will walk through what is and isn't necessary for continual improvement and growth and discuss what tactics, technologies, and approaches to the future state of cyber warfare are most beneficial if adopted now. Buckle up; the ride into battle is always a bit bumpy.

What good are laws in war?

Fair question. After all, war, by its very definition, is what happens when laws have been violated and the structures that surround good order and discipline have fallen into chaos. So why laws? Well we don't necessarily mean "law" in the traditional sense of the word. We aren't thinking about laws in the sense of constraints that hold back our capacity to engage; rather, what we mean in this context is laws for survival and continued operational capability in a space that is dangerous. We mean laws that are solid approaches to the problems that you face in this arena that are based on an analysis and real-world experiences gained while being engaged in actual conflict.

Adoption of these "laws," or guiding principles, or best practices, or whatever you would prefer to call them, is meant to help you stay ahead of the threats that are active in this domain and to help translate the subtle nuances between two domains – cyber and physical. In any conflict zone, there is a seriousness that must be adopted by those that are living and breathing as they transit threatened areas. In war, there are always those that are left behind and must continue to try and live their lives as normally as possible while fire fights and combat rage around them. There are also the ground troops and those that are engaged in the fight that must operate and function without fail, or they will suffer severe causalities. And there is the enemy that is operating with a focus on imposing their will, whatever it may be, on their perceived adversary and targets of opportunity as they continue their chosen campaigns.

Each of those differing groups is always working to simply survive. Everyone in those groups always has the thought in the back of their mind that they want to get on with their lives and be anywhere else but where they are at that dangerous moment. The way an effective combatant does that is to adopt practices and approaches best suited to dominating their enemy to ensure that they are the one that comes out on top. This does not happen by accident. In order to be the last one standing, history has shown us time and time again that those who realize the requirements for the space in which they operate, and abide by well-thought-out strategic approaches to the problems they encounter, are the ones that win and survive.

In cyber warfare, this is no less applicable than in physical warfare. In cyberspace, we operate in a domain with no boundaries, no walls, no clear delineations for rules of engagement, and all of our weapons move at the speed of light. By adhering to, or hopefully at least thinking about, the "laws" provided in this chapter, those of us that are active on the front lines of cyber warfare can have the best chance to "RTB," that is, return to base.

"Law 1" – Default means dead

One of the main issues with technology in the space today is the prevalence of default configurations and accounts. Manufacturers today always set the default configurations of new software and devices to be as open and functional as possible, to enable ease of use and hopefully promote adoption of their particular product. Routers, for example, often will have a predefined password and default username. For other devices, this might mean applications that come preinstalled, again usually having "hardcoded" default login credentials available to the tool or technology.

The reason for this is because it is easier and more convenient to start using new devices or software if it has easy-to-configure default settings. But this does not help the tool or application to be secure. Default settings that are never changed and made safe creates serious security issues and provides adversaries with easy, authorized access to data and networks. Web servers, containers, and application server configurations can also be configured with default accounts that will lead to a variety of security problems.

To demonstrate just how easy this is, during the research for this chapter, I created a custom script containing thousands of Google dorks, simple requests on Google that are crafted to send back specific responses, and ran a few of them to see how many easy targets were available. In a matter of less than 3 minutes, hundreds of vulnerable applications and logins for a wide variety of devices and applications were found. A sample (with all pertinent identifying data removed) is provided here:

www█████████ › FireWeb-UserIDRequestForm-Jun█████████ ▼ XLS

User Ids & Client IDs for Access to Industry Online Services

1, **User ID** Request Form. 2, Required ... (XXX) XXX XXXX, **Email** Address, Address ... Unable to authenticate with your **user name and password**): contact SRD.

```
201. Cisco BBSD MSDE Client 5.0 and 5.1 Telnet or Named Pipes bbsd-client NULL database The BBSD Windows Client password will match the BBSD
     Client password
202. Cisco BBSM Administrator 5.0 and 5.1 Multi Administrator changeme Admin
203. Cisco Netranger/secure IDS 3.0(5)S17 Multi root attack Admin must be changed at the first connection
204. Cisco BBSM MSDE Administrator 5.0 and 5.1 IP and Named Pipes sa (none) Admin
205. Cisco Catalyst 4000/5000/6000 All SNMP (none) public/private/secret RO/RW/RW+change SNMP config default on All Cat switches running the
     native CatOS CLI software.
206. Cisco PIX firewall Telnet (none) cisco User
207. Cisco VPN Concentrator 3000 series 3 Multi admin admin Admin
208. Cisco Content Engine Telnet admin default Admin
209. cisco 3600 Telnet Administrator admin Guest
210. Cisco AP1200 IOS Multi Cisco Cisco Admin This is when you convert AP1200 or AP350 to IOS
211. cisco GSR Telnet admin admin admin
212. Cisco CiscoWorks 2000 guest (none) User
213. Cisco CiscoWorks 2000 admin cisco Admin
```

\"phpremoteview\" - mysql dump

CPDMW8 <a href="http://█████████████/">████████</a>, [url=http://██████████.com/]jtsbnrtptfmy[/url], [link=http://████████████/]ysvvysetrmhh[/link], ...

Terminal Logon

Windows **Registry** Editor Version 5.00 [HKEY_LOCAL_MACHINE\SOFTWARE\ Microsoft\Windows NT\CurrentVersion\Winlogon] "AutoAdminLogon"="1" ...

████████amazonaws.com › data › █████████████ ▼

E-mail,Name,ID,Revenue in $,Customers ████████

E-**mail,Name**,ID,Revenue in $,Customers █████████████████**name**████████cb46cba9-5865-48d7-8f54-6ef454d02f88,"[349, 411, 422, 404, 353, 435, ...

████████████████aster-fast-wordpress-theme-launching ▼

De webvpn - ████████████

████████ - O DEPARTAMENTO DE POLICIA FEDERAL. O de Tecnologia da Informa? **please enter your** username and open web proxy online password.

Figure 1: A number of screenshotted samples of exposed vulnerable applications and logins

While the information found might seem somewhat non-threatening at first glance, what should be evident is the fact that with no more than an hours' worth of time, a researcher working from home was able to find large amounts of misconfigured, open, touchable resources and logins with just a script. Odds are that with a bit more time, and some targeted programming, the results could be infinitely better. And because of the interconnected nature of most networks and the usual lack of internal security controls, any one of those potential accesses could have led to further exploitation.

A point of note is that in the sample screenshots that were provided, some of the results had VPN login credentials, email and user IDs, login information, and a variety of other intelligence that could have been used for attack vectors. And all those results were based on the script looking for default configurations and user accounts, nothing spectacular. Were this script to be better programmed and tied into an automated ML backend that could expedite and tailor the commands and parse the responses, the potential for problems increases exponentially.

Looking at GitHub, one popular tool is `changeme.py`:

`https://github.com/ztgrace/changeme`

`Changeme.py` focuses on detecting default and backdoor credentials, and not just common account credentials. The tool's default mode is to scan HTTP default credentials, but it can scan for other credentials if the script is modified slightly. `Changeme.py` stores collected credential data in yaml files. `Changeme.py` can gather information or intel from almost every protocol that is used on systems today. Targets can be specified by using a single IP address or host, a subnet, a list of hosts, a network scanner output like an Nmap xml file, or a Shodan (a popular device polling database for hackers and penetration testers) query:

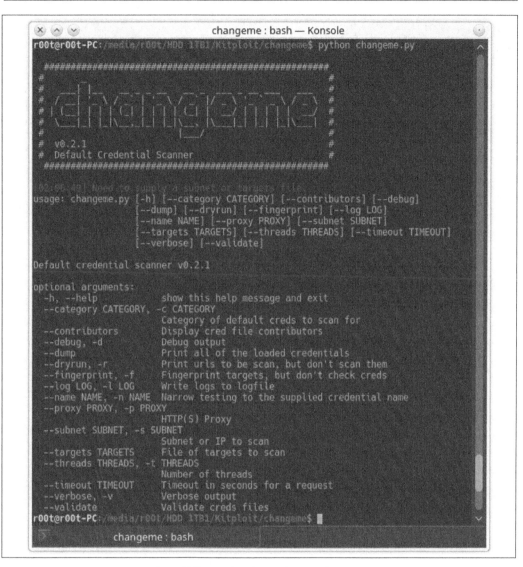

Figure 2: Screen showing options on changeme

Figure 3: Logs on changeme

The following are common scan examples:

- Scan a single host: `./changeme.py 192.168.59.100`

- Scan a subnet for default creds: `./changeme.py 192.168.59.0/24`

- Scan using an Nmap file: `./changeme.py subnet.xml`

- Scan a subnet for Tomcat default creds and set the timeout to 5 seconds: `./changeme.py -n "Apache Tomcat" --timeout 5 192.168.59.0/24`

- Use Shodan to populate a targets list and check them for default credentials: `./changeme.py --shodan_query "Server: SQ-WEBCAM" --shodan_key keygoeshere -c camera`

- Scan for SSH and known SSH keys: `./changeme.py --protocols ssh, ssh_key 192.168.59.0/24`

- Scan a host for SNMP creds using the protocol syntax: `./changeme. py snmp://192.168.1.20`

The point of these examples is that if it is this easy for someone conducting research to find access to such resources, it should be evident to anyone that it should be a matter of the highest priority to remove default configurations. Not doing so threatens the entire network that the default item is connected to, and almost guarantees that a compromise will occur.

Bots and automated AI/ML tools are available to make this intelligence collection even easier and do not require nation state-level capabilities to use.

"Law 2" – Think strategically, move tactically

In warfare, the importance of the need for movement within the battlespace is accepted as critical to survivability. Most of the time, the chaos of the space and the ever changing, and innovating, enemies' actions dominate the thoughts and plans of the defenders. The ways in which actions are being taken by each party result in a constant game of cat and mouse. It is only when one side recognizes that they must more cautiously engage in strategic thinking while enabling tactical movement that the balance of power begins to shift.

This is especially true in cyber warfare. For the last two decades, the major power player nation states on the planet have been engaging with one another in the tactical sense. A constant back and forth of who has the best intelligence and which unit has the newest and most powerful exploitation solution has continually been part of the tactical firefight between nation states. While there could be some argument that the strategy side of these engagements have been part of the equation, in reality the strategic outcomes from those tactical engagements have been tangential to the never-ending game of chess in cyber warfare. No major "wins" have been realized for any nation to date. Yes, there have been some gains and some losses, but, if you look at what has resulted from nation state-level strategic engagement in cyber warfare, no real net gain has been realized.

For any unit or organization to survive – and hopefully thrive – in a warfare environment, there must be an adoption of a strategy at the grandest level. Failure to realize the overarching intricacies and dependencies that are present between actors and their command and control systems and infrastructures is an exercise in failure.

A classic example of how tactical movements based on a lack of patience and strategic thinking can lead to exceptionally bad outcomes can be found by observing the scenario of Custer's Last Stand. On June 22, 1876 General Terry sent Colonel George A. Custer and his 7th Cavalry in pursuit of the Indian leader, Sitting Bull. That pursuit would lead to Little Bighorn Valley. General Terry's plan was for Colonel Custer to attack the Lakota and Cheyenne Indians from the south. This would splinter the Indian forces into a smaller force that could be dominated by Custer's more mobile cavalry forces. On June 25, Custer's scouts discovered the location of Sitting Bull's forces. Colonel Custer maneuvered to a position that would allow his forces to attack Sitting Bull's forces at dawn the following day. Unfortunately for Custer, Sitting Bull's scouts spotted Custer's forces moving into position and moved to inform Sitting Bull of the coming attack.

Instead of retreating at the realization that he'd been discovered, reorganizing his forces, and strategically planning his next move, Custer attacked. At noon on June 25, a day earlier than his planned attack, Custer split his regiment into three battalions. Custer split his forces and sent three companies straight into the village. He then dispatched three companies to the south to cut off the Indian retreat, and he used five companies to attack the village from the north. Those tactical choices proved to be disastrous. By reacting and splitting his forces, Custer left its three main components unable to provide each other support.

As the Battle of the Little Bighorn unfolded, Custer and the entire 7th Cavalry fell victim to a series of surprises, not the least of which was the number of warriors that they encountered. Custer's intelligence group estimated Sitting Bull's force at fewer than 800 fighting men. The real number was over 2,000 Sioux and Cheyenne warriors. His intelligence also stated that the Indian warriors likely only had hand weapons and bows and arrows for their defenses. This was incorrect intelligence as well. Sitting Bull's soldiers had procured advanced repeating rifles and had a large contingent of cavalry as well.

General George Armstrong Custer made a strategic underestimation of the forces he was about to engage with at the battle of Little Big Horn and was outflanked and overrun by a force of over 10 to 1. The intelligence he had gathered was faulty and led his decision making to be flawed. A tactical judgement based on only partially validated data points and best estimates resulted in a folly that has transcended military history for over a century. His rush to respond to perceived actions of the enemy and to engage them in a tactical pursuit played directly into the hands of his adversaries and cost him and all his men their lives.

In Custer's case, he acted tactically based on partial data about the enemy, and he and his forces never had a true understanding of what they were facing. They did not know how large the enemy force was, they did not know about the technology they were facing, and they had little, if any, actual knowledge of what areas of the battlespace were defensible. They just reacted tactically to the stimuli they had received, and everything went to hell. Avoiding that same engagement model is what should be the focus of those who are engaged in cyber warfare

The key to survival for any group is to adopt the concept of strategy first, and then tactics, not the other way around. Far too often, it is apparent that the organization that is outed as being breached or exploited has focused on implementing tactical controls that are adopted because of vendor marketing, not necessarily the realities of the space. It is rare that the leadership and the defenders can cite a singular statement that details the organizational strategy to secure the infrastructure. In physical warfare, that statement might have been "we will win the war on terror" or "dominate the air, control the battlespace." These statements sound simplistic, but that is the point of a good strategic statement. Clarity of vision and simplicity.

In cyber warfare, this must happen as well. An organizational strategic statement might be as simple as "we secure our users as we secure our infrastructure," or "we defend the edge and entity first." Those are not perfect, but they are simple, concise, and are easy to detail for the defenders who will engage with that strategy.

Once that strategy is shared and understood by the entirety of the defender group, the tactics that align and help to tactically make that strategy employable can be adopted. The strategy should be continually updated and adapted as the space and the tactics and tooling evolves, but there should always be a clear and useful strategy in place. And, contrary to Custer's example, the strategy should be based on a slow and careful response to actual enemy actions based on applied data points from a variety of validated sources. In cyber warfare, functional strategic defense is the correct approach, not half-baked tactical responses.

"Law 3" – Details, details

In warfare, the smallest detail can be the difference between life and death, victory and failure. Throughout history, wars have been won or lost because of details that were ignored. Benjamin Franklin is famously quoted as saying *"For want of a nail, the shoe was lost. For want of a shoe, the horse was lost. For want of a horse, the rider was lost. For want of a rider, the battle was lost. For want of a battle, the kingdom was lost, and all for the want of a horseshoe nail"*. He also said, *"A little neglect may breed great mischief,"* in Poor Richard's Almanack in 1758.

There are concrete historical examples of the truth behind that proverb. On the bloodiest day in American history, September 17, 1862, the Civil War Battle of Antietam resulted in nearly 23,000 casualties. After crossing the Potomac River into Maryland on September 9, 1862, Confederate General Robert E. Lee divided the 45,000-man Army of Northern Virginia and spelled out the location for each group on handwritten dispatches for delivery to his commanders. Those dispatches were delivered by couriers on horseback to the commanders, except for one that was accidentally dropped from the courier's pocket when he stopped along the way to relieve himself. That dispatch was found by a Union soldier just a few days later, in an envelope wrapped around three cigars near a fence. This misplaced secret dispatch reached Union Army Commander George B. McClellan, giving him and his 90,000-man army the exact locations of their enemy.

That information led to a strategic Union victory that would ultimately impact the course of the war.

In cyber security and cyber warfare, the focus for most infrastructures has been to focus on the macro. The aim of most of the defenders across systems has been to continue to propagate the failures of the past, namely big perimeters with high "walls." As we described in the section on the failure of the perimeter, this is counter to what needs to happen for security.

Micro-focusing also requires a switch from defending those high walls on the perimeter to one where the focus and the "optics" are aimed into the core of the infrastructure and then maneuvered outward. Host-based isolation, ringfencing for data stores and databases, granular access controls, and vectored analytics that are based on behavioral anomalies are necessary to bolster defenses from the inside out. Those small details that are indicative of potentially threatening activity should be part of the response and remediation protocols that enhance the defender's ability to remediate potential threats. Without the details and a focus on using powerful, specific analytics that enable a fix to the problem, the best "big firewall" in technology won't help better secure the system. As we'll see in the next section, the strongest and tallest wall is worthless if an enemy can simply go around it.

"Law 4" – Kill the password

> *"The weakest link in any chain of security is not the technology itself, but the person operating it; iron gates have no compassion to appeal to, nor fears to exploit, nor insecurities to use to one's advantage. They are, however, operated by us – by beings of unlimited vulnerability and limited energy. Why waste time brute forcing what can easily be circumvented by a clever façade and a crimson tongue?"*

> – *A.J. Darkholme, Rise of the Morningstar*

One of the biggest obstacles any organization will face is their own staff. In studies on cyber security, nearly 84% of leaders noted employee negligence as their biggest security risk. Many were also found to believe the risk of a data breach is higher when employees work remotely. Data collated from a variety of studies indicates that almost 3 out of 4 data breaches reported by leaders stated that users were at least partly responsible for a breach of the infrastructure due to their negligence in relation to basic cyber security practices. As hackers and nation states move "downstream" to continue their attack activities, as discussed earlier in this book, this will impact small businesses more and more. Those small businesses and contractors will face a bigger challenge, as they often operate with limited budgets and restricted security tooling.

Users and their devices now represent the furthest edges of an infrastructure's security apparatus. They are the "front line" in the war that is raging in cyberspace and they are the first place that an attacker can reach into an infrastructure for an exploitation. Consider that in the chapter on this topic, we pointed out the reality of how exploitations have happened and provided specific data that shows that in nearly every instance in history, it has been a user that at some point was the activator of the exploitation life cycle. Data from those same references also shows that training and education do not "fix" users. Even a 1% click rate on an enterprise with a hundred thousand users is too large a likelihood that something will be compromised.

With the reality being that most users are reliant on their password to act as their primary means of security, the issues for user security become even more evident. Users are beholden to the paradigm of passwords and, as stated in the chapter on this topic, relying on the password is not only a management nightmare but it is also a practice that will lead to a failure at some point.

To help better secure this front line, there are a few methods and technologies that might be employed.

- **Biometrics as part of an authentication program** – While a password is nothing more than a string of numbers and letters and, in some cases, special characters, biometric data can be much more specific and useful. There are a variety of biometric authentication protocols and tools that might be applied to help eliminate the password. Some of the more innovative types are new to the market and are primarily in a research phase, but soon they might be available as part of an identity and access management tool set.

- **Brain wave-based authentication** – By using sensors to capture electroencephalograms (EEGs), or the measurement of brain waves, computers can authenticate identity. Scientists at Binghamton University in New York recruited 45 volunteers and measured how each person's brain responded to certain words. The researchers recorded each brain's reaction, which were all different. That information was then used by a computer system to identify each person with 94% accuracy. That system was then applied to a login mechanism and users were asked to log in with nothing more than a thought about a specific word. Obviously, this method is far fetched at the current time, but with the reduction in costs and the size of the sensors required ever decreasing, this approach may be viable in the near future:

Figure 4: A brain wave authentication device in use by researchers

- **Heartbeat-based authentication** – Users have a smart watch, or similar device, and the band or sensor features an ECG sensor or sensors, one on the interior of the band touching the wrist, and another on the outside of the band. A user's ECG, echocardiogram, also known as heartbeat, data is captured. That user would then activate the sensor on the band or smartwatch. After a user sets up their login profile, they then would use the band or device to verify their identity. That unique heartbeat acts as their biometric authentication mechanism to unlock certain devices while the users are wearing it:

Figure 5: The Nymi heartbeat authentication tool

- **Voice and ambient noise authentication** – Another form of biometric data is using sound to enhance security for authentication. Users can use their voice print to log into their bank accounts, make transfers, and check balances using the app, which is powered by voice-recognition technology by the company Nuance. Other sounds can also be used to help secure traditional login systems and can be combined with voice printing solutions to bolster this approach. A team of researchers at the Swiss Federal Institute of Technology in Zürich, Switzerland, revealed a tool they had created called Sound-Proof, which uses ambient noise to enhance the security of multi-factor authentication.

In this approach, access to a site that has Sound-Proof employed requires an app on the user's phone to start recording. Then the microphone on the computer also begins recording a few seconds of ambient noise in the room near the computer requesting access. The software creates a digital signature for the recording from each device and then instantly compares them. If they match, or are within very narrow tolerances, the system grants the user access to the site without them having to enter a second pin because the system assumes that the user's smartphone is in the same room:

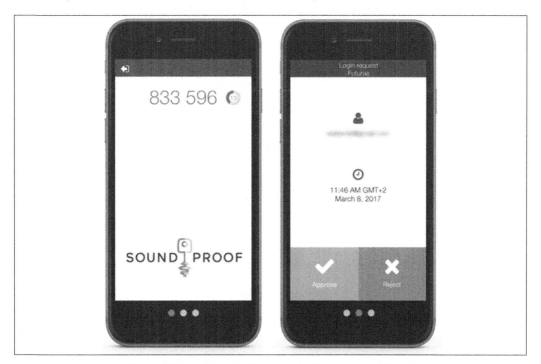

Figure 6: The ambient/voice authentication app, Sound-Proof

There are certainly ways that a well-focused and capable nation state actor or threat group could attack and possibly circumvent these approaches, but to do that would require concerted efforts and is not nearly as failure prone as simply relying on the password. The takeaway for the defenders here is to employ the simplest technologies that offer the biggest "bang for your buck."

If users are where the enemy will first operate and represent the further extension of the edge of the secure infrastructure, then logically, this is a primary point of focus. Employing technologies and tooling that eliminate the issues that a user has regarding them having to be responsible for their own security management and that eliminates the obvious issues that a password-based authentication protocol puts in place should be a key piece of any defense efforts.

"Law 5" – Limit the blast radius

If we accept the points – facts really – that have been presented throughout this book that speak to the reality of cyber warfare, then it is pivotal that we also adopt a position that states that at some time, we will get "hit." Transiting a warfare environment is an inherently dangerous proposition. At any time, a random chunk of metal can come flying across the space and forever impact your survival in that space. When everything we do, all of the time, is situated on that battlefield and is constantly transiting that environment, the chances of that negative outcome increase by the second. The digital space is fraught with danger, and it is the only space that humanity has ever seen that in some way touches everything, and where every power that exists can actively engage one another on a relatively level playing field. To be blunt, in war you can expect things to inevitably hit the fan.

It is not the actual attack, infection, or exploit that is what is so negatively impactful in this battle space. In reality, if those infections and exploits were contained and limited in their ability to propagate, they would be not much more than an inconvenience for the IT teams to reimage and "fix" the exploited machines. It is when that nuisance infection becomes a global pandemic that things go from bad to worse. That is when a digital flesh wound becomes a binary arterial bleed. It is that metamorphosis that must be stopped at all costs. The blast radius of the exploit must be contained in order to have a hope of survivability.

If there was an "explosion" in the infrastructure, how far would that damage go before it could be stopped? How much "blood" would be spilled before the gushing could be assuaged? A secure infrastructure that is correctly segmented should be able to limit that explosion, and it should be strong enough to do so without harming that infrastructure's ability to function. To reach this position of being "armored up," as tank operators in the Army say, there are a few principles that should be part of the infrastructure and strategy:

- **The hackers are already here** – The enemy is already inside the gates. The perimeter model of security has fundamentally and epically failed to secure infrastructure and has allowed nation states and hackers to gain access to infrastructure across the globe for decades. Assuming this position and recognizing that the enemy is already inside is a key strategic point that can help leaders and technicians better address infrastructure security. Just as in physical warfare, the approach to addressing the issue must be based on the truth of the space, and the truth of this space is that everything is probably already compromised and keeping the enemy beyond the wire is an exercise in futility.

- **Eliminate keys to the kingdom** – Nation states and hackers attack the traditional administrators because of the power of that role for an organization. They do this to get those valuable "keys to the kingdom." One administrator login or account is worth 1,000 users who have no real authority across infrastructure components. That elevated set of permissions allows an administrator to do almost anything. Those accounts and those users must be defended and their access closely monitored and tracked at all costs. One compromised admin is akin to a potential tactical nuclear warhead detonating inside a network. The best approach here is to limit and control administrator accounts and accesses as if they were radioactive material. Nothing short of total caution and care should be afforded those volatile assets.

- **Segmentation at a grand scale** – If an intrusion occurs, the exploitation or compromising of one component must not result in the entire system getting taken over. Multiple layers of defense should be applied to "up-armor" the infrastructure from the inside out to eliminate movement; controls regarding role-based access control applied at multiple levels, strict limits on account privileges, monitoring, granular asset segmentation on servers and hosts, and anti-malware and updated patches for all assets. Whitelisted software is the only software that should be allowed to execute, and native tools like PowerShell should be strictly controlled or limited.

- **Use hardened assets** – To date, hardening systems have generically relied on the **Security Technical Implementation Guide (STIG)**, which dictates what should be done to harden an asset and reduce vulnerabilities. The US DoD has released 461 STIGs and continues to release more on a semi-regular basis. STIGs are published and are available for a variety of software packages, including operating systems, database applications, open source software, network devices, wireless devices, virtual software, and mobile operating systems. Using these tried-and-tested guides from an organization such as the DoD that has been fighting the good fight in cyber warfare longer than any other organization can help to secure infrastructure quicker and with a more formulaic approach. A full listing of STIG-suggested configurations can be found at `https://stigviewer.com/`.

A sample of STIG hardening for a Windows 10 machine is presented. Note that for conciseness the information is not presented in full; if you'd like to see the full details, you're encouraged to check out the stigviewer website previously cited. The sample follows:

Finding ID	Severity	Title	Description
V-63797	High	The system must be configured to prevent the storage of the LAN Manager hash of passwords.	The LAN Manager hash uses a weak encryption algorithm and there are several tools available that use this hash to retrieve account passwords. This setting controls whether or not a LAN Manager ...
V-63651	High	Solicited remote assistance must not be allowed.	Remote assistance allows another user to view or take control of the local session of a user. Solicited assistance is help that is specifically requested by the local user. This may allow ...
V-63869	High	The Debug programs user right must only be assigned to the Administrators group.	Inappropriate granting of user rights can provide system, administrative, and other high-level capabilities. Accounts with the "Debug Programs" user right can attach a debugger to any process or ...
V-63325	High	The Windows Installer Always install with elevated privileges, must be disabled.	Standard user accounts must not be granted elevated privileges. Enabling Windows Installer to elevate privileges when installing applications can allow malicious persons and applications to gain ...

| V-63353 | High | Local volumes must be formatted using NTFS. | The ability to set access permissions and auditing is critical to maintaining the security and proper access controls of a system. To support this, volumes must be formatted using the NTFS file ... |
| V-63667 | High | Autoplay must be turned off for non-volume devices. | Allowing autoplay to execute may introduce malicious code to a system. Autoplay begins reading from a drive as soon as you insert media in the drive. As a result, the setup file of programs or ... |

While there are always other techniques, strategies, or tactics that can be part of your "laws" for surviving in combat space, the preceding basic laws are meant to help provide a basic few points to always think on. As with anything in survival situations, it will always be the simple things that matter most first. If you ignore the basics, surely the advanced issues will be even more problematic.

Impact from failure

Apart from causing substantial economic loss to businesses and monetary systems, cyber warfare can harm critical national infrastructure in a variety of ways. In one way, cyber warfare can affect the delivery of essential services to the populace. This has been shown with cyber attacks against electrical grids and the healthcare sector over the past decade. Second, there is the potential to cause physical damage. This was demonstrated by the Stuxnet attack against Iran a decade ago. Cyber warfare tactics may affect the delivery of healthcare as well.

Compromising healthcare

As healthcare sectors continue to move toward increased digitization and interconnectivity, the likelihood of this type of action becomes more real on an almost daily basis. New medical devices are now almost categorically connected to a hospital's information technology system to enable automatic actions and help with healthcare insurance filing, and to enhance patient care. That increased digital dependency, combined with the ever expanding "attack surface," has not corresponded with vast improvement in more secure infrastructure, or better cyber security practices. That infrastructure is particularly vulnerable and has potentially life and death consequences for patients and those who are connected to those devices.

The WannaCry ransomware attacks in 2017 affected a hospital in Hollywood, California, as well as a hospital in Singapore, and another large hospital in the UK. The resulting post-attack investigation into the Singapore attack revealed that the exploit on that hospital's network was in place for more than 10 months. Using their specialized malicious software, attackers were able to query databases for specific patients, including the prime minister. Over time, there was also the potential for attackers to tamper with prescriptions and shut off connected systems. In the cases of the WannaCry Hollywood and UK hospitals, the attacks stopped the medical facilities from operating normally by stopping uptime and impacting data availability.

Patients were literally turned away and denied care because of these exploits. As more digital dependencies are ingrained into healthcare and hospital systems, the more difficult it will become for those critical facilities to operate when those dependencies stop functioning. Other healthcare facilities may soon be under attack as well. Pharmaceutical companies may be targeted for intellectual property theft or may be infiltrated and have their formulas or cures tampered with or possibly rendered unreadable. While it is possible that those operations may not always be destructive in nature, they might still cause damage beyond property theft.

If medication supply lines or vaccines are impacted, the entire medical industry, and the faith that consumers have in those providers, might be called into question. The potential also exists for attacks on research facilities that store dangerous materials, like viruses or diseases.

Bringing down ICS (Industrial Control Systems)

Cyber attacks against industrial control systems have typically been less frequent than other types of cyber operations. However, the frequency of those actions is reportedly increasing, and the severity of the potential impact in this sector is plainly evident. A few days without light and power, and the civilized world will tumble into the dark ages; chaos will follow. Because of the growth of connected capabilities and the potential benefit for humanity with internet-enabled ICS systems, this area is particularly ripe for an attack. Because of the interconnected nature of infrastructure, and the increasingly refined capability of nation state actors and their weapons' capabilities, it is extremely possible that there are already several undetected actors present in ICS systems across the globe.

Nation state threat groups will work to cause large-scale harm to industrial control systems via firmware and supply chain vectors. It is also possible that malware used on industrial control systems could cause unintended collateral damage to other unprotected industrial control systems. There is also the risk that nation states have already installed self-propagating malware that is lying in wait for the command to "go loud" and exploit the system. When considering the impact that an ICS or SCADA system exploit might have, it is important to focus on the reality that even a small-scale attack could have cascading consequences on such systems.

Threatening the fates of nations

When it comes to the added issues of **artificial intelligence (AI)**, cyber warfare, and the impacts those issues might have on national security, there are more uncertainties than answers. One of the primary issues that should be part of that line of questions is how does cyber warfare, AI, and cyber security affect nuclear security and even the fabric of democracy?

AI-augmented cyber capabilities are already in play. There are potential military risks associated with emerging technologies and especially inadvertent or accidental escalation within those circles. Consider the increasing potential vulnerabilities thanks to the interconnected nature of global networks and the focused nation state efforts to impact nuclear systems.

AI has the very real potential to make existing cyber warfare weapons exponentially more powerful. Faster advances in AI technologies and increasing capabilities in autonomous systems could amplify future attacks. To avoid hype and provide clarity to the understanding that is needed, here are a few specific, but possible, ways that AI and cyber warfare might combine in these areas.

Advances in autonomous systems and machine learning means that more networked and physical systems are vulnerable to cyber warfare. As nation states and their associated threat actor groups leverage more AI, capable systems and tools can offer attackers access to cyber attacks to be executed on an infinitely grander scale. The speeds at which those attacks will proliferate also will accelerate across disparate civilian and military domains. The speed and breadth of the next generation of AI cyber tools could have destabilizing effects on entire countries.

Outside of simply attacking via cyber weaponry, a nation state or threat actor could also use AI or machine learning techniques to target the systems that backend common data-specific applications. Those attacks could work to spoof critical data points or inject incorrect data at scale into those critical systems. An attack like that could cause unpredictable and undetectable errors, system malfunctions, or behavioral manipulation to a system's controls. Those civilian systems that use AI or machine learning as part of their decision engine rely on high-quality data to enable their algorithms to function properly. By attacking those backend data repositories and injecting bogus data into those datasets, those unsecured systems would continue to operate "normally" but would, in reality, be making decisions based on faulty data, which could be cataclysmic for systems such as nuclear control actions or hospital patient tooling.

Were that to happen in a nuclear system, or a nuclear-related weapons system, the perceived ability of the state to defend itself from a physical attack could be compromised. Additionally, the faith in the system and the reliance by other nations that those systems are safe to operate would be called into question. The entire nuclear gambit could be called into question with an invalid data action.

The previous section focused on what the larger issues are regarding cyber warfare and ICS, healthcare, and other critical systems. In the following section, we will detail a few potential attack scenarios to try and provide some clarity on what is more realistic in future cyber warfare engagements.

Threat scenario – DeepFakes

Nation state 1 uses outside agents and hackers to send DeepFake video or audio to nation state 2's rival leadership. Those videos indicate that senior military commanders of state 3 are conspiring to attack nation state 2. In short order, those DeepFakes are leaked onto the internet with specific Twitter and Instagram influencers targeted for reposting. This causes civilian panic in the area and escalation of defensive positioning.

Nation state 2 reacts to the perceived threat with actual physical or kinetic actions, which lead to war. AI and ML tooling could be injected into this scenario to either escalate the tensions or to speed the delivery of social media, which would fuel discourse.

Threat scenario – Data manipulation

Nation state 1 uses an ML-based cyber attack to spoof data for nation state 2's civilian air control and tracking system. The fake data injected causes air traffic control to interpret a valid track as a potential threat. Military action is taken to prevent casualties and the valid track (airplane or jetliner) is kinetically eliminated. The security and veracity of the systems and the components that power it is called into question. An entire industry is impacted, and the global economic impact is felt. Civil unrest and discord are also likely to follow as the population reacts to the outcomes of the attacks. Social unrest is potentially widespread.

Threat scenario – Attacking democratic processes

Thanks to the poor state of security of voter registration databases and local, state, and national election systems, and the increased circulation of voter information available in the underground community, nation state 1 attacks the voting process. By using voter registration records, nation state 1 builds out a targeted, localized disinformation campaign. In that campaign, vectored tweets and postings are put online that show elected officials touting inflammatory campaign slogans. At the same time, a campaign is launched with narratives that indicate that voting systems have been compromised and all votes will be calculated for opposition parties regardless of the voters' input.

Those are simply a few examples of what might be possible if these sorts of actions are taken in cyber warfare engagements. While it should be noted in this regard that in no instance did the attacking nation engage in what would be considered a kinetic cyber attack, the results would still be felt by the target nation. By using "softer" tactics powered by targeted cyber activities and coordinated by malicious command and control entities, the attackers can still impact the adversary.

The nature of warfare and the realities surrounding cyber impacts are ever changing and will be a difficult beast to manage if ever unleashed in a coordinated manner.

Conclusion

Providing true cyber warfare survivability requires a fully committed leadership, technical team, and partner alignment. Surviving these types of conflicts is a technically, politically, financially, and procedurally complex issue. In combat, the ability to move and maneuver and the adoption of basic concepts and solid practices is what will help an entity survive. Survival is the goal; anything better than that is simply icing on the cake. Those that survive the longest win.

The goal of cyber defense is to minimize the magnitude of the attacker's effect, increase costs to the attacker, increase the uncertainty that the attack was successful, and increase the chance of detection and remediation. Survivability is the ability of a system, subsystem, equipment, process, or procedure to function continually during and after a disturbance. This must be the focus of our attention as the digital battlespace continues to be transited. As long as the critical functions of the entity can continue, and the entirety of the infrastructure is not rendered useless, the ability to "fight through it" remains.

The aim of this book was to try and provide some real insight into the true history of what cyber warfare looked like in the past and what it will resemble in the future. In doing that, and providing a real-world look into the strategies, tactics, and tools that are active in this space, the author hopes that you have found some nuggets of knowledge that can be used to better defend your organization.

If any one thing should be taken away from this book, it should be that the battlespace in cyber warfare is ever changing, and those that stagnate and focus on what is the current threat are missing the coming onslaught. In digital combat, everything can be a weapon, and everything can be a shield. It all depends on how that item is used and how skillfully the strategy for the use of that shield or spear is applied by those who wield them.

Appendix – Major Cyber Incidents Throughout 2019

November 2019

- Iranian hackers targeted the accounts of employees at major manufacturers and operators of industrial control systems. (**Nation State Industrial Espionage Campaign**)

- An alleged non-state actor targeted the UK Labour party with a major DDoS attack that temporarily took the party's computer systems offline. (**Nation State Disinformation and Election Interference**)

October 2019

- An Israeli cyber security firm was found to have sold spyware used to target senior government and military officials in at least 20 countries by exploiting a vulnerability in WhatsApp. (**Nation State Espionage and Intelligence Collection**)

- A state-sponsored hacking campaign knocked offline more than 2,000 websites across Georgia, including government and court websites containing case materials and personal data. (**Nation State Disinformation and Intelligence Collection**)

- India announced that North Korean malware designed for data extraction had been identified in the networks of a nuclear power plant. (**Nation State Industrial Espionage and Intelligence Collection**)

- Suspected North Korean hackers attempted to steal credentials from individuals working on North Korea-related issues at the UN and other NGOs. (**Nation State Intelligence Collection**)

- The NSA and GCHQ found that a Russian cyberespionage campaign had used an Iranian hacking group's tools and infrastructure to spy on Middle Eastern targets. (**Nation State Industrial Espionage and False Flag Operations**)

- Russian hackers engaged in a campaign since 2013 targeting embassies and foreign affairs ministries in several European countries. (**Nation State Intelligence Collection**)

- Iranian hackers targeted more than 170 universities around the world between 2013 and 2017, stealing $3.4 billion worth of intellectual property and selling stolen data to Iranian customers. (**Nation State IP Theft and Intelligence Collection Operations**)

- Chinese hackers engaged in a multi-year campaign between 2010 and 2015 to acquire intellectual property from foreign companies to support the development of the Chinese C919 airliner. (**Nation State IP Theft and Intelligence Collection Operations**)

- A Chinese government-sponsored propaganda app with more than 100 million users was found to have been programmed to have a backdoor granting access to location data, messages, photos, and browsing history, as well as remotely activate audio recordings. (**Nation State Disinformation and Intelligence Collection**)

- The Moroccan government targeted two human rights activists using spyware purchased from Israel. (**Nation State Intelligence Collection**)

- A state-sponsored hacking group targeted diplomats and high-profile Russian speaking users in Eastern Europe. (**Nation State Intelligence Collection Operations**)

- Chinese hackers targeted entities in Germany, Mongolia, Myanmar, Pakistan, and Vietnam, individuals involved in UN Security Council resolutions regarding ISIS, and members of religious groups and cultural exchange nonprofits in Asia. (**Nation State Intelligence Collection**)

- Iranian hackers conducted a series of attacks against the Trump campaign, as well as current and former U.S. government officials, journalists, and Iranians living abroad. (**Nation State Disinformation and Intelligence Collection**)

- State-sponsored Chinese hackers were revealed to have conducted at least six espionage campaigns since 2013 against targets in Myanmar, Taiwan, Vietnam, Indonesia, Mongolia, Tibet, and Xinjiang. (**Nation State Intelligence Collection**)

- The Egyptian government conducted a series of cyberattacks against journalists, academics, lawyers, human rights activists, and opposition politicians. (**Nation State Intelligence Collection**)

- Chinese hackers were found to have targeted government agencies, embassies, and other government-related embassies across Southeast Asia in the first half of 2019. (**Nation State Intelligence Collection**)

September 2019

- The United States carried out cyber operations against Iran in retaliation for Iran's attacks on Saudi Arabia's oil facilities. The operation affected physical hardware and had the goal of disrupting Iran's ability to spread propaganda. (**Nation State Industrial Espionage Campaign**)

- Airbus revealed that hackers targeting commercial secrets engaged in a series of supply chain attacks targeting four of the company's subcontractors. (**Nation State IP Theft and Intelligence Collection Operations**)

- A Chinese state-sponsored hacking group responsible for attacks against three U.S. utility companies in July 2019 was found to have subsequently targeted seventeen others. (**Nation State Industrial Espionage Campaign**)

- Hackers with ties to the Russian government conducted a phishing campaign against the embassies and foreign affairs ministries of countries across Eastern Europe and Central Asia. (**Nation State Intelligence Collection**)

- Alleged Chinese hackers used mobile malware to target senior Tibetan lawmakers and individuals with ties to the Dalai Lama. (**Nation State Disinformation and Intelligence Collection**)

- North Korean hackers were revealed to have conducted a phishing campaign over the summer of 2019 targeted U.S. entities researching the North Korean nuclear program and economic sanctions against North Korea. (**Nation State Industrial Espionage Campaign**)

- Iranian hackers targeted more than 60 universities in the U.S., Australia, UK, Canada, Hong Kong, and Switzerland to steal intellectual property. (**Nation State IP Theft and Intelligence Collection Operations**)

- Huawei accused the U.S. government of hacking into its intranet and internal information systems to disrupt its business operations. (**Nation State Industrial Espionage Campaign**)

August 2019

- China used compromised websites to distribute malware to Uyghur populations using previously undisclosed exploits for Apple, Google, and Windows phones. (**Nation State Disinformation and Intelligence Collection**)

- Chinese state-sponsored hackers were revealed to have targeted multiple U.S. cancer institutes to take information relating to cutting edge cancer research. (**Nation State IP Theft and Intelligence Collection Operations**)

- North Korean hackers conducted a phishing campaign against foreign affairs officials in at least three countries, with a focus on those studying North Korean nuclear efforts and related international sanctions. (**Nation State Industrial Espionage Campaign**)

- Huawei technicians helped government officials in two African countries track political rivals and access encrypted communications. (**Nation State Disinformation and Intelligence Collection**)

- The Czech Republic announced that the country's Foreign Ministry had been the victim of a cyberattack by an unspecified foreign state, later identified as Russia. (**Nation State Intelligence Collection**)

- A suspected Indian cyber espionage group conducted a phishing campaign targeting Chinese government agencies and state-owned enterprises for information related to economic trade, defense issues, and foreign relations. (**Nation State Intelligence Collection**)

- Networks at several Bahraini government agencies and critical infrastructure providers were infiltrated by hackers linked to Iran. (**Nation State Industrial Espionage Campaign**)

- A previously unidentified Chinese espionage group was found to have worked since 2012 to gather data from foreign firms in industries identified as strategic priorities by the Chinese government, including telecommunications, healthcare, semiconductor manufacturing, and machine learning. The group was also active in the theft of virtual currencies and the monitoring of dissidents in Hong Kong. (**Nation State IP Theft and Intelligence Collection Operations**)

- Russian hackers were observed using vulnerable IoT devices like a printer, VoIP phone, and video decoder to break into high-value corporate networks. (**Nation State Intelligence Collection**)

- A seven-year campaign by an unidentified Spanish-language espionage group was revealed to have resulted in the theft of sensitive mapping files from senior officials in the Venezuelan Army. (**Nation State Intelligence Collection**)

July 2019

- State-sponsored Chinese hackers conducted a spear-phishing campaign against employees of three major U.S. utility companies. (**Nation State Industrial Espionage Campaign**)

- Encrypted email service provider ProtonMail was hacked by a state-sponsored group looking to gain access to accounts held by reporters and former intelligence officials conducting investigations of Russian intelligence activities. (**Nation State Intelligence Collection**)

- Several major German industrial firms including BASF, Siemens, and Henkel announced that they had been the victim of a state-sponsored hacking campaign reported to be linked to the Chinese government (**Nation State Industrial Espionage Campaign**)

- A Chinese hacking group was discovered to have targeted government agencies across East Asia involved in information technology, foreign affairs, and economic development. (**Nation State Intelligence Collection**)

- The U.S. Coast Guard issued a warning after it received a report that a merchant vessel had its networks disrupted by malware while traveling through international waters. (**Nation State Intelligence Collection**)

- An Iranian hacking group targeted LinkedIn users associated with financial, energy, and government entities operating in the Middle East. (**Nation State Intelligence Collection**)

- Microsoft revealed that it had detected almost 800 cyberattacks over the past year targeting think tanks, NGOs, and other political organizations around the world, with most attacks originating in Iran, North Korean, and Russia. (**Nation State Intelligence Collection**)

- Libya arrested two men who were accused of working with a Russian troll farm to influence the elections in several African countries. (**Nation State Disinformation and Election Interference**)

- Croatian government agencies were targeted in a series of attacks by unidentified state sponsored hackers (**Nation State Intelligence Collection**)

- U.S. Cybercommand issued an alert warning that government networks were being targeted with malware associated with a known Iran-linked hacking group. (**Nation State Industrial Espionage Campaign**)

June 2019

- Western intelligence services were alleged to have hacked into Russian internet search company Yandex in late 2018 to spy on user accounts. (**Nation State Intelligence Collection**)

- Over the course of seven years, a Chinese espionage group hacked into ten international cellphone providers operating across thirty countries to track dissidents, officials, and suspected spies. (**Nation State Intelligence Collection**)

- The U.S. announced it had launched offensive cyber operations against Iranian computer systems used to control missile and rocket launches. (**Nation State Industrial Espionage Campaign**)

- Iran announced that it had exposed and helped dismantle an alleged CIA-backed cyber espionage network across multiple networks. (**Nation State Intelligence Collection**)

- U.S. officials reveal ongoing efforts to deploy hacking tools against Russian grid systems as a deterrent and warning to Russia. (**Nation State Industrial Espionage Campaign**)

- U.S. grid regulator NERC issued a warning that a major hacking group with suspected Russian ties was conducting reconnaissance into the networks of electrical utilities. (**Nation State Industrial Espionage Campaign**)

- China conducted a DoS attack on encrypted messaging service Telegram in order to disrupt communications among Hong Kong protestors. (**Nation State Disinformation and Election Interference**)

- A suspected Iranian group was found to have hacked into telecommunications services in Iraq, Pakistan, and Tajikistan. (**Nation State Industrial Espionage Campaign**)

- Chinese intelligence services hacked into the Australian University to collect data they could use to groom students as informants before they were hired into the civil service. (**Nation State Intelligence Collection**)

May 2019

- Government organizations in two different Middle Eastern countries were targeted by Chinese state-sponsored hackers. (**Nation State Industrial Espionage Campaign**)

- A Chinese government-sponsored hacking group was reported to be targeting unidentified entities across the Philippines. (**Nation State Intelligence Collection**)

- Iran developed a network of websites and accounts that were being used to spread false information about the U.S., Israel, and Saudi Arabia. (**Nation State Disinformation and Election Interference**)

April 2019

- Amnesty International's Hong Kong office announced it had been the victim of an attack by Chinese hackers who accessed the personal information of the office's supporters. (**Nation State Intelligence Collection**)

- Ukrainian military and government organizations had been targeted was part of a campaign by hackers from the Luhansk People's Republic, a Russia-backed group that declared independence from Ukraine in 2014. (**Nation State Disinformation and Election Interference**)

- Hackers used spoofed email addresses to conduct a disinformation campaign in Lithuania to discredit the Defense Minister by spreading rumors of corruption. (**Nation State Disinformation and Election Interference**)

- The Finnish police probed a denial of service attack against the web service used to publish the vote tallies from Finland's elections. (**Nation State Disinformation and Election Interference**)

- Pharmaceutical company Bayer announced it had prevented an attack by Chinese hackers targeting sensitive intellectual property. (**Nation State IP Theft and Future Espionage Intelligence Collection Operations**)

March 2019

- An Iranian cyber espionage group targeted government and industry digital infrastructure in Saudi Arabia and the U.S. (**Nation State Industrial Espionage Campaign**)

- State supported Vietnamese hackers targeted foreign automotive companies to acquire IP. (**Nation State IP Theft and Future Espionage Intelligence Collection Operations**)

- Iran's intelligence service hacked into former IDF Chief and Israeli opposition leader Benny Gantz' cellphone ahead of Israel's April elections. (**Nation State Disinformation and Election Interference**)

- North Korean hackers targeted an Israeli security firm as part of an industrial espionage campaign. (**Nation State Industrial Espionage Campaign**)

- Russian hackers targeted a number of European government agencies ahead of EU elections in May. (**Nation State Disinformation and Election Interference**)

- Indonesia's National Election Commission reported that Chinese and Russian hackers had probed Indonesia's voter database ahead of presidential and legislative elections in the country. (**Nation State Disinformation and Election Interference**)

- Civil liberties organizations claimed that government-backed hackers targeted Egyptian human rights activists, media, and civil society organizations throughout 2019. (**Nation State Disinformation and Election Interference**)

- The UN Security Council reported that North Korea has used state-sponsored hacking to evade international sanctions, stealing $670 million in foreign currency and cryptocurrency between 2015 and 2018. (**Nation State IP Theft and Intelligence Collection Operations**)

- Iranian hackers targeted thousands of people at more than 200 oil-and-gas and heavy machinery companies across the world, stealing corporate secrets and wiping data from computers. (**Nation State IP Theft and Intelligence Collection Operations**)

- Following an attack on Indian military forces in Kashmir, Pakistani hackers targeted almost 100 Indian government websites and critical systems. Indian officials reported that they engaged in offensive cyber measures to counter the attacks. (**Nation State Industrial Espionage Campaign**)

- U.S. officials reported that at least 27 universities in the U.S. had been targeted by Chinese hackers as part of a campaign to steal research on naval technologies. (**Nation State IP Theft and Intelligence Collection Operations**)

February 2019

- The UN International Civil Aviation Organizations revealed that in late 2016 it was compromised by China-linked hackers who used their access to spread malware to foreign government websites. (**Nation State Industrial Espionage Campaign**)

- Prior to the Vietnam summit of Kim Jong Un and Donald Trump, North Korean hackers were found to have targeted South Korean institutions in a phishing campaign using documents related to the diplomatic event as bait. (**Nation State Intelligence Collection**)

- U.S. Cybercommand revealed that during the 2018 U.S. midterm elections, it had blocked internet access to the Internet Research Agency, a Russian company involved in information operations against the U.S. during the 2016 presidential election. (**Nation State Disinformation and Election Interference**)

- Hackers associated with the Russian intelligence services had targeted more than 100 individuals in Europe at civil society groups working on election security and democracy promotion. (**Nation State Disinformation and Election Interference**)

- State-sponsored hackers were caught in the early stages of gaining access to computer systems of several political parties as well as the Australian Federal Parliament. (**Nation State Disinformation and Election Interference**)

- European aerospace company Airbus reveals it was targeted by Chinese hackers who stole the personal and IT identification information of some of its European employees. (**Nation State Intelligence Collection**)

- Norwegian software firm Visma revealed that it had been targeted by hackers from the Chinese Ministry of State Security who were attempting to steal trade secrets from the firm's clients. (**Nation State IP Theft and Intelligence Collection Operations**)

January 2019

- Hackers associated with the Russian intelligence services were found to have targeted the Center for Strategic and International Studies. (**Nation State Intelligence Collection**)

- Security researchers reveal that Iranian hackers have been targeting the telecom and travel industries since at least 2014 to surveil and collect the personal information of individuals in the Middle East, U.S., Europe, and Australia. (**Nation State Intelligence Collection**)

- The U.S. Democratic National Committee revealed that it had been targeted by Russian hackers in the weeks after the 2018 midterm elections January 2019. South Korea's Ministry of National Defense announced that unknown hackers had compromised computer systems at the ministry's procurement office. (**Nation State Disinformation and Election Interference**)

- The U.S. Securities and Exchange Commission charged a group of hackers from the U.S., Russia, and Ukraine with the 2016 breach of the SEC's online corporate filing portal exploited to execute trades based on non-public information. (**Nation State Intelligence Collection**)

- Iran was revealed to have engaged in a multi-year, global DNS hijacking campaign targeting telecommunications and internet infrastructure providers as well as government entities in the Middle East, Europe, and North America. (**Nation State Industrial Espionage Campaign**)

- Hackers release the personal details, private communications, and financial information of hundreds of German politicians, with targets representing every political party except the far-right. **(Nation State Disinformation and Election Interference)**

Other Books
You May Enjoy

If you enjoyed this book, you may be interested in these other books by Packt:

Cybersecurity – Attack and Defense Strategies

Yuri Diogenes, Erdal Ozkaya

ISBN: 978-1-83882-779-3

- The importance of having a solid foundation for your security posture
- Use cyber security kill chain to understand the attack strategy
- Boost your organization's cyber resilience by improving your security policies, hardening your network, implementing active sensors, and leveraging threat intelligence
- Utilize the latest defense tools, including Azure Sentinel and Zero Trust Network strategy
- Identify different types of cyberattacks, such as SQL injection, malware and social engineering threats such as phishing emails

- Perform an incident investigation using Azure Security Center and Azure Sentinel

- Get an in-depth understanding of the disaster recovery process

- Understand how to consistently monitor security and implement a vulnerability management strategy for on-premises and hybrid cloud

- Learn how to perform log analysis using the cloud to identify suspicious activities, including logs from Amazon Web Services and Azure

Cyber Minds

Shira Rubinoff

ISBN: 978-1-78980-700-4

- The threats and opportunities presented by AI
- How to mitigate social engineering and other human threats
- Developing cybersecurity strategies for the cloud
- Major data breaches, their causes, consequences, and key takeaways
- Blockchain applications for cybersecurity
- Implications of IoT and how to secure IoT services
- The role of security in cyberterrorism and state-sponsored cyber attacks

Leave a review - let other readers know what you think

Please share your thoughts on this book with others by leaving a review on the site that you bought it from. If you purchased the book from Amazon, please leave us an honest review on this book's Amazon page. This is vital so that other potential readers can see and use your unbiased opinion to make purchasing decisions, we can understand what our customers think about our products, and our authors can see your feedback on the title that they have worked with Packt to create. It will only take a few minutes of your time, but is valuable to other potential customers, our authors, and Packt. Thank you!

Index

Indian Nuclear Plant campaign 139
The US and Libya election interference
campaign 142-144

D

Data Loss Prevention (DLP) 183
data manipulation 285
DeepFakes
about 108, 284
applying 116-118
defining 108
DeepMastersPrints 117
Defense Advanced Research Projects Agency
(DARPA) 70
Defense Information Systems Agency
(DISA) 206
defensive tooling and strategic enablers
about 196
Infection Monkey 197, 198
Software-Defined Perimeter 206
demilitarized zone (DMZ) 211
democratic processes
attacking 285
Denial of service (DoS) attacks 82
Department of Defense (DoD) 7, 73
Distributed Denial of Service
(DDoS) 13, 80, 137
drones
security 64-70
DTrack 140
Duqu 18
dynamic firewalls (DFs) 210

E

Edge and Entity Security (EES)
strategy 186, 188
effective strategy, cyberspace
about 184
concepts, modifying 185
edge, defending 186-189
EES strategy 189, 191
orchestration 191, 192
ElasticGroovy 199

F

False Flag Operation 138
Federal Bureau of Investigation (FBI) 246

G

General Adversarial Networks
(GANs) 109-115
Google Voice Builder
URL 122
Government Communications Headquarters
(GCHQ) 15
governments
perimeters failure 34, 36

H

H8mail 223
hacker 1, 2
Hash Based Message Authentication Code
(HMAC) 211
hashtag
about 90
example 91-97
heartbeat-based authentication 274
Hewlett Packard Enterprises (HPE) 40
High Ground
reclaiming 239-243
hoaxing 155-160

I

Identity and Access Management (IAM) 191
identity provider (IdP) 241
impact from failure, cyber warfare
about 280
compromising healthcare 281
Industrial Control Systems 282
Improvised Explosive Devices (IEDs) 69, 168
Indian Nuclear Plant campaign 139
Industrial Control Systems (ICS) 282
Infection Monkey tool
about 197, 198
advanced uses 203-205
offerings 201, 202

Made in the USA
Monee, IL
03 April 2021